Women and Management: An Expanding Role

Edited by Donald O. Jewell, Ph.D.
Department of Management
Georgia State University

Publishing Services Division
School of Business Administration
Georgia State University
Atlanta, Georgia
1977

Library of Congress Cataloging in Publication Data

Main entry under title:

Women and management.

    Bibliography: p.
    1. Women executives--United States--Addresses, essays,
lectures. 2. Women--Employment--United States--Addresses,
essays, lectures. I. Jewell, Donald O., 1940-
HF5500.3.U54W64   331.4'81'6584   76-30748
ISBN 0-88406-103-5

Published by:

Publishing Services Division
School of Business Administration
Georgia State University
University Plaza
Atlanta, Georgia 30303 USA

Printed and bound in the United States of America

Cover Design by Fredd Chrestman

Foreword

SINCE THE enactment of Title IX of the Civil Rights Act of 1976, which provided protection for minorities and women against discriminatory employment practices, the enactment of protective legislation has increased dramatically. Executive Order 11246, Title VII of the Civil Rights Act of 1964 (amended by the Equal Employment Opportunity Act of 1972), and the Equal Pay Act of 1973 now serve to provide a strong basis for equal access to economic opportunity for women.

Women and Management: An Expanding Role is a declaration of faith that women are and will be capable and competent in the managerial role. There is a clear acknowledgement that there are problems and that there will be problems in the future for women moving into the realms now dominated by men. Not only are there physical, psychological, and interpersonal difficulties between male and female, but there will also be problems of inner conflict within the female and sociological values and barriers with which to contend.

Business and industry, all institutions for that matter, resist change. Like the human personality, there is a clinging to the old way of behaving, to the old way of viewing a potential or present employee, to the old way of selection, promotion, and reward. A change in these values of an institution is as difficult as a change in the human personality, but it is possible.

Gendlin (1964) postulates that becoming aware of the values, attitudes, and stubborn contents in the personality system allow changes in the personality structure to take place. He stresses that one must get a grasp of what all of the problem feels like since there are many facets of the difficulty, often too many to think of each facet alone.

When the individual, or in this case the institution, has a felt sense of what all of the problem feels like, it allows for a forward movement in the value system which brings about a process of resolution and an awareness which evolves into a new way of describing and dealing with the total problem. *Women in Management: An Expanding Role* allows for the apprehension of the vast factual background needed but more importantly conveys to the student a felt sense of the multifaceted problem of advancing women in management.

If individuals and managers can develop this felt sense of the problem, a new awareness will be present. A new affirmative effort which will effect changes to eradicate the old myths of female inferiority will evolve. Of course, this awareness must include the certain knowledge that "new myths reflecting the inferior status of women will continue to spring up to replace the disproved ones," as Athanassiades says in his chapter on Myths of Management. The manager must be able to use this new awareness and these new perceptions to seek out honestly and objectively the false source of the myths in order to allow women to leave stereotyped woman's work and discrimination behind.

The recognition that human talent and human potential is too valuable an asset to waste is crucial even if the package is marked "F". Managers must become role models for their peers as they demonstrate recognition of potential and talent in women. Also, women who move into managerial positions must become role models for their peers in order to encourage others to follow them and to demonstrate to higher management that they are capable and competent, able to contribute to the economic life of business and industry while at the same time developing their individual abilities and talents.

Dr. Kathleen D. Crouch
Georgia State University

Gendlin, E.T., "A Theory of Personality Change," in *Personality Change*, Philip Worchel and Don Byrne (eds.), New York: John Wiley and Sons, 1964.

Preface

THERE IS NO dearth of material concerning women and management—the topic has been researched and explored by many writers. Unfortunately, many of the books and articles have not been generally available, nor have they been written for practicing managers or students of management. This book is an attempt to bring together, as objectively as possible, ideas, research, and experience that shed light on the problems and promise of the expanding role of women in management.

Following a survey of the literature, several articles were selected for inclusion in the book. In addition, original manuscripts were solicited from authors whose publications demonstrated an interest in the field of women in management. Over 200 articles and manuscripts were considered. On route to completing this text, nine original articles were published in a special issue of the *Atlanta Economic Review*. Seven of these nine articles also appear in this book.

The editor wishes to thank the authors and the publishers who have contributed to this book. A special thanks goes to the

Publishing Services Division of the School of Business Administration at Georgia State University, specifically, Jim Miller, Cary Bynum, Carolyn Pollard, Harriett Jones, Susan Hamilton, Dennis Goodwin, and Fredd Chrestman, whose faith and efforts made this book possible.

Donald O. Jewell

Table
of Contents

I
Perspectives on Women in a Changing Society

a. An Expanding Role

Donald O. Jewell *is Professor of Management* and Sandra Beldt *is Assistant Professor of Quantitative Methods, School of Business Administration, Georgia State University, Atlanta.*

Introduction

Donald O. Jewell and Sandra Beldt

ORGANIZATIONS WILL soon find that competent management candidates are not as available as they have been in the past. In his 1974 book, The Human Constraint, *Dr. John B. Miner predicts a decline in the number of qualified male candidates for management positions, as well as a decline in the male's desire to play a managerial role. These two interacting trends which are predicted to peak in the early 1980s, combined with an increasing emphasis on equal rights issues, will result in organizations turning to relatively untapped sources of managerial talent. Unquestionably, the greatest untapped pool of managerial talent is women.*

The recognition of women as viable candidates for management positions has been a slow, and sometimes, painful process. Today, while few knowledgeable people would question the intellectual competence of women relative to men, many still question the emotional suitability of women for the managerial role. Women are being recruited and hired for management positions, but in many instances, with reluctance and apprehension. We can decry this lack of enlightenment but, if we are to deal effectively with those who question women's worth in management, we must understand the historical development of prevailing attitudes toward women relative to the work environment.

In earlier times, childbearing and child care brought about a division of labor; pregnancy and child care kept women in the home. This proximity to household tasks was a primary contributor to the structure of the "woman's role." In almost every society, men were the providers, while women tended to the children and the house. Functionally, these roles for men and women made sense, and this division of labor was not viewed as inequitable.

However, science and technology have so altered the style of life that traditional male and female role models may no longer be relevant. To be more specific, childbearing is now optional due to better and more widely accepted birth control methods, and automation has decreased the amount of time required to perform household activities. Due to these and other similar changes, women are now freer to pursue realistically long-term careers. Yet work that has been available to women such as teaching, nursing, and secretarial and clerical work tends to conform to the traditional role of women and is really an extension of the role women performed in the home. While these functions are critical to society and provide opportunities for growth and satisfaction, many women feel they can contribute in fields and careers which have been more readily available to men. This persistence of the traditional woman's role into more modern times has created perceived inequities in the opportunities for growth, fulfillment, and satisfaction. Many women feel they have much to contribute in terms of abilities and experience and cannot help but feel dissatisfied and frustrated as they find that the barriers between traditional male and female work roles can, at times, seem insurmountable.

Traditions, particularly those passed on so forcefully by parent to child, are difficult to change. Many women are not in agreement that the traditional female role model should be abandoned. For example, some of the most vocal opponents of the Equal Rights Amendment are women, and books and classes which extoll the virtues of the "traditional woman" apparently enjoy a sizeable market. Obviously, attempts to change role models have alarmed many. Many fear the evolution of a unisex *society where all but the physiological differences between men and women will be lost. Envisioned is a deterioration of the quality and stability of male-female relationships and a disintegration of the nuclear family on which our society is founded.*

We believe that a more accurate characterization of present developments in the realm of sex roles is that the roles are expanding. Role prescriptions are becoming less rigid. For example, in the past the principal avenue for the expression of maleness or femaleness was the performance of the appropriate role. Today, we are moving toward a climate where people can express their femininity/masculinity through interpersonal relationships as opposed to their performance in stereotyped roles. Similarly, role prescriptions requiring behaviors characterized exclusively as "male" or "female" are expanding to include behaviors previously characteristic of the other sex role. For example, men are seeking careers as elementary school teachers and women are driving buses and installing telephones.

By expanding general role prescriptions for men and women, as well as by relating occupational role prescriptions more closely to performance requirements, individuals will have a broader choice of roles to play. They will be free to pursue lives and careers congruent with their interests and talents rather than only those careers that fit traditional male and female role models. A woman may pursue a career outside the home or be a "housewife" depending on her interests, and a man should have similar choices. But while barriers are being broken, most men, like women, are still trapped by traditional role models and are limited in the ways they can develop and use their individual resources. The Women's Movement, one of the primary agents of change relative to woman's role, emphasizes the liberation of women from domination by men. Yet, in reality, the movement is also asking that people be allowed to become what they are capable of becoming. Women and men should be free to develop and use their resources in ways that provide them with a sense of fulfillment and personal satisfaction.

Times are changing, individual needs and values are changing, and so must role models. There was a time when the use of the human resources available to society was maximized by the traditional male and female roles. This is no longer true. Families will never again be large, and even those women who choose to have children will spend a relatively small percentage of their productive lives in activities related to children and the home. As stated earlier, technology and a changing life style have combined to make homemaking less of a burden and less demanding of time. Consequently, the resources of many women are not being fully utilized by society.

With their talents no longer fully required in the home, women are seeking other arenas in which to meet their individual needs for growth and contribution. The movement of women into management is a natural extension of their expanding role in society. If Dr. Miner is correct in predicting a shortage of management talent, the emergence of women as legitimate candidates for management roles is fortuitous. With the problems confronting organizations today, we can ill afford to be caught lacking in the most critical of organizational resources—competent managers. As a society we must admit both the problems and promise of women as a management resource and commit the resources necessary to ensure that women have both the competence and the opportunities necessary to succeed.

Roxann A. Van Dusen *is with the Social Science Research Council, Washington, D.C.* Eleanor Bernert Sheldon *is with the Social Science Research Council, New York, New York.*

This article was the APA Invited Address presented by Eleanor Bernert Sheldon at the meeting of the American Psychological Association, Chicago, August 1975. It appeared in the American Psychologist, *February 1976, pp. 106-116. Copyright 1976 by the American Psychological Association. Reprinted by permission.*

1

The Changing Status of American Women: A Life Cycle Perspective

Roxann A. Van Dusen and Eleanor Bernert Sheldon

THE "LIFE CYCLE," a familiar concept to the public and to the media, has recently been receiving substantial attention from social scientists (Riley, Johnson, & Foner, 1972). The life cycle (or "life course") is a way of conceptualizing the aging process: a sequence of statuses and roles, expectations and relationships, constituting, in the broadest meaning of the word, an individual's "career." While the life cycle is universal, it is also infinitely varied. It is shaped by the variety of roles and opportunities available to an individual, as well as by the resources that individual can marshal at various stages of his or her "career."

In the past decade or so, sociologists and other social scientists have borrowed from demographers the concepts and techniques of cohort analysis for studying the process of social change. To state it simply: Social change has been viewed as the succession of cohorts through various stages of the life cycle. This cohort-analytic perspective highlights three important components of social change: (a) change associated with the aging process; (b) change associated with changes in the "external" environment; and (c) change associated with the replacement of one group of people (usually the succession of age groups) by the next.

Consider, first, the aging process: An individual's life is patterned by a variety of role sequences, probably the most important of which is the family life cycle, but also including sequences of student, career, and community roles. The combination and juxtaposition of various role sequences provide texture to an individual life cycle. Certain roles are traditionally associated with certain ages: student roles with the young; parental roles with the middle years; life alone (whether as a result of divorce, widowhood, or lifelong singleness) with the middle aged and elderly.

Second, the historical times during which an individual matures also affect expectations and behavior: the 1930s Depression, World War II, the Vietnam War—all have an impact on patterns of marriage, fertility, and employment.

Finally, each birth cohort has a unique pattern of experiences as it progresses through the life cycle, experiences that may be seen as the interaction of the aging process and the period during which it occurs. The cohort that grew up and reached maturity during the 1930s bears the mark of the Depression. The baby-boom cohort faces (and will continue to face) sharp competition for education, for jobs, and for a variety of social services—the consequences of belonging to a group that is larger than both the group it follows and the one that will follow it.

The combination of the notion of the life cycle (and subcycles within it) and the notion of cohort succession provides a powerful tool for characterizing and understanding some of the recent changes in the roles and status of American women. Some of these changes have resulted from changes in the perception of appropriate role sequences for women; some are the result of the interaction of social, political, and economic events of the 1960s and 1970s; and some of the changes (and certainly the speed of the changes) may be attributed to the fact that the cohort that reached maturity in the past few years is not an ordinary cohort but rather the baby-boom generation.

Let us examine, briefly, some of these changes. It was noted at the outset that the *family* life cycle constitutes perhaps the most important subcurrent of an individual's life cycle. It is certainly the most important subcycle if that individual happens to be a woman. In fact, the tendency until recently has been to equate the family life cycle with the female life cycle. After all, most women marry at some point in their life, and most married women have children. In 1974, for instance, 95% of all women 35 and older had been married at least once, and all but about 10% of them had had at least one child (U.S. Department of Commerce, 1974d, 1975a). Most women's lives have been regulated by the family life cycle, their "career" choices to one extent or another circumscribed by the responsibilities attending their family roles—the bearing and rearing of children.

From this presumed identity of female and family life cycles, there developed well-defined notions of what activities and roles are appropriate for women of different ages, corresponding to different stages of the family life cycle. These expectations were, to some extent, suspended for women who did not fit the mold: the 5% or 10% who never married, and the ever-increasing number of divorced, separated, and widowed women. Thus there developed the notion that there are two categories of women: those who are married and those with careers.

In fact, of course, such a dichotomy never existed. In 1950, one quarter of all married women who were living with their husbands were in the labor force, and more than one quarter of all women in intact marriages who had school-age children were employed: more than 10% of married women with husband present and preschool children were in the labor force. And the number of women who combine career and family roles has risen steadily since then. Nevertheless, it has only been in the last decade or so that notions about what activities and roles are appropriate for women at each stage of the family/female life cycle have become somewhat less rigid. Slowly, social definitions of women's roles are catching up with reality.

Many have seen this trend as the increasing overlap and similarity of men's and women's life cycles. An alternative is to view this trend as the decreasing salience of marriage and the family in the life choices of women. In a recent article, Presser (1973) examined some of the consequences for women and for the family of perfect fertility control. Many of the changes she envisioned are becoming evident in the trends to be highlighted in this article: continuing education for women, an orientation toward lifelong careers, smaller families, and child-free marriages. This is not to suggest that all of these changes may be directly attributed to greater contraceptive efficiency. But what it does suggest is that the distinction (in terms of roles and expectations) between child-free women and those with children (whether by choice or through contraceptive failure) is gradually disappearing. Or, to phrase it differently, the family life cycle is becoming but one of a number of subcurrents in the lives of American women.

In documenting some of the facets of this general trend, it is important not only to examine changes in several key aspects of women's (and men's) lives—education, marriage and the establishment of a separate household, childbearing, and labor force participation—but also to examine these changes with a view to the variable effects on different age groups at different stages in the life cycle.

Education

It is appropriate to begin the discussion of changes in the status of American women with some information on changes in their educational attainment. Education has traditionally been regarded as an early stage of the life cycle—a stage that is completed before a career (be it job, marriage, family, or whatever) is launched. Furthermore, the educational system plays a major role in influencing the goals and expectations of individuals; it also is a major source of the contacts and training that will enable the individual to pursue those goals. Thus, the education system plays both a formal and an informal role in channeling individuals into certain lifework and life-styles.

That there has been a steady rise in the educational attainment of the U.S. population over the past 35 years is well known: the proportion of Americans between the ages of 25 and 34 with at least 4 years of high school has risen from 35% in 1940 to 80% in 1974. The percentage of female high school graduates 20 and 21 years old who have completed at least some college has risen from 24% in 1940 to 46% in 1974; the comparable figures for men are 30% in 1940 and 49% in 1974 (U.S. Department of Commerce, 1974a).

Yet important differences exist between men and women

both in the level of educational attainment of each group and in the types of educational training each pursues. For instance, though women are somewhat more likely to finish high school than are men, women are less likely to continue on to college. And if they do go on to college, women are less likely to complete all 4 years. In 1974, 47% of all white women between 25 and 34 years old had completed high school but had no college training, and an additional 33% had completed some college. The comparable figures for white males are 38% with only a high school degree, and 44% with at least some college (U.S. Department of Commerce, 1974a).

There are several stereotypic explanations for these sex differences in educational attainment. First, it is argued, a family is more likely to invest in a son's education than in a daughter's, in the belief that the son *must* be able to find a job, but the daughter may not have to. Second, even if the daughter intends to work, most jobs open to her do not require a college degree: skills necessary for secretarial, clerical, and operative positions can be learned on the job. And third, so the argument goes, the daughter will undoubtedly get married and have children, and will in any case stop her education at that point.

Indeed, marriage and childbearing have traditionally been considered sufficient reasons for women to terminate their schooling, though the parallel roles for men (husband and father) did not, in general, preclude a man from continuing to be a student as well. In discussing the results of a recent national survey, Campbell, Converse, and Rodgers state:

> The proportion of unmarried young women who report attending school of some kind (61 percent) is twice as high as that of their married age cohort [18–29] (29 percent), but the proportion of unmarried men of this age [who report attending school] (47 percent) is virtually identical to that of married men (48 percent). When asked why they had terminated their formal education when they had, almost half of the married women referred to their marriage; this response was far less common among young married men.[1]

These explanations for sex differences in educational attainment have taken a rather severe beating in the past decade. First, the argument that women need not support themselves: Increasing numbers of women are the sole wage earners for their families or are economically independent. In

March 1973, 42% of all women in the labor force were single, widowed, divorced, or separated, and thus (to a greater or lesser extent) economically on their own; another 19% of the female labor force were married to men with less than $7,000 annual income (U.S. Department of Labor, 1975). Increasingly, women must face the likelihood that at some point in their lifetime they will have to support themselves or contribute to the family income.

Second, the argument that women's work does not require extensive training or educational degrees fails on two counts: (a) women are bringing more education to their traditional jobs and thus making that training a requirement of the position (most secretaries, for instance, are now expected to have some college training); and (b) women are beginning to challenge the rigidity with which "women's work" has been defined, and in seeking entrance to "male jobs," they have had to acquire the prerequisite educational background.

And third, the argument that women will give up their schooling for marriage and family: Increasing numbers of women, in examining their prospects for entering or reentering the labor force, are not abandoning their educational careers upon marriage and the advent of children. The composition of the student population of the United States—in terms of both age and sex—is rapidly changing. Between 1970 and 1974, the number of women in college increased by 30%, while the number of men only increased by 12%. Furthermore, although overall graduate school enrollment has dropped 9% since 1969, the proportion of women in graduate school continues to rise. In 1971, women earned 42% of all BAs and 40% of all MAs. Although women constituted only 14% of all PhDs awarded in 1971, that number is likely to rise quickly in the next few years, for the pool of candidates from which they are drawn is growing rapidly (both in actual numbers and compared with men) (U.S. Department of Labor, 1975).

Not only is the proportion of women seeking education beyond the high school diploma fast approaching that of men, women are also beginning to compete with men to gain entry to the high-prestige occupations that were traditionally closed to them. The proportion of women enrolled in professional schools for such fields as law, medicine, architecture, and engineering, although still low, has risen steadily since 1960.

For instance, of the total enrollment in law schools, women accounted for 4% in 1960, 12% in 1972, and 19% in 1974. The same trend may be seen in total enrollments in medical schools, in which women represented 6% of the total in 1960, 13% in 1972, and 18% in 1974. The increasing proportion of women in the first-year class of these programs suggests that these trends will continue (McCarthy & Wolfle, 1975; Parrish, 1974).

Finally, evidence exists that fewer women are abandoning their educational plans upon marriage and childbearing, or they are setting aside these plans only temporarily. This trend may be seen in the number of women 25 years and older who are in school. Between 1970 and 1974, for instance, the college enrollment of women between the ages of 25 and 34 rose from 409,000 to 831,000—an increase of 102%. The comparable increase for men between 25 and 34 was 46%: from 940,000 to 1,371,000 in 1974. Of women in college between the ages of 16 and 34, those 25 years and older rose from 14% in 1970 to 21% in 1974 (U.S. Department of Commerce, 1975c).

During the period 1970-1974, part-time enrollment in college increased 50%, compared with a 10% increase in the number of full-time students. The role that the older college students play in this trend toward part-time continuing education is evident: 63% of the 25-34-year-olds were enrolled on a part-time basis in 1974, compared with only 17% of those in the traditional college cohort (18-24-year-olds) (U.S. Department of Commerce, 1975c).

These changes have had two important effects on the lives of American women. First, the young women in the age cohort that traditionally constituted the student population (those under age 25) are facing much less resistance—social and institutional—in their efforts to gain access to the training that is a prerequisite for career mobility. Second, and perhaps more important, those women *not* in the traditional student cohort—those who are older, who are married, or who have children—are no longer deemed to have "missed the boat" by having taken on family roles before completing their schooling. "Student" is no longer synonymous with "pre-adult."

In the following sections, some of the push and pull factors associated with the return of older women to school will be discussed: changes in the marital and childbearing patterns that have made continuing education more easy to arrange and changes in the labor market that have made that education more desirable to acquire—at least for women.

Marriage and Childbearing

Three of the most remarkable trends in the past two decades have all had a direct effect on the phasing of what was traditionally considered the main portion of a woman's life cycle—namely, marriage and childbearing. Specifically, women are postponing marriage, postponing childbearing within marriage, and reducing their family size expectations.

Take marital patterns, for instance. The median age at first marriage for women has risen from 20.3 in 1950 to 21.1 in 1974. Furthermore, in the age group in which most men and women traditionally marry (20-24), the percentage of women remaining single has risen from 28% in 1960 to 39% in 1974—an increase of one third. In general, while the percentage remaining single is up sharply for persons under 35, it continues to decline for persons 35 and over (U.S. Department of Commerce, 1974d). The long-term effect of the trend among the 20-24 cohort to remain single may be a later marriage age, or it may be a growing commitment to lifelong singleness: it is too early to say.

There are many explanations for this dramatic change in marriage patterns in the last 25 years. First, the expansion of educational opportunities for women has provided them with alternatives to their traditional life choices, and they are postponing (sometimes indefinitely) parental roles in favor of occupational careers. Second, there is increasing acceptance of nontraditional living arrangements; couples who might have bowed to social pressure to marry no longer feel compelled to do so. Third, the 1960s saw a dramatic rise in the number of young marriage-age men inducted into the armed forces, and thus made relatively inaccessible to the marriage market. But, in addition to these and other explanations for delayed marriage, demographers have given us one other: *the marriage squeeze.* Since women tend to marry men two or three years older than themselves, the women of the baby boom reached marriage age before the comparably large male marriage cohort. Or, to put it another way, there were not enough men in the appropriate age groups for the marriage-age women. For some women, then, the postponement of marriage may have been involuntary—the demographic fallout of the baby boom (Glick & Parke, 1965; Parke & Glick, 1967).

In part as a consequence of postponed marriage, in part for other reasons, women are postponing childbearing. For instance, 70% of white women married between 1955 and 1959 had their first child in the first 24 months of marriage; 10 years later (i.e., among women married between 1965 and 1969), only 60% had had their first child within 2 years of marriage. The same trend is seen for later-order births as well. It should be noted, however, that in the same 10-year comparison for black women, the trend is reversed (U.S. Department of Commerce, 1974c).

Not only are women having their children later, they are also having, and planning to have, fewer children. This phenomenon has given us another term in the popular lexicon on the changing life cycle: *the birth dearth*. Between 1960 and 1974, the percentage of ever-married women between the ages of 15 and 19 who were child free increased by 25% (from 44% to 56%); for ever-married women 20-24, those child free rose by two thirds (from 24% to 41%); and for ever-married women 25-29, the rise was close to 60% (from 13% to 20%) (U.S. Department of Commerce, 1975a). It is interesting to note that this drop in births since 1960 will produce a reverse marriage squeeze in the next five years or so: young men will be locating mates from a *smaller* cohort of women.

In 1974, the birth rate in the United States reached a point lower even than the level reached during the 1930s Depression: 14.8 per 1,000 population. Not only the birth rate but the fertility expectations of women have dropped dramatically and quickly. In 1955, 38% of women aged 18-24 expected to have four or more children (U.S. Department of Labor, 1973); between 1967 and 1974, the proportion of women in this age group who expected to have four or more children dropped by more than two thirds: from 26% in 1967 to 8% in 1974. At the same time, the number of women anticipating *two* children rose dramatically: from 37% of the women 18-24 in 1967 to 56% in 1974—an increase of 50%. For women in the 25-29 age range, the increase in the number expecting only two children was even more dramatic: from 29% in 1967 to 52% in 1974 (U.S. Department of Commerce, 1975a).

At the same time that family size expectations are decreasing, there is an increasing proportion of childless women who expect to *remain* childless: in 1974, 11% of childless married women 14-24 and 27% of childless married women 25-29 did not expect to have any children. These figures represent an increase of 23% in just 3 years in wives under 30 who do not plan to have children (U.S. Department of Commerce, 1975a).

In short, then, women have been entering the traditional family cycle more slowly, and because of their smaller families, they have been spending less time in that phase of their life.

Female Heads of Households

One way to examine some of the changes that have taken place in family living arrangements in the past two decades is to look at changes in female-headed households.[2] Between 1954 and 1969, the number of female heads of families increased by about 40%; this number grew another 22% between 1970 and 1974, so that by 1974 female-headed households represented 10% of all households in the United States, and approximately 15% of all families with children. Much of this change reflects the increase in the number of black female family heads. Since 1960 there has been a 10% increase in the number of white female family heads, and a 35% increase in the number of black female family heads. In 1973, black women represented 28% of all female family heads (U.S. Department of Commerce, 1975b).

Female heads of households are younger (on average) than previously, and more apt to be divorced, separated, or single, rather than widowed. Between 1960 and 1973, the median age of women who headed families declined by about 5 years, from 50.5 in 1960 to 45.1 in 1973, with black female family heads about 9 years younger than their white counterparts (U.S. Department of Commerce, 1974b). The shift toward younger, divorced, or separated female family heads (from older, widowed family heads) will no doubt continue as a result of the continuing and rising rate of divorces and separations. In 1973, 37% of female family heads were widowed, 13% unmarried, and 50% divorced or separated. This is in contrast with 1960, when 50% of them were widowed and 36% divorced or separated (U.S. Department of Commerce, 1974b).

There are two fundamental reasons for interest in and

concern for increases in the number of households headed by women. First, as a group, these households are particularly disadvantaged. Two thirds of all female household heads have less than a high school education. In 1972, more than half of them had incomes below the poverty threshold ($4,254), compared with less than 10% of male heads of households. In 1973, a higher proportion of children under 18 years of age lived in fatherless families than ever before: about 10% of white children and 38% of black children. Nearly one half of all female family heads between the ages of 25 and 44 have three or more children. In short, increasing numbers of children are experiencing the economic disadvantages which attend households headed by women (U.S. Department of Commerce, 1974b; U.S. Department of Labor, 1975; Waldman & Whitmore, 1974).

The second major reason for interest in the growth of female-headed households is that increasing numbers of women have experienced or will experience this status at some point in their lives. The shift toward later marriage age, when combined with the ability and inclination of young single women to leave their parent's home and set up their own household, has been a major element in the increase in households of "primary individuals" who are female. The rise in the number of children born to unmarried women, coupled with the tendency for these women to set up their own household rather than move in with relatives, has also contributed to the trend.

But the major factor in the rise in the number of households headed by women is the increasing likelihood that a marriage will end in divorce or separation. The number and rate of divorces increased in 1974 for the 12th straight year. The ratio of divorced people to those in intact marriages has risen from a level of 35 per 1,000 in 1960 to 63 per 1,000 in 1974, with approximately 50% more divorced women than divorced men in 1974—an indication of the greater likelihood that divorced men will remarry. Perhaps the most important element in this trend has been the shift in the age patterns of divorce in recent years. In 1974, the ratio of divorced persons to persons in intact marriages was higher for those under 45 years old (66 per 1,000) than for those 45 years and over (59 per 1,000), representing a reversal of the situation a decade earlier (U.S. Department of Commerce, 1974d).

It has been argued that the rise in the number of families

headed by women represents not a preference for single-parent families but rather a transitional status which increasing proportions of women will enter (and leave) at some point in their lives (Ross & MacIntosh, Note 2). The vast majority of the individuals who are postponing marriage today are likely to marry at some point; a growing proportion of them will experience separation and divorce; and an increasing proportion of those divorced will experience remarriage. Between 1960 and 1969, the rate of remarriage of divorced women rose by almost 11% (from 122.1 per 1,000 divorced women to 135.4). In contrast, the remarriage rate for widows has remained fairly constant: 36.1 per 1,000 widows in 1960 to 39.3 per 1,000 in 1969. Thus, the major group of women who are likely to remain in female-headed households are widows. But, as noted earlier, widows represent a shrinking proportion of the total female household heads (NCHS, 1973).

If, in fact, there has been a decrease in the importance of marital status in predicting or determining the sorts of activities and roles a woman adopts, part of the reason is that marriage is not eternal. More and more women are spending more and more time in roles that lie outside the traditional family life cycle. The length of time after childhood and before marriage is growing, as is the number of women spending time between marriages.

It is not really surprising that the social perception of appropriate female roles is catching up with the reality of post-World-War-II America. It is rather more surprising that it has taken so long to recognize that the "career woman" and the mother may be one and the same person. But then, as Keller (1972) has noted, the working woman is "one of America's best kept secrets."

Labor Force Participation

The contrast between the female labor force of 1920 and that of the 1970s is striking.[3] In 1920, the typical working woman was single, under 30 years old, and from the "working class." Today, most working women are married; over two thirds of them have child-rearing responsibilities in addition to their jobs; they represent the entire socio-economic spectrum; and more than half of them are 40 or over.

Between 1950 and 1973, overall labor force participation of women rose by one third. Although women who have never married have been and continue to be much more likely to work, the distinction between never married and other categories of women in terms of their labor market activity is rapidly disappearing. While the labor force participation of never-married women rose 13% between 1950 and 1974 (from 50.5% to 57.2%), it rose over 80% for married women who were living with their husbands (from 23.8% to 43.0%).

Since the mid-1960s, the greatest increase in labor force participation of women has been among those in the 25-34 age range—the ages during which women are most intensively involved in child-rearing, and the ages at which female labor force participation has traditionally been lowest. Among women 25-34, the proportion in the labor force has risen from 36% in 1960 to 50% in 1973—an increase of close to 40% in 13 years (U.S. Department of Labor, 1975).

Several reasons can be given for the changing composition of the female labor force over the past several decades, some of which have already been highlighted. The rise in the educational attainment of young women in the past several decades has given women access to jobs that were previously inaccessible to them because they lacked the requisite training. Demographic trends have also played a role in encouraging increasing numbers of women to enter the labor force, and to stay there. Because young women have been postponing marriage, and postponing childbearing within marriage, they experience a relatively long period of time after completing high school or college during which they may advance in their careers. And increasingly, women are finding it difficult to give up the economic independence, as well as the challenge, recognition, and satisfaction they derive from their jobs. Over a third of married women with preschool children were in the labor force in 1974, as contrasted with only 12% in 1950.

In a study of female labor market activity using data from the 1960 U.S. Census, Sweet (1973) found that women with more education were more likely to be in the labor force while their children were preschoolers than were those women with less than a high school education. Sweet suggests two reasons for these findings: differences in child-spacing patterns and differences in previous labor market experience. If women with less education are likely to have the second child relatively quickly, they will be pregnant again while the first child is still a preschooler, and thus less interested in returning to the job. And with good reason: The jobs less educated women perform tend to be more hazardous than the jobs open to women with a college education.

Well-educated women are more likely to have worked both before marriage and before childbearing, and for a longer period of time. This fact has two consequences: (a) the family's consumption patterns have become adapted to two incomes, a level of living difficult to abandon; and (b) these women, with their relatively recent work experience, have greater contact with the labor market and knowledge of job opportunities and are more likely to find employment when they want it.

In addition to affecting the number of women in the labor force, demographic trends have also affected the composition of the female labor force, more particularly the shift from a young, unmarried female labor force to a middle-aged, married one. This shift has been explained, in part, by the concept of a *life cycle squeeze* (Gove, Grimm, Motz, & Thompson, 1973; Oppenheimer, 1974). Expenses are particularly high two times during the typical family life cycle: the first occurs soon after the couple is married, when the acquisition of home and other accoutrements of married life usually takes place; the second occurs when children reach adolescence. Both are times when the husband's income alone is not likely to be sufficient to cover these expenses: the first because he is at the beginning of his career at the time that he is beginning his marriage; the second because the time when the costs of maintaining the family are highest (adolescence of children) may not coincide with the time when his income reaches its peak. Oppenheimer (1974) finds that men in occupations where the peak median earnings in 1959 were $7,000 or more were much more likely to have their incomes rise roughly in proportion to increases in the cost of maintaining their families. However, men in occupations with peak median incomes under $7,000 in 1959 were likely to experience peak child-care costs at a time when they were not earning much more, and sometimes less on average, than were younger men with younger and therefore less expensive children. These situations create strong economic pressures for an additional income, and are undoubtedly one reason why young brides continue to work after marriage, and why women in their forties and fifties have entered or reentered the labor market in record numbers in recent years.[4]

Changes in the U.S. economy in the 20th century have also encouraged women to enter and remain in the labor force. The industries and occupations that have expanded most rapidly (particularly during the period after 1940) are those that were the major employers of women. This trend has been characterized as a shift from the goods-producing economy prior to World War II to the service-producing economy of the 1970s (Waldman & Whitmore, 1974). The post-World-War-II baby boom created the need for an expansion of a wide variety of services—educational, medical, governmental, and recreational among them—services in which most women workers were concentrated.

But while the demand for female labor was rising, the women who traditionally filled these jobs—the young and the single—constituted a stable or declining population, at least until the late 1960s. The dramatic expansion and changing composition of the female labor force in post-World-War-II America, then, are seen in part as the response of older married women to the growing demand for female labor (Oppenheimer, 1970).

Let us consider for a moment the notion of a demand for female labor and the question of the sex labeling of jobs and professions. It is well known that women are highly concentrated in a few occupations in which they constitute an overwhelming majority of all workers. For instance, in 1960, elementary school teachers and registered nurses accounted for almost 54% of all female professional employment; in 1970, they were still just over 46% of all female professionals (Fuchs, 1975). Oppenheimer (1970) has argued that the U.S. labor market is actually two markets—male and female—and that men and women in most cases do not really compete for the same jobs. The expansion of "women's" occupations after World War II led not to a demand for additional labor but to a demand for additional *female* labor.

The principal employer of women today, as it was in 1940, is the service industries and, more particularly, professional services (medical and health, education, and legal) (Waldman &

McEaddy, 1974). As Oppenheimer (1970) has suggested, a number of reasons can be given for the persistence of sex labels on certain jobs:

1. Such "women's jobs" as teaching, nursing, and secretarial work depend on skilled but cheap labor in fairly large quantities—and women who are entering the labor force for the first time, or reentering after a long absence, are willing to accept pay that is not commensurate with their skills or training.

2. Most of the training for these occupations is acquired *before* employment. Thus the employer does not bear the risk of investing time and money training women, with the attendant possibility that they will soon leave.[5]

3. These "women's jobs" do not require a long-term commitment, or extensive sacrifice of time, and thus women, who have traditionally been seen as secondary earners who lack high career aspirations, are attracted to them.[6]

4. These jobs exist all over the country, and thus women are not usually handicapped by their mobility (if their husbands must move frequently in their jobs) *or* their immobility (if their husbands must stay in one place).

5. Finally, these jobs have traditionally been held by women. The jobs are thought to call on skills that are innately female (the greater manual dexterity often attributed to women) or on skills that are acquired in the home (the patience to work with children!). Furthermore, these traditional female jobs rarely put women in a supervisory position over men—a situation that is thought to create rebellion among male underlings.

Considerable debate continues as to whether there has been any change in the sex labeling or sex segregation of occupations in recent years (Fuchs, 1975; Gross, 1968; Hedges & Bemis, 1974; Knudsen, 1969). Gross (1968) has argued, for instance, that what small decrease there may be in occupational segregation is due not to the entrance of women into traditionally male occupations but the reverse: a "decreased resistance by female occupations to the entry of males" (p. 198). Fuchs (1975) has argued that the trend is much more complex. A drop in an index of occupational segregation could occur either as a result of a change in the average amount of segregation within occupations or as a result of differential rates of growth of occupations. Using a simple index of sex segregation, which may be interpreted as the proportion of people who would have to shift to occupations dominated by the opposite sex in order to eliminate sex segregation, Fuchs finds a drop of 7 percentage points between 1960 (66.2%) and 1970 (59.2%). Fuchs notes that between 1960 and 1970 some occupations became less segregated: the greatest changes were among elementary school teachers and registered nurses (in female-dominated professions) and among engineers, accountants, and science technicians (in male-dominated professions). At the same time, the less sex segregated occupations (e.g., college and secondary school teachers, computer specialists, health technologists) were growing more rapidly.

If there is today less resistance to female employment in traditionally male-dominated occupations, it has not been without its adverse consequences. In the present recession, women workers have accounted for significantly larger proportions of the unemployed—a fact that underscores their recent entry and consequent low status in a range of occupations (U.S. Department of Labor, 1975). And among women who have been able to keep their jobs, there seems to be no decrease in the income differentials between men and women. The grim news in the 1975 *Manpower Report of the President* was that "nearly two-thirds of all full-time, year-round female workers earned *less* than $7,000 in 1972" while "over three-quarters of full-time, year-round male workers earned *over* $7,000" (p. 55). Even when earnings are adjusted for hours worked and level of education of the worker, the large differentials in earnings between male and female workers persist. For instance, Suter and Miller (1973) found, in working with income data from 1966, that "if women had the same occupational status as men, had worked all their lives, had the same education and year-round full-time employment in 1966, their income would be . . . 62 percent of that received by men" (p. 962).

The sex labeling of jobs, the occupational segregation of women, and the consequent income differentials between men and women have been remarkably persistent in the face of dramatic demographic and socioeconomic changes. But it is precisely these changes that will inevitably restructure the career experiences and labor market activity of women in the next several decades. The present female occupational distribution, as is noted in the 1975 *Manpower Report*, is the result of myriad influences, some in early childhood: "Role differentiation in early life later affects educational and occupational choices, hours and location of work, and other factors which relegate women to lower level positions in the lower paying industries" (U.S. Department of Labor, 1975, p. 63).

The change that is coming can already be seen in the choices young women have been making in their educational and their family "careers." Because marriage is no longer an end in itself; because so many women spend time outside of marriage or in between marriages; because family/parental roles occupy a relatively short portion of a woman's total life in today's two-child society; because women are receiving the education and training (and with it the career aspirations) to cause them to plan for and expect employment opportunities parallel to those of men; and finally, because all of these conditions represent changes from the recent past, to note that the pattern of female labor force participation is likely to change is anticlimactic.

However, despite all these changes, nowhere is it suggested that the pattern of female occupational choices, earnings, or job mobility will approximate that of men, and certainly not in the near future. The reasons have nothing to do with women's skills or aspirations, and surprisingly little to do with the prospects for economic recovery in the United States in the next few years. The reasons have everything to do with the life cycle concerns discussed previously. Although marital status and parental responsibilities are likely to become less salient in women's career choices, women will continue to bear the major responsibility for children, and it is their career that will continue to be marked by the need to accommodate both parental and occupational roles.

Whether female labor force participation will approximate that of males, or even whether it should—given that the distribution of mothers, and most of the responsibilities that accompany that role, is 100% female—is not a particularly fruitful line of inquiry. More productive of insight will be some close attention to the social and economic lags created by these recent social and demographic trends. Two examples come readily to mind: the "two-career family" and the "dual career" woman.

The two-career family is one in which both the husband and the wife are employed; it characterizes a growing portion of all U.S. families. Traditionally, career mobility has involved some geographic mobility. A family with school-age children and headed by one wage earner is not particularly mobile; the two-career family is even less so. What will be the effects on the labor market of the increased reluctance or inability of talented young people to move to further their careers? Or, alternatively, what will be the effect on marriage and divorce patterns on the continued importance of a certain amount of geographic mobility in furthering one's career?

Second, "dual careers": Dual careers refer to the combination and juxtaposition of parental and occupational responsibilities which confront increasing numbers of women. As more and more women with family responsibilities enter the labor force, certain institutional changes may be necessary—among them, the improvement of child-care facilities, increased flexibility of work schedules, and better provisions for job training. At what cost will these changes to accommodate the dual career woman be made? Or, alternatively, what will be the costs (social and otherwise) of *not* making the necessary institutional changes?

Conclusion

At the outset it was suggested that one way of summarizing these various trends was in terms of the declining importance of the family life cycle in the woman's total life cycle—the diminishing social importance of the distinction between married women and those who are unmarried (never married, no longer married, not yet married). In examining this general proposition, recent changes in a number of areas which have a direct impact on a woman's life choices were highlighted: education, marriage, childbearing, and employment.

The essential message has been: The traditional family life cycle for women has been slowly disappearing for the past quarter century; the rapid-paced changes of the past decade have released the secret, and another sacred myth is being dispelled. With the death of the myth, little doubt now exists that during the last decades of the century these trends will exert a profound effect on family, economy, social values—and, of course, the changing bases of self-identification and of sex roles.

Footnotes

1. Campbell, A., Converse, P.E., & Rodgers, W. *The perceived quality of life.* Ann Arbor: University of Michigan, 1975. (Prepublication draft)

2. Any woman 14 years old or older may head a family if she is not married and living with her husband. She may or may not live alone, and if she lives with others, they may or may not be related to her. If she lives alone or with nonrelatives, she is called a primary individual. If she lives with others who are related to her by blood, marriage, or adoption, she is the head of a primary family. For a detailed discussion of households headed by women, see Ross, H.L., & MacIntosh, A., *The emergence of households headed by women.* Washington, D.C.: Urban Institute, June 1973. (Unpublished paper)

3. For a discussion of trends in female labor force participation in the United States in the 20th century, see Oppenheimer (1970). For additional information, see the annual publication of the U.S. Department of Labor, *Manpower Report of the President.*

4. Comments by A.J. Jaffe and Murray Gendell on Oppenheimer's article appear in *Demography* (1975, *12*, 331-336). Gendell notes that it may be the financial squeeze that propels middle-age women into the labor force (as Oppenheimer suggests), or it may be the decreased childcare responsibilities associated with adolescent children which *enables* women to seek outside employment.

5. A recent study examines patterns of quitting for men and women, and finds that quitting to exit the labor force is larger for women, and quitting to move to another job is larger for men. Barnes and Jones (1974) also find that total female quitting is usually greater than male quitting, but male quitting is more variable from year to year.

6. For a discussion of the assumptions about female career aspirations, see Crowley, J.E., Levitin, T.E., & Quinn, R.P. *Facts and fictions about the American working woman.* Ann Arbor: University of Michigan, Institute for Social Research, January 1973. (Mimeo)

References

Barnes, W.F., & Jones, E.B. Differences in male and female quitting. *Journal of Human Resources*, 1974, *9*, 439-451.

Fuchs, V.R. A note on sex segregation in professional occupations. *Explorations in Economic Research*, 1975, *2*, 105-111.

Gendell, M. Further comment on V.K. Oppenheimer's "The life-cycle squeeze: The interaction of men's occupational and family life cycles." *Demography*, 1975, *12*, 333-336.

Glick, P.C., & Parke, R., Jr. New approaches in studying the life cycle of the family. *Demography*, 1965, *2*, 187-202.

Gove, W.R., Grimm, J.W., Motz, S.C., & Thompson, J.D. The family life cycle: Internal dynamics and social consequences. *Sociology and Social Research*, 1973, *57*, 182-195.

Gross, E. Plus ça change . . . ? The sexual structure of occupations over time. *Social Problems*, 1968, *16*, 198-208.

Hedges, J.N., & Bemis, S.E. Sex stereotyping: Its decline in skilled trades. *Monthly Labor Review*, 1974, *97* (May), 14-22.

Jaffe, A.J. Comment on V.K. Oppenheimer's "The life-cycle squeeze: The interaction of men's occupational and family life cycles." *Demography*, 1975, *12*, 331-332.

Keller, S. The future status of women in America. In C.F. Westoff & R. Parke, Jr. (Eds.), *Demographic and social aspects of population growth* (Research Reports of the Commission on Population Growth and the American Future, Vol. 1). Washington, D.C.: U.S. Government Printing Office, 1972.

Knudsen, D.D. The declining status of women: Popular myths and the failure of functionalist thought. *Social Forces*, 1969, *48*, 183-193.

McCarthy, J.L., and Wolfle, D. Doctorates granted to women and minority group members. *Science*, 1975, *189*, 856-859.

National Center for Health Statistics. *Remarriages, United States* (Series 21, No. 25, Vital and Health Statistics). Rockville, Md.: Author, December 1973.

Oppenheimer, V.K. *The female labor force in the United States: Demographic and economic factors governing its growth and changing composition* (Population Monograph Series, No. 5). Berkeley: University of California, 1970.

Oppenheimer, V.K. The life-cycle squeeze: The interaction of men's occupational and family life cycles. *Demography*, 1974, *11*, 227-245.

Parke, R., Jr., & Glick, P.C. Prospective changes in marriage and the family. *Journal of Marriage and the Family*, 1967, *29*, 249-256.

Parrish, J.B. Women in professional training. *Monthly Labor Review*, 1974, *97* (May), 40-43.

Presser, H. Perfect fertility control: Consequences for women and the family. In C.F. Westoff et al. (Eds.), *Toward the end of growth*. Englewood Cliffs, N.J.: Prentice-Hall, 1973.

Riley, M.W., Johnson, M., & Foner, A. (Eds.). *Aging and society*. New York: Russell Sage Foundation, 1972.

Suter, L.E., & Miller, H.P. Components of differences between the incomes of men and career women. *American Journal of Sociology*, 1973, *79*, 962-974.

Sweet, J.A. *Women in the labor force*. New York: Seminar Press, 1973.

U.S. Department of Commerce, Bureau of the Census. Educational attainment in the United States: March 1973 and 1974 (P-20, No. 274). *Current Population Reports*. Washington, D.C.: Author, December 1974. (a)

U.S. Department of Commerce, Bureau of the Census. Female family heads (P-23, No. 50). *Current Population Reports*. Washington, D.C.: Author, July 1974. (b)

U.S. Department of Commerce, Bureau of the Census. Fertility histories and birth expectations of American women: June 1971 (P-20, No. 263). *Current Population Reports*. Washington, D.C.: Author, April 1974. (c)

U.S. Department of Commerce, Bureau of the Census. Marital status and living arrangements: March 1974 (P-20, No. 271). *Current Population Reports*. Washington, D.C.: Author, October 1974. (d)

U.S. Department of Commerce, Bureau of the Census. Fertility expectations of American women: June 1974 (P-20, No. 277). *Current Population Reports*. Washington, D.C.: Author, February 1975. (a)

U.S. Department of Commerce, Bureau of the Census. Population profile of the United States: 1974 (P-20, No. 279). *Current Population Reports*. Washington, D.C.: Author, March 1975. (b)

U.S. Department of Commerce, Bureau of the Census. School enrollment—Social and economic characteristics of students: October 1974 (P-20, No. 278). *Current Population Reports*. Washington, D.C.: Author, February 1975. (c)

U.S. Department of Labor. *Manpower report of the President*. Washington, D.C.: U.S. Government Printing Office, annual.

Waldman, E., & McEaddy, B.J. Where women work—An analysis by industry and occupation. *Monthly Labor Review*, 1974, *97* (May), 3-13.

Waldman, E., & Whitmore, R. Children of working mothers. *Monthly Labor Review*, 1974, *97* (May), 50-58.

Judith B. Agassi *is Senior Lecturer, Ruppin Institute for Kibbutz Management, Israel.*

Reprinted with permission of Macmillan Publishing Co., Inc. from The Quality of Working Life, *Vol. I by Louis E. Davis and Albert B. Cherns. Copyright* © *1975 by Louis E. Davis and Albert B. Cherns.*

2

The Quality of Women's Working Life

Judith B. Agassi

THERE IS A fundamental difference in female and male work roles and a need for examination of the nature of these socially accepted sex-bound roles. Although no society is without a sex-based division of labor, there is an extraordinary variety of sex typing of occupations across cultures suggesting that the sex typing is not based on unchangeable, genetic, physiological, or psychological differences between the sexes, but is and has been a social construct. Industrialization brought a huge expansion of service occupations which, accompanied by increased education for girls, has created many more work opportunities and brought to the fore problems concerning "women's two roles." In all countries, to varying degrees, women's jobs remain inferior in matters of skill, pay, prestige, and authority. The main vehicle for maintaining this inferiority is the stereotype of femininity, held widely by members of both sexes—a stereotype in sharp conflict with women's actual success in the world of work. It is not only the pressure of norms which weakens women's commitment to work; it is also the inequality and low quality of their jobs. Several societal trends, however, are weakening these latter norms: the rise of the women's movement and concern over population growth. Women at work are not equally distributed within the economy. While some differences in sex distribution are understandable, others are due to prejudice and to the vested interests of the present predominantly male incumbents in many kinds of jobs. There is an erroneous impression in some quarters that most women's jobs are somehow better than men's: less difficult, more refined, and involving more service to others. However, women in industry are now performing the most fragmented and stressful jobs which require high levels of accuracy but offer little intrinsic interest. Most women do not compete in an open labor market; most are shunted into "women's work"—a matter of inequality and discrimination which, until recently, has been both widespread and legal.

New anti-discrimination laws in Western countries have brought some redress, but de facto discrimination is still rampant. Needed are more real choices for women in and out of the home: community support services, career ladders, and development of meaningful rewarding job designs.

It is futile to discuss the quality of women's working life without analyzing the very basic difference between the female and male work role. This requires an examination of the nature of the socially accepted sex roles today as well as an evaluation of the chances for their alteration in the future. At present, both sex roles in general and sex-based work roles in particular are in a considerable state of flux all over the Western world; not only is there intense criticism leveled against the status quo, and increasing experimentation with divergent patterns, but statistical evidence shows that we are now witnessing considerable changes in the work behavior of a large part of the female population.

The Female Work Role: Its History

One feature of the present division of labor of the sexes appears to be basic: women almost universally have the care of the children, especially infants and small children at least up to age 6 or 7. The physical care of small children does not necessarily involve either confinement to a nuclear family home or exclusive pursuit of the domestic chores of food preparation and the making and care of clothes; yet the female work role nearly always involves these services for the children and, with the exception of men who live outside a family-type household, for the male members of the family as well. In agricultural societies women also pursue "productive activities"—ranging from the gathering of food or its cultivation through horticulture, agriculture, and animal husbandry to food processing—not only for their own household but also for exchange or sale.

One thing is clear: As varied and extensive as the work activities outside the domestic sphere may have been in different societies and in various periods in time, it has been taken for granted that a married woman would first fill the domestic and child-care role, either by doing the work herself or by supervising other women doing it.

The Emergence of Women's Two Roles

Industrialization brought far-reaching changes in the world of work. On the one hand, the proportion of small independent self-employed entrepreneurs, farmers, artisans, storekeepers, merchants, and manufacturers in the population declined drastically. On the other hand, the numbers of those working for wages and salaries increased.

One immediate result of the Industrial Revolution was that masses of girls and women went into the new factories, just like men. Thus, the place of economic activity and the home became separated, and the old economic partnership between husband and wife, parents and children, became increasingly rare. Girls and women in great numbers worked in factories and in mines, for long hours under the harsh conditions of the time, often at great detriment to their own health and that of their children.

With time, however, parallel and coeducational schools began to offer formal education for girls, similar to that for boys. In addition, high industrialism brought with it the enormous expansion of the tertiary or service sector of the economy, with jobs for which girls and women often were at least as well qualified as men and which did not involve harsh physical conditions or night work that progressive labor legislation had meanwhile made illegal for women. In the United States unmarried girls streamed into offices, stores, banks, schools, and hospitals. Since World War II they ceased leaving automatically upon getting married, and those who did leave often returned several years later. More and more middle-class women married; the ratio of married women rose considerably and, also, of working married women. The problems of women's two roles—reentry into the labor market, part-time work, sex typing of occupations, widespread inequality and discrimination in hiring, training, promotion, pay, and fringe benefits—have now come to the fore.

Some Statistical Signposts toward Equalization

In industrialized countries today, the most important factor determining the rate of female participation in the labor force is society's attitude toward the employment of married women and especially of mothers: in the Netherlands and rural Norway, the opposition to their employment is still strong and only 7 and 9.5 percent of married women go out to work; the rate of female labor participants is 22.6 and 23.8 percent, respectively. In the United States and Great Britain, where norms have adapted to the "two roles," the figures are 41 percent and 39 percent, respectively. In Sweden and Finland, countries which have openly encouraged and favored their economic activity, 53 percent and 60 percent, respectively, of married women work.[1]

While everywhere more married women enter the labor force, the percentage of young girls in the labor market is declining in all those countries that have recently raised the age of compulsory and free education and increased the number of their student populations. In most Western countries, age curves of female labor participation still show a peak during the ages 15 to 25. Yet there is a change: before World War II there was a continuous decline after the age of 25, and no older age group achieved as high a labor participation; nowadays most countries still show a steep dip in the 25 to 30 age groups, but they also show a steady climb from age 35 upward. Female labor participation remains on a plateau until about age 55 or 60, the difference being largely determined by the official retirement age of women. In some countries this middle-age plateau is now as high and even higher than the peak participation of young women before motherhood.[2]

Though at present there are still many women in Western countries who do not work outside their own households, the percentage of employed married women, including mothers with children of school age, is constantly rising. Even at the present level of labor market participation, nine out of each ten baby girls will be employed during their lifetime. While these statistics point toward an equalization of women's worklife with that of men, it would be wrong to underrate the still existing inequalities and basic differences.

The Norms of Female Roles and Their Effect on Women's Commitment to Nondomestic Work

Statistics point to the increasing participation of women in productive work whose value is included in the GNP. Yet the degree of their participation remains less extensive—51 percent of the population making up 24-43 percent of the labor force in Western countries—and less intensive; many more women than men work part time. In addition, women's position in the world of "productive labor" is inferior in matters of skill, pay, prestige, and authority. It is argued here that the average intrinsic quality of women's jobs is also inferior to that of men's jobs. An obvious explanation of this situation derives from the fact that women are late-comers in the relatively open, competitive labor market; and, as usual, incumbents try to exclude newcomers from the better positions. The main vehicle for keeping them out and down has always been the stereotype of femininity, held widely by members of both sexes. This stereotype is in sharp conflict with women's success in the world of work.

Women's Preparation for Work

Women's education was until recently based on the assumptions that women's major achievement is marriage and children, not work and career; that proper feminine characteristics are supportive, nurturing qualities; that women are or should be noncompetitive, nonaggressive, passive, averse to taking responsibility and authority, concerned with nest-building but unadventurous and devoid of the capacity for abstract thinking. Therefore, the domestic sphere of activity is deemed more appropriate to women than the labor market; and if in the labor market, their proper position is in supportive, service, and routine activities.[3] The education of women results in less aspiration for careers and fewer marketable skills than that of men. Thus, for example, though more than half of the graduates from U.S. high schools are girls, they are considerably less than half of the graduates from college. Similarly, most women with higher education are either not trained for any occupation or trained for one of three major sex-typed occupations: grade-school teaching, office work, or nursing. There are few women in apprenticeships and vocational programs except domestic and secretarial subjects. Parents, counselors, and teachers have long neglected and discouraged the intensive and prolonged preparation of girls for highly skilled occupations and professions on the assumption that (1) these occupations and professions are unsuitable to feminine nature, and (2) the investment and effort are not worthwhile because of the expected short worklives of women. Employers have denied women training for positions of higher skill and responsibility using (1) the femininity argument, (2) the short worklife argument, and (3) the argument that men resent working for a woman. As a result, women are relatively less skilled, especially for positions of responsibility in technical and executive occupations, and in the professions.

Stages in Women's Life Cycle: Marriage

In several Western countries, even until quite recently, public and private employers used to dismiss female employees on marriage.[4] But, even without such drastic action, marriage very often seriously disrupts the worklife of women. Consequently, marriage for women has often meant a comedown from more skilled to less skilled work; it has tended to lessen women's aspirations and commitment to work as a career.

Birth of Children

In Western countries, in recent decades, the birth of the first child marked the stage in most women's life cycle when they left the labor market for a long period or even permanently. At this point, additional strong norms about the proper feminine role come into play, which condemn any desire of the young mother to work outside her home as both unnatural and callous.

In many Western countries a paid maternity leave of several weeks' duration, covering the period when the mother is physically unable to work, is part of accepted health and labor regulations. In the United States this progressive measure has not yet been established by law.

Thus, under present typical conditions in the West, of the nuclear family in its one-family dwelling, the mother of an infant either has to stay at home until the child can attend nursery school, if one is available—when she will barely be able to go out to part-time work or study—or has to find substitute day care by finding somebody to care for her infant in her own home or somebody else's home or an institutional group setting. A publicly supported or subsidized network of crèches (day care centers for infants) is found only in those societies or during those periods where and when the norm condemning the employment of mothers of infants has been breached. The same is true in regard to development and support of nursery school, kindergarten classes, school lunches, afternoon supervision for grade-school children, and even summer day camps.

Reentry

The pressure of the norms against mothers of young children working and the dearth of suitable child care arrangements have been counteracted by the following trends: (1) a reduction of the domestic role, (2) the rising education and expectations of women, and (3) the availability of many more jobs in the service sector. The result is the *reentry* of women at middle age (40-45 years) into employment or refresher study for employment. Since the 1950s labor statistics in many Western countries have pointed to this phenomenon and its growth.

However, more and more younger married women, from age 30 upward, are now reentering the labor market, utilizing the gradually expanding child care services as well as family and paid arrangements. Many of these younger reentrants work part time, at least at the beginning.

According to recent evidence, it may be that a growing number of young mothers in the United States have worklives with hardly any interruption; for them the pattern of an early period of work followed by several years of an exclusively domestic role and subsequent reentry into the labor market does not apply at all. The proportion of working married women in the 20 to 24 age group (husband present) with preschool children increased from 13 percent in 1951 to 33 percent in 1970.[5]

Different Groups of Women and Length of Their Work Life

As a result of the pressures of accepted norms, the most numerous group of women, the *typical* group, those getting married and bearing children with a husband present, tend on the average to have a considerably shorter worklife than men. Other groups have longer and more intensive worklives: women with children who have no husband to support them (divorced, deserted, unmarried, or with a handicapped husband) tend to work longer years, in spite of their heavy domestic and child-rearing responsibilities, because they have a strong economic motive and because society's norms are not opposed to their working—or even demand it to prevent their dependence on welfare. Women who are married, remain married, but are childless have even longer worklives, nearly as long as those of men. Finally, the worklives of single and childless women are even longer than those of men. While this group is also heavily concentrated in women's occupations, it nevertheless contains a larger percentage of women in positions of responsibility, authority, and higher incomes than do working women in general.[6] In the past a good number of women with a strong commitment to work—for example, professionals—remained single for the express purpose of pursuing their careers. As long as the norm prescribed firing women teachers and civil servants when they got married, only single women had a chance to advance to positions of authority in these occupations. And, lastly, men considered the confirmed spinster a woman somewhat outside the conventional norm of femininity and, therefore, more suitable for positions of responsibility.

The Female Role, Commitment, and Motivation to Work

As we have seen, the effect of the pressure of accepted norms about the female role as wife and mother has been and still is weakening women's commitment to work careers. It is, of course, not only the pressure of the norms which weakens women's commitment to work; it is also the pressures of inequality and low quality of jobs. A number of societal trends are weakening these norms, such as the rise of the women's movement, the ecology movement's denouncement of population growth, the establishment of effective methods of birth control, the liberalization of sex mores, and the severe criticism of shortcomings of the contemporary nuclear family. As to the inequality and low quality of women's jobs, these aspects are still rather underrated as factors reducing women's commitment to work.

As to motivation, most working women, as most working men, declare income as the major motive for work.[7] Working women's income is of considerable economic importance, even when it is additional to the husband's. In many families, it is a woman's income which makes the difference between poverty and sufficiency or between lower- and middle-class living standards. Moreover, many working women are heads of families, and often sex discrimination is the major cause of their poverty. Indeed, the major difference between men and women as far as motivation to work is concerned is not their wish to earn money, but the obstacles that society places in the way of women working at all, working full time, and earning a "living wage."

It would be very useful to know more about the factors which influence women's commitment as well as expectations and attitudes toward work. Yet, to this end it would be necessary to (1) examine meticulously women's family situations, their own and their husbands' views about women's work outside the home, their own work history, and the characteristics of their present jobs; (2) relate all this to women's perception and evaluation of the characteristics of their jobs, both "hygiene" and task characteristics; and finally (3) compare results with those of a male control group.

Present Content and Quality of Women's Work

Many have extolled the virtues of the "homemaker's" work role: the relevance of her work to the well-being of those nearest and dearest to her; the pleasant work conditions; the freedom to organize her own work and take breaks, and the variety of her tasks as cook, maid, baby nurse, educator, chauffeur, gardener, and often also bookkeeper. Yet critics from the women's movement condemn this work outright as subordinate, of low skill, limited and limiting, dirty, and unpaid.[8] Being housebound, women feel lonely and out of the mainstream of modern life. The repetitiveness and noncumulativeness of the housewife's work and the nonpermanence of her product, permit her little sense of achievement. In addition, the modern housewife is frustrated because it is hard for her to evaluate her own work performance and because society rewards her work with neither suitable recognition nor pay.

The Unequal Distribution of Women over the Occupations

Women are not equally distributed in the economy.[9] In the United States, official labor statistics divide all occupational groups into eleven categories: for men the two most populous categories (nearly equal in size) are craftsmen and foremen, and operatives, together occupying about 40 percent of all working men. Yet for women, by far the largest category, over 34 percent, is that of clerical workers (only 6.3 percent of men and the seventh category), followed by service workers except in private households, about 18 percent. The most striking difference between men and women here is that the category of craftsmen and foremen ranks ninth for women, comprising only 1.5 percent of all employed women. For men the category of managers, officials, and proprietors is the third largest, accounting for about 13 percent of the male "productive" population; for women this category ranks sixth, not quite 5 percent. Professional and technical occupations constitute the third category for women, 15.1 percent, and the fourth for men, 14.3 percent; this is the fastest growing among all categories. The fourth category for women is operatives, a category which declined slightly in importance during the sixties but has recently increased again. The fifth category for women comprises sales occupations—eighth for men—employing about 7 percent of working women who make up about 40 percent of this entire group. The seventh occupational category for women, about 4 percent, is that of private household workers, a nearly exclusively female occupation where women account for about 96 percent of the total. Significantly, it is the third—17 percent—for black women; it is also the category with the lowest pay, where work tends to be intermittent, and where workers are neither covered by minimum wage and hour laws nor benefit from unemployment and workmen's compensation.

Which other occupational categories are predominantly female? Women hold 73 percent of all clerical jobs, and 57 percent of all service jobs (except private household). Among professional and technical workers and among sales workers, women exceed slightly the average for all occupations.

From statistical evidence regarding these eleven major occupational categories one cannot learn much about the content, characteristics, and quality of women's jobs. One can see, however, that women are nearly excluded from those manual jobs in manufacturing industry that demand higher skill and training, and from industrial jobs that carry some authority and responsibility. One can see also that women in the United States are severely underrepresented in the category of managers, officials, and proprietors, and in that of farmers and farm managers, whose work role is characterized by a considerable degree of authority and responsibility and often also of initiative and autonomy. In the category which increasingly provides the largest number of jobs demanding considerable specific skills and constant use of knowledge, judgment, and initiative—professional and technical jobs—women now seem to keep pace with men.

In official labor statistics the eleven categories are grouped into four large categories: "manual," "white collar," "service," and "farm work." As over 48 percent of all working men (and only 16 percent of women) do "manual" work, as the largest group of working women (nearly 60 percent) perform "white collar" jobs, and as nearly 22 percent of the rest perform "service" jobs, the erroneous impression has been created that most women's jobs are somehow better than men's: less difficult, less dirty, more refined, involving more formal education, and more service to human beings. Yet an examination of the 36 occupations, in each of which more than 100,000 women worked in 1960,[10] reveals that manual jobs amounted to well over 6 million and brainwork jobs to over 4 million, while about 3 1/3 million jobs involved a mixture of both, with the manual part usually predominant. Obviously, all clerical jobs were officially counted as white-collar jobs, whereas in reality some clerical occupations of women are largely manual (typist, file clerk, keypunch operator); most of the female "service" jobs are either semiskilled operatives' jobs—for example, in laundries—or outright unskilled cleaning jobs. Most of the lower—near exclusively female—jobs in education and health services, such as teacher's aide, nurse's aide, and practical nurse, are largely manual. The confusion is enhanced by the fact that the largest male occupational group of "craftsmen and foremen" is traditionally classified as manual, yet nowadays their work often includes a considerable amount of paperwork and even of brainwork. In conclusion, there exists absolutely no evidence for the assumption that the totality of women's jobs is comparatively more stimulating mentally than those of men.

Sex Typing of Occupations and the Dual Labor Market

Women are concentrated in a rather narrow range of occupations; or, in other words, a very large number of working women are employed in occupations stereotyped as female occupations. If we consider not the four or eleven large statistical categories of jobs, but more specific occupations, we shall see that nearly two thirds of working women are concentrated in only 36 out of hundreds of occupations, and one third in only 7 occupations: secretary, saleswoman in retail trade, private household worker, grade-school teacher, bookkeeper, waitress, professional nurse. The first three occupations—secretary, saleswoman, and private household worker—are large groups, each with well over a million workers;[11] the next three, grade-school teacher, bookkeeper, waitress, with over 700,000; the seventh, eighth, and ninth occupations—professional nurse, sewer and stitcher in industry, and typist—each have more than a half million workers. In addition, nearly all the 36 occupations which employ more than 100,000 women are also typical "women's occupations," where women make up over 50 percent of the membership; only 4 have less than 50 percent, and all have more than the 40 percent that would be proportional to the rate of women in the labor force. The sex typing of occupations is extreme: in 19 occupations, women make up 90 percent or more; in 8, from 80-89 percent, and in another 7, from 75-79 percent of the total employed. In 1960 at least 59 percent of the female labor force was in occupations where women comprised 70 percent or more of the workers.[12]

How does an activity or occupation become a female enclave? Much of this development is lost in history, yet we can look at more recent examples whose history we can still trace. A few occupations became women's occupations in times when male labor was short, and female labor was cheaper and sometimes also better qualified. Thus, at the time of the American Civil War, male schoolteachers were in short supply and young women took their jobs at a cheaper rate. At the turn of the century when the typewriter appeared on the scene in America, young men who could spell English were scarce; young women who could spell moved into the new occupations of typist and secretary. Once an occupation is sex typed as "women's work," men tend to shy away from it and the differentiation becomes even more pronounced.

How much did physiological differences contribute initially to this occupational differentiation? With the rise of modern industry new traditions evolved. Those branches of industry which originally demanded much muscle power became male preserves, and have remained so even after further mechanization made such power redundant. In addition, a tradition evolved according to which women (and little girls) should be assigned to those industries where smaller and more delicate fingers seemed more useful, as, for example, in the spinning mills. Thus this part of the textile industry became women's work. Yet the hypothesis that female sex-typed occupations are simply extensions of the domestic role—that is, the processing of food and the manufacture of clothes—is false: the entire "apparel" or "needletrades" industry including shirt making and men's suits became a women's industry only after the old craft skills had become less important and the work had turned into low-skilled, routine production. The few remaining skilled jobs in these industries—namely, maintenance, setting up, pattern making, and cutting—remain reserved for men. Likewise, the technologically-advanced production of flour, bread, beer, and sugar are male enclaves.[13]

The following is an important characteristic of sex-typed jobs, yet one systematically overlooked in industry today: women are concentrated in those branches where the characteristics of the material—such as limp cloth and foodstuffs, or the extreme smallness of the parts to be processed and assembled, as in electric bulbs or electronic circuits—pose considerable difficulties for automation. Women in industry are now performing the most fragmented, accurate, and straining jobs. This has been explained by the contention that women have natural qualities of passivity, like routine and repetition, have a penchant for accuracy, a dislike of initiative and responsibility, and also fear mathematics and mechanics. In fact, these are not "natural" qualities; rather, women are still ready to take low quality and dead-end jobs because their commitment to work as a career is weaker than men's. They are ready to work in the poorly paid jobs of declining industries because frequently their income supplements the larger one of a husband.

The common characteristic of typical female occupations (and of women's specializations in otherwise male occupations and professions) is that of low prestige. Whenever a previously high-prestige occupation becomes female sex-typed—for example, medicine in the U.S.S.R.—it declines in prestige as well as in pay, conditions of work, and quality of task characteristics.[14] Even in those professions which have become women's work (e.g., teaching and social work), the higher, more prestigious positions remain reserved for men.

Sex typing in nearly all cases is unjustifiable—at least, no longer justifiable. Yet, the sex typing of jobs divides the labor market, creating a "dual labor market." Women do not compete in an open labor market; most are shunted into "women's work" and there compete with other women. This dual labor market facilitates inequality and discrimination.

Inequality and Discrimination

Until quite recently, outright and open discrimination against working women was widespread and legal. Women were excluded from entire occupations, from branches of industries, and from the higher reaches of other occupations simply by not hiring them or accepting them for training. Separate job advertising was the rule. The assumption, of course, was that these occupations were unsuitable for women. Likewise, open pay differentials for equal work (e.g., for identical positions in the Civil Service) were the practice; here the official justification was that women "needed" less money.

During the last two decades, however, one Western country after another has signed international and national nondiscrimination laws. Gradually, these laws have led to some practical results. Practices such as open exclusion from hiring and training, separate posting, and open pay differentials are gradually disappearing when challenged in the courts. But de facto discrimination and de facto pay differentials are still rampant. Women's income in the United States is only 62 percent of men's after adjustments have been made for level of education, occupational status, and part-time employment—according to the latest study of income differences.[15] Official figures for those Western countries that publish them range from 60 percent in Great Britain to 79 percent in Sweden, and are usually lower than the national average for women operatives in industry and somewhat higher in clerical and professional and technical jobs.

In Great Britain, even recently, many unions still concluded lower pay agreements for their women members.[16] Some cantons in Switzerland still officially maintain lower salaries for their women employees.[17] Yet today the main devices for paying women less are the hiring and segregation of women into special (all female) wage groups or separate all-female job classifications, so as to avoid the situation where women do "equal work" with men in the same firm; starting all male entrants automatically two or three wage levels above that of female entrants; not giving women chances at training and promotion; not appointing women to supervisory or administrative positions—all these devices, together with the social sex typing of occupations, keep women in a separate and inferior labor market.

What Is Needed to Enhance the Quality of Women's Working Life?

The Problem of Enhancement or Reduction of the Domestic Work Role

Is reduction or compensation for the domestic work role necessary for all women? It is quite likely that a certain number of women with strong domestic and especially strong maternal leanings can be largely satisfied and psychologically well adjusted to a prolonged or even a lifetime domestic work role. It is wrong to denigrate these women and press them into career work roles which do not suit them. Women should be neither pressured nor confined into an exclusive domestic or a full-time lifetime labor market role, but should have the choice between them. It is to be assumed that for the foreseeable future most women will aim at some combination of the two roles; day care centers will greatly facilitate this.

Most women today and in the foreseeable future will still have to fill a considerable domestic work role, and most are no longer satisfied by this role alone. Women, like men, seek work for satisfaction of the psychological needs of self-actualization, achievement, recognition, and social contact, in addition to pay; for many, these needs are no longer met by the exclusive domestic work role. Yet most women's jobs, just like most men's jobs, also fail to satisfy these needs and therefore should be redesigned.[18] Many women's jobs have certain characteristics that are especially harmful because they compound the same characteristics existing in the domestic work role: the domestic role demands very little intellectual exercise, so do most women's jobs; domestic work requires a lot of routine and repetition, women's jobs are the most repetitious in the labor market; the housewife's products are without permanence, women are concentrated in the production of nondurables; domestic work consists largely of personal cleaning and feeding services, women are concentrated in cleaning and feeding jobs; housewives suffer from lack of achievement and recognition, most women's jobs lead nowhere. In order to compensate for the domestic work role, women's jobs should be intellectually challenging: women should design, produce, and maintain more durable artifacts; deliver personal services other than just cleaning and feeding; have built-in chances for achievement, advancement, responsibility, and recognition.

What Is Needed to Eliminate Present Inferior Work Roles?

The low quality of so many women's jobs is a direct outcome of the segregation of women into a separate labor market of separate occupations, branches, and departments. A conscious effort should be made to break the sex typing of occupations; male entrants should be welcomed to the female occupations; women should gain training and entrance into previously closed or restricted occupations, especially those technologically advanced and expanding, into government, business, finance, and the professions. It should become illegal to hire women into separate job groups and pay female entrants less than male entrants. Women should demand open posting of jobs within the firm and information about qualifications needed for all jobs. They should not be excluded from any job because of obligatory overtime or night work. Women in part-time work should not be paid less per hour than in full-time work; they should have the right to proportionate fringe benefits, including pension rights. Paid maternity leave should be incorporated into labor laws of all nations. Women workers should have a right to additional optional unpaid maternity leave with job security. They should also be given the right to a period of optional part-time work without loss of pension, training, and seniority rights.

There are those who claim that as long as most women adhere to the pattern of withdrawal and reentry and/or periods of part-time work, they will not be able to overcome their relatively inferior position. In the light of recent changes in male work patterns, this seems no longer inevitable; the rigid, full-time plus overtime, year-round, uninterrupted worklife in one and the same occupation is no longer sacrosanct. Flexible work time, four-day work weeks, optional overtime, training leaves, sabbaticals, mid-career changes, all these are breaking up the conventional male work pattern. Therefore, it should not be too difficult to gain full legitimation for the female work pattern; discrimination justified by the difference between male and female work patterns should not be tolerated.

Viable Career Ladders for Women

Until now, careers for women were not the norm. That women should acquire more experience and skill and progress gradually to positions of greater challenge, responsibility, status, and pay was not considered necessary.

Women's jobs were considered as simply "jobs," not as steps in a career ladder. A young woman is hired for a sales job as a salesclerk, a young man as a "management trainee"; most young women enter business as typists, file clerks, receptionists, switchboard and telephone operators, keypunch operators, cashiers, bookkeepers, and secretaries with little prospect that their work role will ever become much more challenging and responsible. Reform of women's clerical jobs demands the breaking down of the barrier separating them from management or administrative skills.

The rapidly expanding health and education sectors are rigidly stratified, with women occupying the lowest menial and the middle semiprofessional levels while the top professional, administrative, and research positions are nearly exclusively taken by men. Each level is rigidly separated from the other with no chance to rise upward. In the West, until recently, this was considered perfectly in accord with "nature"—as men should be doctors and women, nurses. Men teach in schools of education, draw up curricula, are school principals, and inspect schools; women carry out their plans and follow their instructions as teachers; women from the working classes act as nurses' aides, teachers' aides, practical nurses, and do the cleaning, laundry, and kitchen chores in schools and hospitals.

In order to improve the quality of the numerous women's jobs in the fields of health and education, it is essential to open up career ladders. First attempts in this field resulted from the realization that recruiting welfare mothers into low-status, low-pay health jobs without any prospects was futile. Therefore, attempts were made through teamwork, on-the-job training, and special training to let low-level workers acquire paramedical and social relations skills and thus enhance their jobs; to open up avenues of advancement to nurses through the acquisition of preventive health and administrative skills and take on responsibility for the organization and administration of entire community health teams.[19] Another attempt was to open up a new avenue reaching into the sacred precincts of the physician through the physician-assistant program. Men and especially women with practical health care experience and a minimum of undergraduate-level science courses can, through an 18-month course, become assistant medical practitioners.[20]

Such breaking down of barriers and establishing of career ladders should also be attempted in the fields of education, social work, and librarianship. Even private household work can be improved through the establishment of a skill ladder; the skills needed for it are at present undefined and it is treated as unskilled work. A Belgian experiment has shown that by training and accreditation for such domestic activities as laundry work, cooking and serving meals, baby care, and so on, and assuring the trainees of placement and wage rates in accordance with the number of skills acquired, even these jobs can be greatly improved in competence, dignity, and pay.[21]

The Improvement of the Mass of Existing Women's Jobs

The large majority of women's jobs in manufacturing, laundries, restaurants, typing pools, keypunching, and billing are fragmented, repetitive, regimented, and mindless, without room for initiative and judgment. Women have a disproportionate share in assembly work, eye-straining work, basic work cycles of a few seconds only, and pay by piece rate. Their knowledge and skills are greatly underutilized. Factory operatives with a high school diploma are treated as if they could neither read nor write, much less think. Clerks with a B.A. degree are not permitted to compose a letter or sign it. Telephone operators are made to use set phrases.

Job enrichment experiments of clerical positions in industry, banks, and telephone companies have shown that without major technical changes many clerical service jobs can be greatly improved by letting the individual employee take over a meaningful portion of the service process, such as comprehensive relations with a number of customers, stockholders, or subscribers, and granting her maximum autonomy within this area. Other clerical jobs have been improved by the autonomous or semiautonomous work group method—encouragement of multiple skill acquisition, rotation of activities, scheduling and responsibility for product or service quality within the group—again without major changes in the physical layout of the office.[22]

A much more comprehensive and exciting model of the improvement of clerical jobs is the office team of the General Foods plant in Topeka, Kansas.[23] Here a team of ten persons (seven women and three men) work according to the autonomous work group method: moreover, they have entirely done away with the traditional status barriers between (1) lower-skill office work, such as switchboard, typing, filing, and keypunching; (2) mid-level secretarial work for management, specialized clerical work such as payroll, materials ordering, or billing; and (3) the semiprofessional work involving corporation law and state labor law problems, usually considered managerial. Everybody performs the low-level chores for herself or himself, takes turns at the switchboard, and is encouraged to train even for managerial skills to the limit of her or his wish and capability.

Experience of the redesign of women's industrial and manual service jobs is still very scanty. Even in progressive firms such as Texas Instruments in the United States,[24] Olivetti in Italy,[25] or Philips in the Netherlands, where considerable efforts have been made to enhance the quality of men's jobs, little or nothing has as yet changed in the women's departments, where tiny, often microscopic components are being spot-welded, assembled, and checked. An interesting exception is the Philips experiment, which let groups of women devise a new group method of assembling tiny electrical bulbs.[26] In assembly of larger components, there is the Norwegian electrical heater experiment in which women of rural background successfully cooperated with men in the operation of autonomous work groups, gradually attempting technically more demanding activities as well as approaching positions of responsibility.[27] In the United States there is the experiment of the Corning Glass plant in Medfield, Massachusetts, where women operatives assemble individually entire hot plates and medical instruments or, in the case of large and more complicated instruments, work in semiautonomous groups—in both cases doing away with the traditional fragmentation and lack of initiative of typical women's industrial jobs.[28]

Areas in which there is still lack of or scant experience and which might pose considerable need of changing the technical system are (1) industrial jobs which involve the handling of microscopic components, such as in electric bulbs and electronic circuits, and accurate eye-hand coordination; and (2) jobs in technically backward and often declining industries such as large parts of the needletrades and food-processing industries. Here women perform enormously fragmented and repetitive activities which involve considerable manual dexterity and speed. In both areas basic improvement may hinge on the automation of many processes now performed by hand using electric hand tools, tending, connecting up, and correcting the work of isolated and often unsatisfactory semiautomated machinery.[29] In both areas, too, competition is keen from Third World countries where both men and women are still ready to perform these low-quality jobs for considerably lower wages than in the West. Therefore, many prosperous United States firms tend to transfer their electronic assembly departments to such countries and declining textile, needletrades, or food industries rely on remaining rural, minority, or immigrant female labor, paying the lowest wages in industry; both groups are reluctant to invest sizeable sums in developing new automated machinery, in spite of the fact that prototypes do exist and that some are already in operation in Japan, Germany, and even Israel.[30] Perhaps some government encouragement such as special tax concessions or, for small firms, the establishment of cooperative modernized facilities, would be necessary to induce management to embark on this needed technological modernization; at this point government tax concessions or other assistance could be made contingent on management's agreement to the redesign and radical improvement of the quality of women operatives' jobs.

Conclusion: Urgent Need for Research and Coordination of Reform Attempts

The reform of women's work life is still in its beginnings; most reformers have not treated it as a specific object with conditions and problems that are different from those of men's work life. Those fighting discrimination against women and struggling to erase women's inequality in the world of work often have not considered sufficiently the wider goal, the enhancement of women's overall working life. Researchers concerned with women's jobs need exchange of experience and coordination among themselves. The efforts of quality of working life reformers need coordination and exchange of experience with fighters for women's rights.

Both groups are in dire need of more reliable information about a wide range of characteristics of women's jobs and women's reactions to them: what characteristics hurt them most; to what extent they are ready to press for changes and train for more responsible jobs; what part of the female population prefers the exclusive domestic role and what are their characteristics; more comparative individual, family, and detailed work histories, in order to better analyze trends of change in women's work behavior; how individual work experience, education, family conditions, national and ethnic background, husband's attitudes, and influence of the views propagated by the women's movement affect women's attitudes toward and expectations from work.

There is still an enormous amount of outright male resistance to the upgrading of women's position in the world of work; but there is also a large amount of simple ignorance and confusion about what different groups of women want and need. And this can and should be overcome.

Footnotes

1. International Labor Organization, Organization for Economic Cooperation and Development, country statistical yearbooks, and censuses. Compiled by Marjorie Galenson, *Women and Work* (Ithaca, N.Y.: Cornell University Press, 1973), p. 18.

2. Based on "Labor-Force Participation Rates of Women by Age," in Galenson, *op. cit.*, pp. 17, 20.

3. A recent and comprehensive statement claiming that this stereotype is based on the genetic inferiority of females in aggressiveness and in abstract thinking and that therefore girls should not be socialized to compete with males is in Steven Goldberg, *The Inevitability of Patriarchy* (New York: Morrow, 1973).

4. Thus in the Netherlands only "the legal requirement that women retire on marriage has been removed in government service and in public school teaching" has recently been abolished, "but there are still clauses in private union agreements giving the employer the right to discharge a female employee if she marries. Teachers in Holland's many private schools are among those subject to such provisions. The maternity protection tax on employers, to finance compulsory maternity leaves, encourages employers to fire married women." In "Switzerland which has failed to ratify the ILO's Equal Remuneration Convention . . . marriage may constitute grounds for discharge from federal employment." Galenson, *op. cit.*, pp. 77, 79. In the period of mass unemployment of the thirties, public opinion in most Western countries was in favor of dismissal of women on marriage.

5. Valerie Kincade Oppenheimer, "Demographic Influence on Female Employment and the Status of Women," in Joan Huber (ed.), *Changing Women in a Changing Society* (Chicago: University of Chicago Press, 1973), p. 185.

6. Elizabeth M. Havens, "Women, Work, and Wedlock: A Note on Female Marital Patterns in the United States," in Huber, *op. cit.*, pp. 213-218.

7. Women's Bureau, U.S. Department of Labor, *Handbook* for 1969, p. 8, reports the economic reason as crucial; also, Canada Department of Labor, *Occupational Histories of Married Women*, 1960, p. 64, comes to the same conclusion.

8. An early yet trenchant analysis of the work of the housewife can be found in Charlotte Perkins Gilman, *Women and Economics* (Boston: Small Maynard, 6th ed., 1913), pp. 67-75, 157 (1st ed., 1898).

9. Subsequent statistics are compiled from *Employment and Earnings*, 20, no. 1 (July 1973).

10. Unfortunately, this detailed statistic has not yet been updated; it appears in U.S. Department of Labor, *op. cit.*, p. 96.

11. These are 1960 figures; the absolute number of private household workers has since declined, but it is still among the six largest.

12. Valerie Kincade Oppenheimer, *The Female Labor Force in the United States. Demographic and Economic Factors Governing Its Growth and Changing Composition*, Population Monograph Series No. 5 (Berkeley: University of California Press, 1970), p. 75; according to Oppenheimer, *op. cit.*, 1973, p. 187, there has been

no decline in the concentration of women in the traditional female occupations and it may even be greater.

13. For the unequal distribution of women over the food industry and its relation to the state of technological development, see *Employment and Earnings*, 20, no. 2 (August 1973), p. 63.

14. Excellent illustrations of this process can be found in Alexander Solzhenitsyn, *Cancer Ward*.

15. Larry E. Suter and Herman P. Miller, "Incomes of Men and Career Women," in Huber, *op. cit.*, p. 208.

16. Galenson, *op. cit.*, p. 41.

17. Ibid., p. 77.

18. Until recently it has been claimed that, notwithstanding the low quality of most women's jobs, surveys demonstrated that women were mostly satisfied with their jobs; it was implied that women were satisfied with jobs that men were not. See Galenson, *op. cit.*, p. 42, quoting a 1967 British Ministry of Labour survey of working mothers, 92 percent stating they were either very or fairly satisfied with their jobs; p. 68, quoting a 1966 Helsinki interview study of married couples: although the wives' earnings were only 60 percent of their husbands', they were nevertheless more satisfied with their work. Yet the recent Michigan University Survey Center's national sample work satisfaction survey, reported in Harold L. Sheppard and Neal Q. Herrick, *Where Have All the Robots Gone?*, found higher rates of job dissatisfaction for women than for men in all age groups. Apparently, there exists as yet no survey of work satisfaction/dissatisfaction of women and men in jobs as similar as possible.

19. See Suzzanne B. Greenberg, "Curriculum Development and Training for Community Health Workers," *Comprehensive Health Services, Career Development, Technical Assistance Bulletin*, 1, no. 7 (May 1970), pp. 1-8.

20. See *Bulletin*, Northeastern University, Physician Assistant Program.

21. Personal observation, in Brussels during the 1950s.

22. Frederick Herzberg, "One More Time: How Do You Motivate Employees," *Harvard Business Review*, January-February 1968, pp. 59-60; see also W.J. Paul and K.B. Robertson, *Job Enrichment and Employee Motivation* (London, Gower Press, 1970).

23. Personal observation, August 1973.

24. Personal observation, 1969.

25. Personal observation, March 1972.

26. Described by its initiator, H.P. Vossen, "Experiment in the Miniature Bulb Department of the Terneuzen Works of Philips in the Netherlands," unpublished paper, April 1972.

27. Described by L.A. Ødegaard, "Summary of Third Field Experiment," Industrial Democracy Project, Phase B, unpublished paper.

28. See Michael Beer and Edgar F. Huse, "A Systems Approach to Organization Development," *Journal of Applied Behavioral Science*, 8, no. 1 (1972).

29. These kinds of typical women's industrial jobs are described by Judith Buber Agassi, "Women Who Work in Factories," *Dissent*, Winter 1972, pp. 233-236. See also Ulrike Marie Meinhof, "Frauen sind billiger," *Frankfurter Hefte*, June 6, 1967, and Jean Tepperman, "Two Jobs: Women Who Work in Factories," in Robin Morgan (ed.), *Sisterhood Is Powerful* (New York: Random House, 1970), pp. 115-124.

30. The introduction of much more advanced textile and needletrades machinery than that used currently in most U.S. plants has been reported from these countries.

Raymond Munts *is professor of social work and assistant director of the Institute for Research on Poverty, and* David C. Rice *is a law student, University of Michigan.*

This article is reprinted with permission from the Industrial and Labor Relations Review, *Vol. 24, No. 1 (October 1970).* Copyright © 1970 by Cornell University. All rights reserved.

3
Women Workers: Protection or Equality?

Raymond Munts and David C. Rice

DURING THE reform period of the decade preceding World War I, states began enacting protective laws for workers. This was acclaimed widely as a public victory over unchecked industrialization. Some of these laws apply only to women, regulating their hours of work and conditions of employment. Now legislatures and courts are taking a new look at women's protective law at the urging of those who feel such legislation restricts women's access to certain jobs and places women at a disadvantage in competing with men. The Equal Employment Opportunity Commission claims that Title VII of the Civil Rights Act of 1964 invalidates women's protective law because it prohibits employment discrimination based on sex. This amendment was added to the Civil Rights Act during congressional debate and was regarded, at the time, as a mere maneuver intended to block passage of the Act, but the ultimate fate of female protective law may turn on the primacy of this federal statute.

State Laws Regulating Aspects of Women's Employment

With the rapid growth of industry, finance, and commerce at the end of the nineteenth century, women entered the labor force in substantial numbers. By 1900 the five million female employees constituted 18 percent of the labor force. Public attention was directed by the National Consumers' League and others to the long hours, low wages, and miserable conditions of many working women. Immigration and rapid urbanization had provided an overabundance of female "help." With few skills, low mobility, and no union protection, women were easily exploited. In the reform movement which began about 1900 as a response to unchecked industrial expansion, legislative protection for women and children laborers was a prominent theme.

The reformers argued vigorously for laws limiting the hours of employment for women. By 1913, twenty-seven states had created maximum weekly or daily hours to protect the "health and morals" of women.[1] The constitutionality of using state police power in this way was upheld in *Muller* v. *Oregon* (1908), the case in which Louis Brandeis as counsel for the State of Oregon first introduced the "sociological brief." He built his case almost entirely on the testimony of doctors, sociologists, and economists. Judge Brewer, speaking for the court, acknowledged the "abundant testimony of the medical fraternity" and added,

> History discloses the fact that woman has always depended upon man. . . . Though limitations upon personal and contractual rights be removed by legislation, there is that in her disposition and habits of life which will operate against a full assertion of those rights. She will still be where some legislation to protect her seems necessary to secure a real equality of right. . . . Differentiated by these matters from the other sex, she is properly placed in a class by herself, and legislation designed for her protection may be sustained . . . her physical structure and a proper discharge of her maternal functions—having in view not merely her own health, but the well-being of the race—justify legislation to protect her from the greed as well as the passion of man.[2]

Although today it has a ring of quaint chivalry, this is still the best statement of principle behind standards governing women's hours of employment. At their peak, in 1967, these laws existed in forty-six states, the District of Columbia, and Puerto Rico.

Some standards were established by statute; others were the orders of minimum wage or industrial commission boards. The standards apply to maximum daily or weekly hours, days of rest, meal and rest periods, and limitations on night work.

Minimum wage legislation for women has a quite different history. Eight laws were enacted in 1912 and 1913 and eight more in the next ten years, but these efforts came to naught in 1923 when they were declared unconstitutional in *Adkins* v. *Children's Hospital*. The decision in this case provides the best statement of the "equality" argument which always has existed as an antithesis to the "protection" argument. Justice Sutherland's argument in the Adkins case occurred in a climate of significant social change brought by World War I. The end of large-scale immigration and war-time pressures for production had brought higher wages, better conditions, and new jobs for women in both the government and private sectors. In addition to their new economic opportunities, women had won the right to vote.

> The Muller decision proceeded upon the theory that the difference between the sexes may justify a different rule respecting hours in the case of women than in the case of men. . . . In view of the great—not to say revolutionary—changes which have taken place since that utterance, in the contractual, political, and civil status of women, culminating in the 19th Amendment, it is not unreasonable to say that these differences have now come almost, if not quite, to the vanishing point . . . *we cannot accept the doctrine that women of mature age, sui juris, require or may be subjected to restrictions upon their liberty of contract which could not be imposed in the case of men under similar circumstances.* To do so would be to ignore all the implications to be drawn from the present-day trend of legislation, as well as that of common thought and usage, by which woman is accorded emancipation from the old doctrine that she must be given special protection or be subjected to special restraint in her contractual and civil relationships.[3]

Thus began a period of fifteen years of ambivalence in public policy with one set of legal precedents supporting state law limiting women's hours and another group denying women minimum wages. The ambivalence was resolved with the crucial one-vote shift on the Supreme Court which followed the 1936 election and the Court "packing" fight. The case involved a hotel chambermaid, Elsie Parrish, who sued for pay due under a hitherto unenforced Washington state minimum-wage. The argument of the court was an echo of the argument in *Muller* v.

Oregon: "What can be closer," said Chief Justice Hughes, "to the public interest than the health of women and their protection from unscrupulous and overreaching employers? . . . how can it be said that the requirement of the payment of a minimum wage fairly fixed in order to meet the very necessities of existence is not an admissible means to that end?"[4] *Adkins* v. *Children's Hospital* was overthrown, and protection of women's wages took its place alongside protection of their hours. As a result of the Parrish decision and the subsequent enactment of the Fair Labor Standards Act, many states adopted minimum-wage laws. In 1970 forty jurisdictions provide minimum wages, of which seven apply to women (or women and minors) only and seven others have some provisions applying to women only. Twenty-six of the minimum wage laws have premium-pay-for-overtime provisions, four of which apply to women only; there are other states in which the premium pay for women is found in separate statutes which limit hours of work for women.[5]

In addition to hours and minimum-wage laws, protection for women workers has found expression in statutes governing industrial homework, regulating employment before and after childbirth, prohibiting female workers from entering some occupations, establishing requirements for seating, and imposing restrictions on weight-lifting.[6]

The critics of this legislative history argue that such laws, by making a distinction based on sex, open the door to discrimination. They point out that the Fourteenth Amendment to the U.S. Constitution guarantees equal protection of the laws, but if sex is a valid basis for classification, the meaning of equal protection of the laws for women is defeated.[7]

Title VII and the Equal Rights Movement

The sixty-year tradition of protective laws for women is being challenged by Title VII of the Civil Rights Act of 1964. The Civil Rights bill was introduced in the House of Representatives without any mention of "sex." While the bill was before the House Judiciary Committee, Howard Smith of Virginia decided to add an amendment which would assure its defeat—equal rights for women. His strategy backfired—both the amendment and the bill passed—and the law became effective July 2, 1965. It is interesting that no women's group petitioned for or supported the sex amendment to Title VII.[8]

The trivial circumstances leading to enactment of the sex provision of Title VII and the profound changes it eventually may bring appear to qualify as historical accident. Such a conclusion, however, would overlook a tradition of "equal rights" which has long been a counterpoint to the prevailing protectionist policy. Every year since 1923 an "Equal Rights Amendment" has been proposed to the federal Constitution. This amendment covers the ground of Title VII but goes beyond, providing that "Equality of rights under law shall not be denied or abridged by the United States or by any state on account of sex." Its proponents have argued that economic progress has made protective legislation for women obsolete and that the real effect of such law now is to disadvantage women by providing a basis for discrimination under the guise of safety and welfare legislation.

Although the amendment has not been enacted, interest has continued, and in 1961 a Presidential Commission on the Status of Women further investigated these questions. The Commission recommended that minimum-wage and working standards be extended to men as well as women and emphasized premium overtime pay as the way of limiting hours. Until universally applicable standards could come into being, the Commission urged retention of present laws. It also asked for greater flexibility in regard to weight-lifting restrictions, night work, and occupational limitations.[9]

The Commission endorsed the idea of an equal pay law, an objective long sought by the labor movement, women's groups, and the U.S. Department of Labor. The Equal Pay Act was enacted in 1963. It amended the Fair Labor Standards Act to require that each covered employer pay equal wage rates to men and women doing equal work.[10] At the state level, some dozen states and the District of Columbia now include clauses prohibiting sex discrimination in their fair employment practice statutes (only two of which were enacted prior to the Civil Rights Act), and twenty-nine states have equal pay laws.[11]

However, it is the amended Civil Rights Act of 1964 which is doing most to bring the equal rights philosophy to bear on labor legislation. Coverage of Title VII, which deals with discrimination in employment, is extended to four major groups: (1) employers of twenty-five or more persons, (2) public and private employment agencies dealing with employers of twenty-five or more persons, (3) labor unions with twenty-five or more members or which operate hiring halls, and (4) joint labor-management apprenticeship programs.

The specifications directly applicable to women are those which prohibit any employer, union, or employment agency from discriminating in hiring or firing; wages, terms, conditions, or privileges of employment; classifying, assigning, or promoting employees; extending or assigning use of facilities; and training, retraining, and apprenticeships.

The most important issue in administering the sex discrimination provision of Title VII has been the interpretation of the "bona fide occupation qualification" exception which provides exceptions to Title VII where the employment of members of only one sex is reasonably necessary for the normal operation of a particular business or enterprise. Immediately after passage, this exception assumed great importance as the only meaningful defense to a sex discrimination complaint and it was interpreted by some to be a "saving exception."[1][2] In fact, however, the Equal Employment Opportunity Commission (EEOC), established by Title VII to interpret and apply its provisions, has construed the bona fide occupational qualification very restrictively. As with the rest of the problems created by Title VII, it ". . . remains for the judiciary to set a final standard for the scope of the exemption, and to pass on the problem of what types of evidence will be relevant in establishing a bona fide occupational qualification."[1][3]

Enforcement by the EEOC

In an attempt to end some of the confusion arising from the interaction of Title VII and state laws, the EEOC has issued guidelines for compliance with Title VII. These guidelines have gone through several stages. The EEOC began (on December 2, 1965) with a position relative to state protective legislation as follows:

The Commission will not find an unlawful employment practice where an employer's refusal to hire women for certain work is based on a State law which precludes the employment of women for such work: *Provided*, that the employer is acting in good faith and that the effect of the law in question is to protect women rather than subject them to discrimination. However, an employer may not refuse to hire women because State law requires that certain conditions of employment such as minimum wages, overtime pay, rest periods, or physical facilities be provided.[14]

On August 19, 1966 the EEOC changed its position and adopted a new policy stating that it ". . . would not make determinations on the merits in cases which present a conflict between the Act and State protective legislation . . . that in such cases the Commission would advise the charging parties of their right to bring suit. . . ."[15] But in February 1968 the Commission rescinded this policy and reaffirmed the earlier one.[16]

In August 1969 the EEOC went further and declared that state laws prohibiting women from certain occupations or limiting their hours of work "have ceased to be relevant to our technology or the expanding role of the female worker in our economy . . . such laws and regulations do not take into account the capacities, preferences, and abilities of individual females and tend to discriminate rather than protect. . . ." In this, its strongest statement, the Commission asserts that all such laws are in conflict with Title VII "and will not be considered a defense to an otherwise unlawful employment practice or as the basis for the application of the bona fide occupational qualification exemption."[17]

The importance of the EEOC guidelines does not lie in enforcement powers of the Commission but in its role as the administrative agency which interprets the law. It has no power to issue cease-and-desist orders not to go to court to enforce its recommendations. It can only investigate, recommend, and attempt to conciliate; and when that fails, the original complainant is entitled to go to court. Here the EEOC guidelines become significant: the EEOC may file *amicus curiae* briefs in these cases, and the courts give the Commission's views great weight on the ground that the EEOC has responsibility to interpret and apply the statute.[18]

Accommodation by States

Since 1965 a pressing question has been how states could reconcile their protective laws with Title VII. A Task Force on Labor Standards was created in the federal government to study the issues. It recommended that states with minimum wage and prescribed rest period laws extend the same privileges to men as well as women, and that states incorporate their statutes pertaining to lunch periods, weight-lifting limits, and occupational hazards into a comprehensive safety and health program applicable to men and women alike. The Task Force urged removal of current restrictions, including prohibition on night work. Lastly, it recommended hour limits be replaced with overtime provisions when agreed to by employees. The AFL-CIO representative on the Task Force, Ann Draper, dissented on the grounds that past experience showed voluntarism would not work and that the premium pay provisions are insufficient leverage against excessive weekly hours.[19]

There now exists a clear trend in the states toward eliminating and changing women's hours and weight-lifting restrictions.[20] Delaware has repealed all its women's protective laws, and Nebraska repealed its maximum hours law in the 1969 legislative session. Also in 1969, the legislatures of New Mexico, New York, Puerto Rico, Massachusetts, Connecticut, and Maryland amended their hours laws, allowing more flexibility for women to work longer hours or to work at times previously forbidden. Since 1965, nine states have eliminated or diminished restrictions on women's hours where the women workers are subject to the standards of the federal Fair Labor Standards Act. Many states have considered bills which were not enacted. Some proposals have been made to apply hours legislation to men as well as women, but the direction of most bills is toward diminishing or abolishing restrictions on women. More states probably will take such action during the odd-year state legislative sessions of 1971.

Meanwhile, decisions by state law enforcement officials also are undermining the state statutes.[21] In February 1969 the South Dakota attorney general held that a state law limiting the hours of women was superseded by Title VII. The North Dakota attorney general made a similar decision the next month. In December, following the new EEOC guidelines of August, the attorney generals of Michigan and Oklahoma ruled their laws invalid because of conflict with Title VII. In January 1970 the Department of Industrial Relations in Ohio stated it would no longer enforce its law as did the Corporation Council of the District of Columbia in April—both because of Title VII. The Wisconsin attorney general ruled in July that the state hours law is superseded by Title VII with respect to employers covered by the Act.

Intense feelings are generated about the questions involved. These can be found on opposite sides of the issue even within the same organization. An example is the United Automobile Workers union. The general counsel of the UAW has called protective state laws "undesirable relics of the past. . . . Only a square confrontation with these so-called protective state laws can do the job. The point is, very simply, they do not protect women, they injure them."[22] However, when the issue came up in Michigan, an Ad Hoc Committee Against Repeal of Protective Legislation, led by representatives of the Hotel and Restaurant Workers' union, sought to prevent termination of the hours limitations. Among the witnesses were women members of the UAW who worked in a Chrysler plant.[23]

The Michigan experience is of interest because it produced evidence of what can occur in some companies when hours limitations are suspended. The Michigan law limiting hours to fifty-four a week and ten a day was repealed in 1967 and almost immediately reinstated; the legislature decided instead of repeal to establish an Occupational Safety Standards Commission which was empowered to make an administrative decision on women's hours limitations. In the confusion created, it appears that a Chrysler plant demanded considerable overtime from its employees. A female employee of Chrysler testified before the Commission that she had to work sixty-nine hours a week—six days at ten hours and nine on Sunday. She further testified that women dropped over from fatigue and exhaustion daily and had to be removed by stretcher. Other Chrysler female employees corroborated her testimony. Another witness from a packing company reported, "my boss ordered us to work 12 hours a day, seven days a week."[24]

The dangers of too much overtime also were described by telephone operators who were members of the Communications

Workers of America. Expert medical testimony was presented, recalling many of the same issues which arose in the *Muller* case of 1908.[2 5] An Ad Hoc Committee Against Repeal of Protective Legislation issued a statement saying:

> Exemptions can be made for executive, administrative and professional women since they frequently find that limitations on hours adversely effect their opportunities for employment and advancement. But the overwhelming majority of the women working in this state need and demand the freedom from forced overtime.[2 6]

The Occupational Safety Standards Commission chose nevertheless to remove any limit on daily hours. Later, its ruling was successfully challenged in court by the Chrysler women.[2 7] Still later the attorney general of Michigan declared that state's law invalid, as noted previously.

The Michigan experience may or may not be the only instance of a "grass roots" revolt against repeal of a protective hours law, but it indicates that long hours on a compulsory basis still can occur. Since overtime is rarely subject to the controls of collective bargaining, protective law is the main preventive constraint against excessive work demands.

Reaction of the Courts

Three separate cases appear, at this writing, to be headed for eventual resolution by the Supreme Court.

In the *Mengelkoch* case,[2 8] three female plaintiffs, all heads of families, alleged that the California maximum-hours law conflicts with Title VII and the Fourteenth Amendment. The defendant corporation admitted the women were denied overtime and promotions to positions requiring overtime but urged as justification the state's maximum-hours law, under which no administrative exceptions are available. There is no suggestion that the health or welfare of the charging parties would be affected adversely. The case is now pending in the Court of Appeals.

Another case in the Central District of California, *Rosenfeld* v. *Southern Pacific Company*,[2 9] also involved the question of whether a company discriminated against a woman on the basis of her sex. The court held that the "bona fide occupational qualification" clause of Title VII could not be applied in this case. It further held that the California hours and weights legislation discriminates against women on the basis of sex and is therefore void because of the supremacy of the federal law. A summary judgment was granted ordering the company to consider the employee for any position sought—without regard to her sex and without regard to the California law. This case also has gone to the Court of Appeals.

Perhaps the case most likely to reach the Supreme Court is *Weeks v. Southern Bell.*[30] The District Court had held that Southern Bell had not violated Title VII of the Civil Rights Act when it refused to promote Mrs. Weeks to a job which required lifting thirty-one pounds. At the time of this ruling, Georgia had a regulation prohibiting women from lifting more than thirty pounds. By the time the case was heard by the Circuit Court of Appeals, the regulation had been restated more generally: no weight limit was specified, and weights were to be limited "so as to avoid strain or undue fatigue." Furthermore, the regulation applied equally to men and women.

The Circuit Court of Appeals, therefore, based its ruling entirely on whether the company could refuse to assign Mrs. Weeks on the basis that there was here a "bona fide occupational qualification" under Title VII. In interpreting this clause, the court said

> . . . that in order to rely on the bona fide occupational qualification exception, an employer has the burden of proving that he had reasonable cause to believe, that is, a factual basis for believing, that all or substantially all women would be unable to perform safely and efficiently the duties of the job involved.[31]

This goes far toward plugging any major exception.

Understandably, the EEOC is pleased with the *Rosenfeld* and *Weeks* cases as well as with the general drift of state legislative and executive decisions. The embattled posture of the EEOC is impressive, and its effectiveness beyond question. We are assured there is much more to come. In a recent weight case[32] which did not involve a state protective law, the chairman of the EEOC stated that this case

> . . . will simplify the law concerning discrimination based on sex, making it easier for employers to understand their obligations under the law, and the court's decision regarding back pay relief should result in substantial encouragement for potential discriminators to obey the law.[33]

Comment and Conclusion

In his study of the legal status of women, Leo Kanowitz has concluded that there has been improvement. Some of the common law doctrine that disparages married women relative to their husbands has been abrogated by statutes; unmarried women also have made legal gains. "The legal status of American women," he says, "has risen to the point that it is not now far below that of the American men."[34] But he notes that discrimination continues flagrantly in law regulating sexual conduct and in the employment area. The authors agree that much needs to be done in the world of work to assure equality of treatment for women. We question whether eliminating all protective legislation for women is either a necessary or proper means to that end.

A suspicion persists that the more ardent advocates of "equal rights" care nothing for protective labor legislation, for either men or women. For example, this language of the court in the *Weeks* case has been cited jubilantly by equal rights advocates:

> Moreover, Title VII rejects just this type of romantic paternalism as unduly Victorian and instead vests individual women with the power to decide whether or not to take on unromantic tasks. Men have always had the right to determine whether the incremental increase in remuneration for strenuous, dangerous, obnoxious, boring or unromantic tasks is worth the candle. The promise of Title VII is that women are now to be on equal footing. . . .[35]

This is exactly the argument which was advanced earlier against workmen's compensation and other labor legislation. It is a statement of Adam Smith's principle of "equal net advantages," which Smith himself pointed out could function only in the theory of a free market.[36] The notion that any intervention by the state distorts the unfettered interplay of supply and demand factors has been used improperly against labor legislation from the beginning. The recurrence now of such an argument, even in vestigial form, carries the discussion beyond the issue of equal treatment of women to the heart of protective legislation itself. The point that equal rights advocates are overlooking is that under many circumstances employers can and do exercise controls over the labor market, particularly in the lesser skilled factory and service employments.

The origins of protective legislation are rooted in the

recurring crises which have characterized the growth of industrialization. What was required was use of state police power to assure degrees of freedom for employees through minimum wages, maximum hours, safety codes, and social insurance.[37]

The idea of balance and mutuality in the employer-employee relationship still remains an important objective. The search for equality among employees—particularly women and racial minorities—should be sought within this framework and not at its expense. Nevertheless, a noteworthy aspect of the current situation is that instead of protectionist legislation being extended to include men, it is being rooted out altogether.

It is possible unwittingly to destroy the foundations of protective legislation. There seems to be little awareness of this risk, probably because the tight labor markets of the last eight years have diminished public sensitivity to the multiplicity of interests operating. The danger of depending solely on economic forces is obscured while the opportunities are emphasized. It is not coincidental that employer groups have encouraged the repeal of women's protective legislation and opposed its extension to men.[38] The issue is now maximum hours; will it be minimum wages next?[39]

The hours question is more complex than equal rights advocates paint it. Overtime work is attractive for men and women alike as a way of solving pressing financial problems, but prolonged compulsory overtime usually brings a reaction as the family, social, and psychic cost becomes clear.[40] When one is exhausted with compulsory overtime, he or she is of course free to quit, but this cannot by itself be an argument against protective legislation. The availability of alternative employment must be a consideration. At this time it is premature indeed to base a policy on the assumption that future labor markets always will be tight. Furthermore, a new phenomenon in recent history is the high cost of hiring, due in part to health and welfare programs and other fringe benefits which are employee-related rather than hours-related.[41] It also has been noted that finding, interviewing, processing, and training people often cost several hundred dollars per employee and that labor layoffs and downgrading through seniority systems can cost additional amounts in lost time and training.[42] Under these conditions overtime even at premium rates is cheaper for employers than hiring new employees. Employers have a heavy stake in unilateral control of overtime policy.

In the current discussions one is struck by the abstract nature of the arguments and the paucity of information on possible effects of rooting out protectionist law. This is somewhat ironic, since the legal precedent for women's hours law was the *Muller* case in which Brandeis filed the brief which attempted to bring the realities of economic life into the apparatus of legal thought. If the courts have erred in the past in not being sensitive to discriminatory aspects of protectionist law, it is equally dangerous to block one's vision to the dangers of compulsory overtime. It does not appear that enough attention is being directed toward legislation requiring that overtime must be voluntary for *both* men and women. If hours limitations for women are to be repealed rather than extended to men, the only remaining way to achieve both equality and protection is through laws which require the employee's consent in assigning overtime work. However, as a remedy for the all-at-one-blow extirpation of protective hours law by Title VII, the enactment of voluntary overtime law state-by-state is a difficult and therefore unlikely remedy.

Although further research is required in those states where women's protective law has been repealed, the Michigan experience indicates that some women may still fall victim to compulsory overtime. Such women should not be denied hours protection until voluntary overtime statutes are enacted. On the other hand, there are some women who are qualified to perform jobs requiring lifting weight or working hours beyond the statutory limits. These women should not be denied the opportunity to fill such positions in reliance on state protective laws.

Thus, the question is whether state law which protects some women from the hardships of compulsory overtime must fall under Title VII in order to provide equal employment opportunity for other female workers. It is suggested that until voluntary overtime laws are enacted or until protective legislation is extended to cover men equally, protective laws be retained with administrative exemptions for women desiring positions requiring more overtime. In this way, women desiring protection would be covered while women desiring more strenuous positions would not be denied such employment because of their sex.

However, in light of cases currently pending, the Supreme Court may have to determine whether the abolition of female protective legislation is, as the EEOC contends, a *sine qua non* for eliminating discrimination and whether equality for some women must necessarily entail misery for others.

Footnotes

1. The most complete account of this activity is still Elizabeth Brandeis' "Women's Hours Law," in John R. Commons, *et al., History of Labor in the United States, VoL III* (New York: Macmillan, 1935), pp. 457-500.

2. Muller v. Oregon, 208 U.S. 412 (1908).

3. Adkins v. Children's Hospital, 261 U.S. 525 (1923). (Italics added.)

4. West Coast Hotel Company v. Parrish, 300 U.S. 379 (1937).

5. U.S. Bureau of Labor Standards, *State Minimum Wage Laws*, Feb. 1, 1970 (Washington: G.P.O.).

6. U.S. Department of Labor, *Summary of State Labor Laws for Women* (Washington, D.C., March 1969).

7. Pauli Murray and Mary O. Eastwood, "Jane Crow and the Law: Sex Discrimination and Title VII," *The George Washington Law Review*, Vol. 34, No. 2 (December 1965), p. 238.

8. The House debate on Smith's amendment turned "ladies afternoon" into a comic discussion. Smith read a letter from a woman constituent decrying the excess of two million [sic] more males than females. Congressman Tuten argued that no southern gentleman would support legislation discriminating against women. Congresswoman St. George spoke in support of the amendment, "We outlast you, we outlive you, we nag you to death. So why should we want special privileges? . . . We are entitled to this crumb of equality." This debate suggests the difficulties the courts have since had in discovering the legislative intent behind the sex discrimination provision. See United States Equal Employment Opportunity Commission, *Legislative History of Titles VII and XI of the Civil Rights Act of 1964* (Washington: G.P.O., 1968), 3213 ff.

9. President's Commission on the Status of Women, *American Woman* (Washington: G.P.O., 1963), pp. 35-38.

10. The Equal Pay Act was a major step forward in ending sex discrimination in employment. The most obvious limitation of the act is the fact that a guarantee of equal pay is of little value to a woman who cannot get the job in the first place due to sex discrimination.

11. Demands for government action for equal pay date back to the Knights of Labor Convention in Philadelphia in 1868, where a resolution was passed urging federal and state governments "to pass laws securing equal salaries for equal work to all women employed under the various departments of government." Public attention was focused on the problem of equal pay for women during World War I when large numbers of women were employed in war industries on the same jobs as men. The National War Labor Board enforced the policy of "no wage discrimination against women on the grounds of sex." In 1919, two states—Michigan and Montana—enacted equal pay legislation. For nearly 25 years, these were the only states with statutes providing for equal pay for women. However, stimulated by the Second World War, 10 additional states passed similar laws. Seventeen others have acted since World War II.

12. Anthony R. Mansfield, "Sex Discrimination in Employment under Title VII of the Civil Rights Act of 1964," *Vanderbilt Law Review*, Vol. 21, No. 4 (May 1968), p. 495.

13. Ibid., p. 496.

14. 21 *Fed. Reg.*, p. 1 (1968).

15. Ibid.

16. Ibid.

17. 34 *Fed. Reg.*, p. 11,367 (1969).

18. See Weeks v. Southern Bell Telephone and Telegraph Co., cited in fn. 30, below.

19. Task Force on Labor Standards, *Report* (Washington: G.P.O., 1968).

20. Ora G. Mitchell and Clara T. Sorenson, "State Labor Legislation Enacted in 1969," *Monthly Labor Review*, Vol. 93, No. 1 (January 1970), pp. 48-56.

21. Bureau of National Affairs, *State Labor Law Reporter*, 1.32-1.34, March 16, 1970.

22. United Automobile Workers Women's Department, *Statement of Stephen Schlossberg, General Counsel, International Union, UAW, to the EEOC at the Public Hearing* (May 2, 1967), Washington, D.C.

23. Others persons associated with the Ad Hoc Committee came from such groups as the American Federation of State, County, and Municipal Employees, Amalgamated Clothing Workers, Building Service Employees, Council of Catholic Women, Council of Jewish Women, Michigan Credit Union League, YWCA State Council, Musicians Union Local 5, and some 13 other groups.

24. *Detroit Free Press*, Jan. 21, 1969.

25. Testimony of Dr. E.R. Tichauer, professor of biomechanics, Institute of Rehabilitation Medicine, New York University Medical Center.

26. "Statement of Policy of the Ad Hoc Committee Against the Repeal of Protective Labor Legislation for Women Workers in Michigan," mimeo, undated.

27. This decision was based primarily on the court's estimate of the powers of the commission. It argued that the commission did not have the power to rescind the act, and that furthermore it was an employment safety body and did not deal with the field of discrimination. But the decision also ranged over the basic issues of whether women's health and safety required differential treatment, and noted that the commission could have, within its powers, offered some compromise such as "allowance of excess overtime by consent of the woman worker," an approach, the court noted, that seemed to find favor among women who testified in the trial. Stephanie Prociuk v. Occupational Safety Standards Commission. 3rd Circuit Court of Michigan, Wayne County, Michigan, June 20, 1969.

28. Mengelkoch, *et al.* v. Industrial Welfare Commission of California and North American Aviation, Inc. (C.D., California, 1968).

29. 293 F. Supp. 1219 (C.D., California, 1968).

30. Weeks v. Southern Bell Telephone and Telegraph Co., 408 F. 2d 228 (C.A. 5, 1969) *reversed* 279 F. Supp. 117 (S.D. Ga., 1967).

31. Ibid.

32. Bowie v. Colgate Palmolive Co., 408 F. 2d 711 (7th Cir., 1969) *reversed*, 272 F. Supp. 332 (S.D. Ind., 1967).

33. Bureau of National Affairs, *Labor Relations Reporter*, 72 Analysis 25, Oct. 13, 1969, pp. 227-228.

34. Leo Kanowitz, *Women and the Law, the Unfinished Revolution* (Albuquerque: University of New Mexico Press, 1969), p. 197.

35. Cited in fn. 30, above.

36. Adam Smith, *Wealth of Nations* (New York: Random House, Modern Library, 1937), p. 99 ff.

37. See John R. Commons and John B. Andrews, *Principles of Labor Legislation* (New York: Harper, 1927).

38. In the 1969 session of the Wisconsin legislature, for example, two bills were considered, the one extending hours limitation to men, the other removing hours limitations for female enployees. Employers strongly opposed the first and favored the latter.

39. The recent EEOC guideline abolishes the former specific distinction made between laws which require "benefits" for women (such as minimum wages, premium pay for overtime, rest periods, or physical facilities) and laws which "prohibit" the employment of women. There is in the guideline no longer a specific direction that an employer may not refuse to employ or promote in order to avoid providing a "benefit" for a woman as required by law.

40. This generalization is based on experience of one of the authors (Munts) in the Textile Workers Union of America.

41. Joseph W. Garbarino, "Fringe Benefits and Overtime as Barriers to Expanding

Employment," *Industrial and Labor Relations Review*, Vol. 17, No. 3 (April 1964), pp. 426-430.

42. Herbert R. Northrup, "Reduction in Hours," in Clyde E. Dankert, Floyd C. Mann, and Herbert R. Northrup, eds., *Hours of Work* (New York: Harper, 1965), chap. 1, p. 14.

Patricia T. Carbine *is Editor-in-Chief and Publisher of* Ms. Magazine.
This article is taken from an address to the General Motors Public Relations Conference at the General Motors Technical Center in Warren, Michigan. Reprinted with permission from The Changing Challenge, *General Motors Quarterly, Vol. 2, No. 4, 1975, pp. 10-15.*

4

Where the Women Are

Patricia T. Carbine

COMING ALONG FROM the airport today, I was trying to remember my first assignment at the GM Tech Center. I finally decided that it was 1958 as a reporter/journalist for *Look*. And I must tell you that I never dreamed on that day that I'd ever return to speak to so august a group in such a beautiful room and about this of all topics. The height of vanity I guess, is the title that I submitted: "Where the Women Are."

I would like to point out very quickly that I don't think there is a person in the United States of America, indeed the world, who knows "where the women are." And I sure don't.

What I am going to presume to share are some insights that I gathered as a journalist, as a reporter, as a woman, as a feminist, and as a business person. Insights. And that's really all. Because, I think, the worst mistake we could ever make is to think that all women are in the same place any more than all men are in the same place.

What I am going to try is to take a huge step back from the problems facing you as a corporation. I want to trace for you what, I think, has happened, is happening, to 51% of the population. How it came about. And what the implications are.

I want to begin by asking you to think about a symbol in your mind's eye. I don't know if it's distributed in Michigan, but I hope you've seen the advertising symbol of Ballantine beer. Three rings that interlock. There is a small area in the center where they overlap. Ballantine, as you know, calls those rings: purity, body, and flavor. (When I say that, I think it may have been something invented by the Sisters of Mercy, who educated me.)

However, having suggested the symbol I now want to ask you to substitute another notion. Look at those three rings. Suppose one of these circles represents the person I think I am. And the second circle, the person I really am. And the third circle, the person others think me to be.

Look at those three rings and think about the small area in the center where they overlap. Now, I suggest that we also look at Carl Rogers' concept of personal congruence. Dr. Rogers says that "congruence is the term we have used to indicate an accurate matching of experience and awareness. And it may still further be extended to cover a matching of experience, of awareness and communication."

Carl Rogers writes, "An individual has within herself," (actually he said himself, I think it only fair to point out), "the capacity and the tendency, latent if not evident, to move forward toward maturity. In a suitable psychological climate this tendency is released and becomes actual rather than potential. It is evident in the capacity of the individual to understand those aspects of her life and herself which are causing pain and dissatisfaction; an understanding which probes beneath her conscious knowledge of herself into those experiences which she has hidden from herself because of their threatening nature. It shows itself in her tendency to re-organize her personality and her relationships to life in ways which are regarded as more mature. Whether we call it a growth tendency, a drive toward self-actualization or a forward-moving directional tendency, it is the mainspring of life. It is the urge that is evident in all organic and human life: to expand, to extend, to become autonomous, to develop, to mature. It is the tendency to express and activate all the capacities of the organism in order to enhance the organism or the self. The tendency may become buried under layer after layer of encrusted psychological defenses. It may be hidden behind elaborate facades which deny its existence. But it is my belief," concludes Dr. Rogers, "that it exists in every individual and awaits only the proper conditions to be released and expressed."

I'd like to suggest that we can agree on one thing today. And that is that the proper conditions have coalesced to produce activity among women to expand, to extend, to become autonomous. To develop in a way that is without precedent, that is in fact revolutionary.

It is interesting to consider the role of women when this country celebrated its first birthday, since we're thinking so hard about our 200th. It is fascinating to look at the extent to which roles have been assigned to us by society.

Two hundred years ago, we were, of course, very important producers in this country. We made the fabric, soap, medicine. We helped to tend the animals. We helped to shape the pots and pans. And we certainly helped with the farming. Most importantly, we helped produce human beings. We were producers of children, of workers. The country needed a lot of them. It is interesting to look at the history of those families. Often there was one husband and two wives. The burdens of childbearing having been the tolltaker all those generations ago.

Women were producers. We were, I think, at a point were there was virtually no difference between the importance of men's work and women's work. And, I think it also fair to say that we had every reason to believe that our role of producer would continue. We'd stand side by side with our mates, our men, and continue to contribute equally to our community, to our growing society.

I'm going to telescope a lot of history. But I'm going to jump to 1852 to illustrate what then seemed to be the role that society had assigned to us. The subject then was women's suffrage. An editorial in the *New York Herald* went this way: "How did woman first become subject to man as she now is all over the world? By her nature, her sex, just as the Negro is and always will be to the end of time, inferior to the white man and, therefore, doomed to subjection. But woman is happier than she would be in any other condition, just because it is the law of nature."

What we had been dealt, as women, was the role of *servicing* the needs of husband and children. We were forced not to think of ourselves as producers anymore, for something extraordinarily important had happened in this country. There was the incredible breakthrough in the organizing of work, putting it under the same roof, and discovering profit (and I know it was a white male who discovered it).

What happened was fascinating. What had been women's work suddenly became man's work. Men became the soapmakers and distributors. Men became the fabric makers and sellers. Men even came to own the diaper wash companies! And what could be more womanly work than diaper washing?

We were no longer producers of goods; we had become consumers. The roles had shifted. What we thought we were, that is to say, producers of goods, was no longer true. But we were at least producers of children. That at least was our own true nature.

Clare Boothe Luce describes what happened to that reality: "The only world that ever was really women's world, the world where she was dominant, was the nursery. It was the only place where she was ever really needed. There she was, when the cradle was full, irreplaceable. The only place where she was superior and was looked up to and not looked down on. Where someone was inferior to her and where she had authority. Where others were deeply dependent on her. Where her love was freely given and freely returned." Where she could be herself, the person she really was, her second circle you could say.

"At the core of that ugly phenomenon that came along in the twentieth century called 'momism,'" says Mrs. Luce, "lay woman's fear of her loss of status as mother, and her return to the inferior status of wife. If women had to leave the nursery and a lifetime career of keeping the cradle full, what was she to do? What could she do that would let her esteem herself and cause man to esteem her in return?"

We were cast in the role of the inferior person. And if women really understood that, and if we were smart or strong, if we were artists or thinkers, we understood that we had better work hard to hide it. We knew perfectly well that smart women, strong women, tended to alienate men. And we needed men to choose us, to reaffirm us. Don't forget we grew up as our father's daughter, and we hoped to exchange that identity and become our husband's wife and then our children's mother. And the last thing we ever questioned was the ceremony of marriage itself, which included the moment when our father *gave* us to the groom. Or that when we were pronounced man and wife, he was pronounced a person and we were pronounced a role. For weren't we by nature subject to man and happier that way? Weren't we naturally passive, and dependent, and less responsible? More emotional? Possessors of smaller brains? and wasn't the belief that all of this was true somehow reassuring?

Cynthia Ozick says it very beautifully, when she writes about women and creativity. She says that "female infantilism is a kind of pleasurable slavishness. Dependency, the absence of decision, the absence of responsibility, the avoidance of risk, the shutting out of the gigantic toil of art. All of these are the comforts of contented subjects."

Well, of course, what we have been confronting—those of us who represent more than half the population in this country—is that our role as producers of children, the one area where we were still productive, is no longer the role that society expects of us. Or demands of us. Quite the reverse. For if we are now to cooperate with our community, our society, our planet, we are encouraged to produce fewer children, not more. But that leaves us rather bereft as human beings. The roles that we understood as being truly and naturally ours no longer seem to fit.

That brings me to where, I think, women are. For what we have been involved in, in these last four or more years—bravely, endlessly, and in the face of much ridicule—is a gigantic effort to become congruent persons. To question, in other words, the reality of that three ring symbol. Until women began to ask hard questions of themselves and tried to figure out just what it is we are, and what it is we are worth, the reality is that the person we thought we were had a very, very small area of overlap with the person it turns out we really are. And what we have been deeply involved in is a huge effort to bring those two circles into phase.

What, I think, is out of phase and dramatically so, is that third circle. The person society thinks us to be. There are many ways of looking at it. But, probably one of the most productive I have seen recently was an examination that the advertising community made of itself, a study that came out this past spring from the National Advertising Review Board called, "Women and Advertising."

It is dramatic for any number of reasons. To begin with it is the industry looking at itself. And, since so much of your work is involved in trying to understand where women are, not just inside your various divisions but in terms of the consumers whom you're trying to meet and satisfy, the conclusions of this study are very telling. And it goes to the heart of trying to understand why it is that women have suddenly gotten uppity.

If it is true that we are trying to integrate those three facets of ourselves to become truly congruent human beings, then the image the world has of us becomes very, very important. The NARB panel was examining the basis for complaints about advertising that portrays women or is directed to them. It analyzed a broad sampling of current advertising as well as reviewing in depth the current literature on the subject both supportive and critical of what is known as the Women's Liberation Movement.

The panel interviewed people from both ends of the spectrum. The concern was based upon a belief in the power of advertising, and the panel concluded that the problem expressed is indeed real. "To deny that the problem exists, in fact, is to deny the effectiveness of the advertising message. What critics are saying very simply is that advertising, in selling a product, often sells a supplementary image as well. Sometimes in women-related advertising that image is negative and deprecatory. Unfortunately such images may be accepted as true to life by many men, women, and children. Especially when they reinforce stereotypes of a time gone by. Seen in this light, advertising must be regarded as one of the forces molding society.

"Those that protest that the advertising merely reflects society must reckon with the criticism that much of the current reflection of women in advertising is out of date. To the extent that it is true, advertising is neglecting its responsibility to be fair, to be accurate, to be truthful."

Studies being made of the image of women in all media are going forward in this country at a clip that would, I think, make your heads reel. I'm especially aware of it as Chair of the Media Committee of the Presidential Commission on International Women's Year. We are in the process of rounding up all studies—be they graduate theses, institutional studies, or professional women's group studies—of the image of women in the media. The number of studies all by themselves, becomes, I think, a dramatic comment. How society sees us is an incredibly important issue for women.

I want to point out that one of the reasons women have become more and more determined to share in the decisions controlling our lives is because of the support of men who have understood that women have been trapped by old myths and have set them aside.

I want to share with you a portion of a speech that Arthur Taylor, president of CBS, made to a school in New Jersey. He is the father of three young women, and he said some very, very valuable things that might well be shared with men who are trying to understand and promote women as business colleagues.

Mr. Taylor says, "Let me tell you some of the assumptions that have long been made about women that I now reject. I reject the assumption that you will work for only a few years, and that you have little interest in a long-term career. I reject the assumption that you do not care about salary, that you do not need as much money as men do. I believe that you want to earn recognition, status and power. I do not believe that women want to work only to help people. I reject the idea that women are unable to ask, 'What's in it for me?' I reject the idea that because you are women you do not belong in the management ranks of industry. Instead, I'm going to be talking to you today from my belief that women are full, complete people."

This kind of reinforcement from the folks in power has been extremely, extremely important to women. It cannot be overestimated.

Considering the educational level that women have now achieved in this country (between 1960 and 1970 the number of women who attended college increased 160%); considering the fact that we who choose to marry and have children will probably have two, and that those children will be in school by the time we're 30 or 32 years old; and considering the fact that we're going to be living until we're 75 (you know you men have seven fewer years. Not incidentally, part of this revolutionary scheme of ours involves splitting it so that you gain 3½ and we give up 3½); what we are talking about is some 40 years of a human being's life. We are talking about a natural resource that has been wasted in this country. We're talking about an incredible effort that is underway wherein women are beginning to discover that we are not naturally passive or less able or less intelligent or less determined or less ambitious or less able to participate in the decisions that control our lives. We're talking about the gigantic effort of realizing that the person we thought we were was not indeed the person we really are. And the wrenching effort involved in bringing those two circles into phase is what this movement is all about.

I'm also talking about the bottom line for you. It seems to me that the better you understand your market and what's happening to it, the better you're obviously going to realize that extraordinary innovation for which I give you full credit: profit. Women need mobility. Women need freedom. Women need an efficient way to begin to realize this new life of ours. An automobile becomes extraordinarily important to us . . . and it better work.

There was a study done recently by a psychologist of racial stereotyping in ghetto schools, dealing with two to five year olds. Having completed that study she thought it would be interesting to see what happens in sexual stereotyping and how early we begin our fragmented-role existence.

She asked little boys the obvious question: What are you going to be when you grow up? And the answers were terrific. "I'm going to be an astronaut." "I'm going to be a cowboy." "I'm going to be President."

She reversed the question. She said to the little boys, suppose you were little girls, then what would you be? There was a lot of silence and a lot of squirming. Finally one little boy said, "Well, then I guess I'd have to be nothing."

Then she went to the little girls. What are you going to be when you grow up? Little girls get the message very, very easily and very early. "I'm going to be a stewardess." "I'm going to be a teacher." "I'm going to be a mommy." All of which, believe me, are *worth* being.

The question was reversed. Well, suppose you were boys, then what might you want to be. Excitement. Lots of wiggling around. Lots of hands in the air. And one little girl said, "Then I could be a priest." And another little girl said, "Then I could be President." And a third little girl secretly smiled and she said, "Well, if I were a little boy then I would have wings, and I could fly over the city."

Well, where the women are, in my opinion, is at the point of making a gigantic discovery. Which is that we do have wings. And that we can become congruent persons so that the person we think we are is the person we really are, and we hope that soon it's the person you see us to be.

b. Reactions to Change

FOR MOST PEOPLE change, particularly significant change, is frightening. Change creates uncertainty and threatens our ability to control our destinies. So, we resist change. The movement of women into management roles constitutes a significant change. It threatens men in management, and those men who aspire to management positions, and their wives. The forces of change are powerful, and have generated resistance in many forms and intensities. Dealing with resistance to her expanding role will be part of the life of the woman manager for many years to come.

5
Why Men Fear Women in Business

Jean Way Schoonover

THE PSYCHOLOGISTS say that each one of us is a trio. The psychologists believe that each one of us is a child. Each one of us is a parent. Each one of us is an adult. I hope that it is *my* adult—the adult within me—that speaks to you now.

But before I start in about *sex*, about *fear*, or about the reasons why men fear women, before I do any of those things, I want to take a moment to remember a child, a little girl in glasses and dreams, growing up in Westport, New York, and wishing she had been born a boy.

Me.

That little girl.

So long ago—further in space really than in time. And I mean the space between ideas. The distance between changing mores.

I remember that third of me, that little girl with her head full of dreams, her heart full of a first bitterness, the realization of a nine-year-old girl in an all-American town of forty years ago that her dreams were fun but impossible because she had been born in a man's world.

I want to pause also to remember the final third of me that

psychologists say makes up the whole person. The parent.

Not me as parent.

But my parents as parent—they made the parent in me.

My dad, especially, tall and gaunt with overwork, a country veterinarian, a hell of a man in a man's world; a man who wanted sons, lots of them—a man who got a daughter, me, another daughter, my sister, then finally my brother.

Well, here I am, the threesome that is the child, the parent, the adult.

We've come a long, long way, baby! All of us—and we are, all of us, going much, much further!

If anyone had told that little girl, or if anyone had told my dad, that one day I would talk about sex—S-E-(*my God!*)X!—And not only *s-e-x*, but s-e-x on the job, we would have had that person confined, and talking to a psychologist for real!

But here I am, writing about something I know something about. Women and business. Everyone is going to learn about women. And fast. It's the law.

And it's the most *complex* problem today.

Corporate management is thinking and talking and worrying about women as they never have before: from the neck up!

The future will be spent in a brand-new, unprecedented way: men and women will be hunting together. Not hunting each other, mind you, but hunting together.

All of business is a mighty hunt. Until recently men hunted alone: the game was the customer. The sale. Men, in order to be effective, did what they did millennia ago; they formed hunting tribes. This time they called the tribe the business or the corporation. The women did as they had always done—stayed behind, at home, in the caves of Scarsdale and Westport, raising the children, unable to run with the men, bound by apron strings. A few were closer to the hunt—closer to the cliffs and canyons, hills and valleys of business—and they were called secretaries. Clerks. Typists. And they brought some of the comforts of the cave to the office—steaming cups of coffee, for example.

There are a few men who know about women—about women and business today. Tom Leighton, for one. Tom, senior vice-president of Dudley-Anderson-Yutzy Public Relations Inc., and a renowned New York management counselor, says, "Yes, it's true. Until recently, men were the Chosen People, THE CHOSEN SEX. Mighty hunters."

But now—Uncle Sam—traitor to his sex, has ordered that the hunt be opened to women, that there be equal opportunity, that the Man's World hang out both "his" and "her" signs.

That has given rise to true anguish—the very real, the very understandable anguish—that men are now suffering as they take up *the problem of women in business today*, or perhaps, *business and the new woman*.

What's wrong? Why this real pain? Why this soul-searching? Why all this brow-beating and brain-wrinkling?

Here are some of the things business is learning today about The New Woman, about the problems men and women have on the job, about fear—the fears men have concerning women in business, women on the job, women as peers and as colleagues, women on the hunt.

Why, we ask medical and psychiatric advisors on business problems, why are men having so much difficulty working with women, accepting women?

Fear, to be dispelled, must be understood. Here are some of the reasons men fear women—here are keys to understanding; here are ten reasons why men fear women on the job.

One. Men fear women as peers on the job—the brainworkers in particular—because they believe, and often rightly, that women are unable to free on-the-job relationships of sexual tensions.

Two. Men fear women on the job because the culture, our business society, has not taught them how to work with women whose only relationship to them is that of co-worker, professional colleague.

Three. Men fear women because of their physical need for women and they fear that career women will exploit their need, their vulnerability, and that in the case of competitors, a woman's sex gives her a strong competitive "edge."

Four. The fourth fear men have of business equals who are women is that men do not trust women because they do not trust women's emotions. Most men feel that the emotional responses of women to business problems—problems in general—are unpredictable. Because men cannot predict the responses of women to business stimuli, not with any reliability at any rate, they do not trust women in business. From a lifetime of experience, from boyhood on, the culture teaches the male members of our society the rules of the game, teaches them the perimeters of response, teaches them to predict, with reasonable certainty, the reactions of another man to a given stimulus. Women haven't learned the game. Their responses are not predictable by the men, and because they are not, women are considered untrustworthy.

Five. Men fear women on the job because, with very few exceptions, they have had no "life models" for the business relationship between man and woman. Women are mothers, wives, sweethearts, girl friends, relatives. Women are not co-workers and most men are afraid because they view the working woman through the tunnel of their experience with women, which is very small. Each experience is easily and rigidly "typecast" by a culture which affords men remarkably few opportunities to learn about women other than those in stereotyped, culture-conditioned roles.

Six. The sixth fear so prevalent in executive suites throughout the country today is man's fear of woman's superiority. We all know—and men and women of the insurance industry know better than anyone—the physical superiority of woman. Woman lives longer than man, years longer, and this actuarial truth has given rise to still other fears about woman as a physically superior being. When Masters and Johnson discovered that the "little woman" was a mythic figure sexually, that her appetite was very likely superior to the man of the house, male machismo took a tumble; anxiety was produced.

Seven. Men fear women on the job—in the professions—because of what they believe is woman's ability—the career woman's ability to concentrate on her career, to devote herself utterly to her job. The "career man" usually has a wife, children, home, friends, church, and many other interests beyond his work; he must play many roles imposed by the culture, and this variety, this diffusion of energy, gives his female counterpart a tremendous advantage. He believes that the career woman is free to focus her full force on career goals while he is forced by the culture to spread himself thin, playing a variety of roles.

Eight. The eighth fear, so common today among executives trying to understand women, trying to cope with *the problem of women in business today*, is that they are not dealing with ordinary women on the job, in their careers, but with extraordinary women, work-freaks of some kind, demented amazons who want to be facsimile men. What they have to get used to, what we all must get used to, is that today—thanks to The Pill, perhaps, and to new cultural values, the new woman in business is a normal, an ordinary woman, seeking to make her way in a normal, ordinary way.

Nine. The ninth fear—and a very sharp, very real one, and I must add, a painful one in a mature society—is this: executive America, corporate America fears women because the men who run corporate America are afraid of losing their identities. It is one of America's tragedies that we have come to believe that a man is what he does for a living. Chiefly that. If women also do what he does for a living, is he less than he was? Less than a man ought to be? Are his victories made small because women also enjoy them? What is a man in our society who loses a job? A man who loses his job loses his identity. It is this, far more than income loss—which is usually temporary—that terrifies men. It is one more reason, this critical factor of identity, why men cannot help fearing co-workers who are women.

Ten. The tenth fear—the tenth key to understanding yourself, to understanding women through the eradication of fear—the tenth fear men have of women is a secondhand fear: a "second-person" fear. You women will understand. The tenth reason why men in corporate America fear women is the fear their wives have of the women with whom they work; the woman who serves as co-worker, peer, equal to their husbands. This may be the most difficult fear of all to deal with, the *fear of one woman for another.*

There you have them: ten keys to understanding, ten real, ten common fears in executive America, in corporate America, of the new woman, fears held by the "old man."

The old culture.
The old work ethic.
The old wisdom.
The old fears.
The old *waste*.
Yes, waste.

We see it so often. In board rooms, in executive offices, in clubs and bars, wherever good men gather: the pain, the real anguish, the joylessness of executive America, of corporate America, thinking about, grappling with, *the problem of the new woman—of business and the new woman.*

What waste, what a colossal waste!

America's businessmen are the best in the world, the most creative, the boldest, the most enterprising, and yet they do not see an opportunity of historic proportions, a monumental opportunity to use—to harness virtually untapped energy; to put into the service of this culture, of this business society, limitless new brainpower, a totally fresh perspective—the energy, the brainpower, the perspective of Woman, modern woman, the liberated woman . . . the woman who is free to hunt with the man, free to run with him, build with him, free to build a new way of business, an entirely new way of business life. Better. Different. Richer. Variegated. Male and female.

A society not of free men only, nor of liberated women only, but a society that is totally liberated—a society that liberates humankind from the cave and the loneliness of the hunt.

One way or another, the women are no longer going to stay home.

Not all of them at any rate.

One way or another the women are going to join the hunt.

You men, abandon your fears of women. You have nothing to lose but the chains of the past, the limits to your growth as human beings.

Donald R. Stacy *is Regional Counsel for the Equal Employment Opportunity Commission in Atlanta and Adjunct Professor, University of Georgia Law School.*

This article is reprinted with permission from Atlanta Economic Review, *March-April 1976, pp. 9-14.*

6

The Intrepid Executive's Guide to Avoiding Sex Discrimination

Donald R. Stacy

THERE IS a bevy of federal statutes, executive orders, and agency regulations that forbid discrimination in employment.[a] Yet, whenever we analyze personal income figures and sources, we uncover a stark and tenacious disparity by sex in earnings and vocational dispersal, reflecting both wage and job discrimination. Other articles in this issue will address the matter of how to eliminate those manifestations of sex discrimination which impede the entry of women into management. This article will focus mainly on how courts have dealt with failure to do so.

A chronological inventory of the federal provisions against sex discrimination would have to begin with two sections of the 1871 Civil Rights Act.[b]

---

[a] Several commentators including, most recently, then Secretary of Labor Dunlop have offered the conclusion that the very profusion of provisions in this area may limit their effectiveness. 2 CCH *Fair Employ. Prac. Guide* Paragraph 5333 (1975).

[b] Stressed here is the current (and now settled) construction, inasmuch as the statute was originally construed as no boon to women. In the first sex discrimination case to

99

As currently construed, one section[1]—embracing the nonfederal public sector—forbids invidious employment discrimination on any ground, including sex.[2] The other section,[3] which covers private employment as well, forbids (among other things) conspiracies affecting another's employment which arise out of an animus against a class to which that "another" belongs. A federal district judge in Pittsburgh has twice refused to dismiss a suit brought under this conspiracy section by an outspoken 67-year-old women's rights advocate who contends that officials of Chatham College were prompted to dismiss her by the animus they felt toward her "academic and extracurricular involvement in the struggle . . . for liberation."[4]

Those regulatory agencies born in the 1930s are finding sex discrimination in employment to offend that public interest which they were ordained to safeguard.[c] The National Labor Relations Board (NLRB) has found sex discrimination to arise to an unfair labor practice under section 8,[5] and to be provable to deny certification to a popularly chosen collective bargaining agent under Section 9.[6] Those subject to regulation by the Federal Communications Commission (FCC) know of that agency's published provisions designed to prevent discrimination against women.[7]

---

reach the Supreme Court under this section, the high court upheld Illinois' refusal to license women as attorneys. In an egregious concurrence Mr. Justice Bradley penned the boggling bromide:

"The civil law, as well as nature herself, has always recognized a wide difference in the respective spheres and destinies of men and women.

". . . The natural and proper timidity and delicacy which belongs to the female sex evidently unfits [sic] it for many of the occupations of civil life. The constitution of the family organization, which is founded in the divine ordinance, as well as in the nature of things, indicates the domestic sphere as that which properly belongs to the domain and functions of womanhood. The harmony, not to say identity, of interests and views which belong, or should belong to the family institution is repugnant to the idea of a woman adopting a distinct and independent career from that of her husband. . . . The paramount destiny and mission of woman are to fulfill the noble and benign offices of wife and mother. This is the law of the Creator." Bradwell v. Illinois, 83 U.S. (16 Wall.) 130, 141 (1873).

[c]The Securities and Exchange Commission, a holdout in this trend, was ordered to reconsider its failure to adopt a corporate disclosure regulation requiring companies to report statistics about their equal employment practices. Natural Resources Defense Council, Inc. v. Securities and Exchange Commission. 389 F. Supp. 689 (D.C.D.C. 1974). See also NAACP v. F.P.C., 520 F.2d 432 (D.C. Cir.), cert. granted, 44 U.S.L.W. 3223 (1975).

During the decade beginning in 1963 Congress enacted yet other statutes prohibiting sex discrimination in employment. In 1963 the Equal Pay Amendment[8] was added to the Fair Labor Standards Act, forbidding employers subject to it to discriminate in regard to wages on the basis of sex. The Civil Rights Act of the following year created the Equal Employment Opportunity Commission and forbade discrimination on the basis of race, color, sex, religion, or national origin in Title VII.[9] In 1972 the Education Act of that year was amended to forbid sex discrimination in federally assisted education.[10] The Revenue Sharing Act of the same year banned discrimination in programs funded by federal "block grants."[11]

In addition to the Congressional activity of the decade, the White House in 1965 issued Executive Order 11,246 requiring all those with government contracts of $10,000 or more not to discriminate and further requiring certain larger contractors and subcontractors to undertake affirmative action to employ and promote minorities and women.[12]

The requirements which the private sector manager of a substantial enterprise is most likely to encounter in recruiting and remunerating women in management are those arising under the Equal Pay Amendment to the Fair Labor Standards Act, Title VII of the Civil Rights Act, and Executive Order 11,246.

The other provisions, recited by way of overview, are less likely to be encountered. The Supreme Court put a damper on counsel's incentive to file suit under the 1871 Civil Rights Act last spring when it decided to disallow the awarding of attorneys' fees to prevailing counsel as "private attorneys general."[13] Assuming that managers are not organized into unions, rulings of the NLRB are not relevant. Matters concerning FCC regulatees, educational institutions, and recipient municipalities are not of routine operational concern to most private sector managers.

Discussion of the Fair Labor Standards Act may seem curiously out of place in an article on women in management. For one remembers clearly that executive, administrative, and professional employees are exempted from the minimum wage and overtime provisions. But there the exemption stops; the 1972 amendments granted equal pay coverage to those white-collar workers.[14]

The Equal Pay Amendment pertains only to situations in which employees engaged in essentially similar work are compensated on sexually disparate scales. (To this extent, the Equal Pay Amendment overlaps with the prohibitions of Title VII.) It does not aid anyone in getting hired or promoted or resisting layoff or discharge. That is the domain of Title VII and Executive Order 11,246. Both of these laws forbid discrimination in employment; the latter also requires an employer of 50 with a government contract of $50,000 or more to plan and carry out affirmative action to remedy the underrepresentation of minorities and women in his work force.[d] Title VII relies on the ultimate sanction of publicly or privately brought litigation in federal district court. Executive Order 11,246 relies on the ultimate (but infrequent) sanction of debarment from further government contracts, imposed after an administrative hearing.[e]

Steps necessary to avoid the prohibitions of Title VII will also avoid the prohibitions of E.O. 11,246. For economy of exposition, separate reference to E.O. 11,246 hereinafter will be omitted.

Three Basic Precepts

There are three basic precepts that will serve as a trustworthy guide in interpreting Title VII:

1. Title VII obviously proscribes treating persons differently on the basis of race, color, sex, religion, or national origin.[f]

2. Title VII faults facially nondiscriminatory criteria which

---

[d]The $50,000 contract and 50 employees trigger the affirmation action obligation for nonconstruction contractors. In construction the obligation attaches to contractors or subcontractors performing work on federal or federally assisted projects which are estimated to exceed $500,000 in total cost.

[e]The recent debarment of a Dallas envelope manufacturer was only the fifth contractor debarred in the decade of E.O. 11,246 enforcement. *Woman Law Reporter* 1.31 (1974).

[f]Section 702 excuses religious organizations from the prohibition against discrimination on the basis of religion. Section 703 admits of the possibility that in certain situations sex, religion, and national origin may be shown to be bona fide occupational requirements.

have an adverse impact on a group protected under the Act, unless the criteria are required by business necessity.[g]

3. Even where the respondent has discontinued those practices which discriminated by intent or consequence, the effect of the abandoned practices may be perpetuated by seemingly unobjectionable and routine decisions.

The first precept needs no elaboration save to point out that its force is not limited to faulting only criteria applied against all persons of a sex. If a condition incident only to some members of a sex is responded to differently than that same condition is responded to in a member of the opposite sex, Title VII is violated.[h] Thus an airline's discharge of stewardesses who married was found to violate Title VII where male flight personnel were not discharged upon marriage.[15] Similarly, it violates that same "sex plus" principle to impose different assumptions as to child care upon the mother of preschool age children than upon the father of preschool age children.[16]

The second precept is of greater sophistication. Here intent becomes irrelevant and consequence all important. Job qualifications which operate to exclude a protected class, e.g. females, are forbidden by Title VII unless manifestly related to job performance. For example minimum height requirements and minimum weight requirements have been successfully knocked out by female litigants under Title VII.[17][1] Exclusion

---

[g]The defense of business necessity was approved by the Supreme Court in Griggs v. Duke Power Company, 401 U.S. 424, 432 (1971), to allow an employer to redeem a requirement that has an adverse impact if he can show the requirement to "have a manifest relationship to the employment in question." A leading case from the Fourth Circuit imposes the following additional gloss: "[T]here must be available no acceptable alternative policies or practices which would better accomplish the business purpose advanced, or accomplish it equally well with a lesser differential racial impact." Robinson v. Lorillard Corp., 444 F.2d 791, at 798 (4th Cir.), *cert. dismissed*, 404 U.S. 1006 (1971). But see Albemarle Paper Co. v. Moody, 422 U.S. 405 (1975).

[h]The Courts of Appeal have concluded that this rule does not extend to long hair on male shoulders. Baker v. California Land Title Co., 507 F.2d 895 (9th Cir. 1974), *cert. denied*, 422 U.S. 1046 (1975); Dodge v. Giant Food Co., 488 F.2d 1333 (D.C. Cir. 1973), Willingham v. Macon Telegraph, 507 F.2d 1084 (5th Cir. 1975) (*en banc*), Knott v. Missouri Pacific Railroad Co. ___ F.2d ___ (8th Cir. 1975).

[i] But in Smith v. Troyan, a 5'8" height requirement for police was upheld as manifestly related to ability to intimidate in effecting arrest and thus redeemed from adverse impact. 520 F.2d 492 (6th Cir. 1975).

from consideration of those with illegitimate children also has been found to have an adverse impact on females.[18] Test batteries which have a larger mechanical component than is relevant to the job or the requirement of a degree with a more peculiarly "masculine" major than is necessary to do the job similarly may violate Title VII in closing the doors of the management suite to women.

Rigorous self-audits are required to avoid this unintended and often unperceived exclusion. The problem cannot be successfully finessed by hiring a "satisfactory" number. First of all, there are three different judicially approved formulas for demonstrating adverse impact, each of which may give a different "satisfactory" number.[j]

Secondly, a sexually tainted failure to promote is as much a violation of Title VII as is a sexually tainted failure to hire. Thus to hire a gaggle of employees with an eye to composition rather than to competence is to sow the seeds of future charges.

The third precept faults those "neutral" practices which perpetuate consequences of discrimination, even where such discrimination has been detected and discontinued. An aptly entitled law review note on this concept was waggishly styled "Title VII: How to Break the Law without Really Trying."[19] This standard was used to fault as well-spoken-of a practice as "promotion from within" where the outside applicant was of a group which had not yet internally made its way up the promotion ladder to the level receiving consideration.[20]

In another recent case the court ruled that where a company has historically classified its employees on the basis of sex, it is unlawful for the company to rely on word-of-mouth notice of

---

[j] As was pointed out in Green v. Missouri Pacific R.R. Co.:

"A disproportionate racial impact may be established statistically in any one of three ways. The first procedure considers whether blacks as a class (or at least blacks in a specified geographical area) are excluded by the employment practice in question at a substantially higher rate than whites. [Citation of authorities omitted.]

"The second procedure focuses on a comparison of the percentage of black and white job applicants actually excluded by the employment practice or test of the particular company or government agency in question. [Citation of authorities omitted.]

"Finally, a third procedure examines the level of employment of blacks by the company or government agency in comparison to the percentage of blacks in the relevant geographical area." [Citation of authorities omitted.] 523 F.2d 1290, at 1293-94 (8th Cir. 1975).

job vacancies.[21] That court also found that women had been discriminated against where judgments as to promotability of employees were made by all-male foremen and supervisors without objective criteria to guide them.[22] Since we all tend to see virtue more readily in those who remind us of ourselves, it is imperative to guard against situations which are so conducive to subtle but foreseeable discrimination.

Equalizing Prospects

As the foregoing discussion has hopefully underscored, Title VII requires one to discard many of those rules of thumb of yesteryear which excluded so effectively and to focus—rather empirically—on the individual's ability to perform a job's component tasks. The courts have been emphatically clear that such an inquiry into an individual's fitness must be unencumbered by sexual stereotypes, whether they attach to the requirements of the job or the presumed attributes of an applicant. Assumptions about customer preference is one of those encumbrances.[23] Obviously subsumed within that example are presumptions that male workers would not abide a female supervisor. State protective laws, as they are popularly so-called, and notions as to conditions under which a woman ought not work are other judicially condemned encumbrances.[k] Nor ought women be excluded from consideration because of assumptions as to the lack of a relevant trait: aggressiveness, for example, in the case of sales work.[24]

Turning from those sexually stereotyped selection criteria which violate Title VII *per se*, let us next consider a personnel rule frequently questioned by married females: the rule against nepotism. Given the prevalence of the nuclear family unit and the frequent relocation of families, a rule against nepotism functions in great part as a "no-spouse" rule. Employers who have adopted such a rule speak of it as reducing problems in

---

[k]As Judge Johnson remarked: "Men have always had the right to determine whether the incremental increase in remuneration for strenuous, dangerous, obnoxious, boring or unromantic tasks is worth the candle. The promise of Title VII is that women are now on an equal footing." Weeks v. Southern Bell Telephone and Telegraph Co., 408 F.2d 228, 236 (5th Cir. 1969).

shift assignments, transfers, scheduling of vacations, promotions, incidence of sick leave, and partiality in supervision.

The rule against nepotism has succumbed to judicial attack where a sexually biased history of exceptions could be shown.[2 5] However, assuming unwavering application, the rule would not offend our first precept of intentional discrimination against a sex, nor does it suggest an adverse impact which would engage our second precept since spouses come in matched pairs.[1]

It is in the fact-conscious application of our third precept—"is past discrimination perpetuated"—that the rule against nepotism stands or falls. The most widely discussed case to date involved a suit brought by a female against her husband's employer, an airline.[2 6] The airline won because the woman was unable to show a perpetuation of past discrimination.

Airlines and hospitals predictably will win these cases because they have hired more than a proportionate number of women for a long time. However, if such a suit were brought against a trucking line, the plaintiff likely would stand to win. Inasmuch as teamstering is almost an all-male calling, the impact of a "no-spouse" rule would fall almost wholly upon women.

It should be emphasized that where discrimination is evidenced, "good" motives on the part of the employer do not excuse the violation or mitigate the remedy.[2 7] A trucking line's rule against unmarried male/female teams was found to have a disproportionate impact on females since it was virtually impossible for female truck drivers to find a partner of the same sex. The employer's expressed concern about propriety did not suffice to save the rule.[2 8] Similarly, the discharge of an

---

[1]In public employment where constitutional limitations can be invoked, there is another basis for challenging the "no-spouse" rule. Governmental benefits, such as employment, cannot be conditioned upon the surrender of fundamental rights. The Nebraska Supreme Court recently voided a city personnel rule which conditioned continued employment upon nonmarriage to a fellow city employee. Voichahoske v. City of Grant Island, 231 N.W. 2d 124 (1975).

A private sector rule which restricts a spouse's employment in much the same fashion as the rule against nepotism may deserve comment here. In Emory v. Georgia Hospital Service Association, the court held that a company rule which prohibited the employment of persons whose spouse worked for a competitor was not discriminatory since the policy applied equally to men and to women. 4 EPD Paragraph 7785 (M.D. Ga.), aff'd. per curiam, 446 F.2d 897 (5th Cir. 1971).

unmarried female employee having an affair with a fellow employee violated Title VII where the married male employee was only "talked to."[29] The purportedly benign decision to layoff a "working housewife" with 20 years service and to retain a "family man" with 2 years service, who presumedly had the more pressing need for employment, was nevertheless reckoned sex discrimination.[30]

The identification of the male worker as the "breadwinner" with presumably greater income needs is one of the phenomena to which the Equal Pay Amendment was directed. Disparities in pay encountered in the lower grades may be compounded when a female employee is promoted into the management suite. This is the case particularly when compensation upon promotion is not fixed by the new position but is a percentage increment on prior wage experience. The January 18, 1973, opinion letter of the Acting Administrator of Wage and Hour Division illustrates this problem in the AT&T system.[31]

More subtle but no less endemic are the inequalities which creep into training programs and arise in channeling into slots with less promotion potential. Where training is primarily of an on-the-job, as-time-permits variety, some males to whom the training task falls have been observed to be more comfortable about, and thus to find more time for, showing the new *man* the ropes. Even where training is structured to limit such variations, extra seminar and exposure opportunities have on occasion been seen to be a preserve for the "high potential white male." That is a situation to which one ought to be alert. A pitfall into which financial institutions have been alleged to have stumbled is a channeling of women and blacks into personnel, collections, trusts, and consumer services and away from commercial loans, the lucrative mainstream from which the majority of senior officials are chosen.[32]

Conclusion

This article has sought to equip you to recognize both the salient and subtle barriers to female employment which courts and commissions have condemned. The removal of these and analogous hurdles should allow the more proportionate use of distaff talent. Those who decline to redress the impediments to advancement of females and the consequent paucity of women at the upper levels may well, in time, be confounded by a court's order enjoining discriminatory practices, requiring back pay, and mandating numbers or fractions of female promotees. As we enter the second decade of court enforcement of Title VII, numerical standards are being set for promotion as well as for hiring. In a recent Detroit case a preliminary injunction was entered ordering the promotion of 19 women.[33] The consent decree involving the Steel Industry went the precentage route in reserving promotions into supervisory occupations for females.[34] The management and morale problems which these solutions entail will prompt the astute to set aright those situations upon which such orders could be predicated.

Footnotes

1. 42 U.S.C.A. Section 1983.

2. Johnson v. City of Cincinnati, 450 F.2d 796 (6th Cir. 1971).

3. 42 U.S.C.A. Section 1985 (3).

4. Pendrell v. Chatham College, 370 F. Supp. 494, at 495, and 386 F. Supp. 341 (W.D. Pa. 1974).

5. *Glass Bottle Blowers Assn., Locals 106 and 245*, 210 N.L.R.B. No. 131 (1974), enforcement granted, 520 F.2d 693 (6th Cir. 1975).

6. *Alden Press, Inc.*, 212 N.L.R.B. No. 91 (1974).

7. 40 Federal Register 31625 (July 28, 1975).

8. 29 U.S.C.A. Section 206 (d).

9. 42 U.S.C.A. Section 2000-e *et seq.*

10. 20 U.S.C.A. Section 1681 *et seq.*

11. 31 U.S.C.A. Section 1221.

12. 3 C.F.R. 169 (1974). The ban against sex discrimination was added to E.O. 11,246 in 1967 by E.O. 11,375.

13. Alyeska Pipeline Service Co. v. Wilderness Society, 419 U.S. 823 (1975).

14. P.L. 92-318; 86 Stat. 235, at 375.

15. Sprogis v. United Air Lines, 444 F.2d 1194 (7th Cir.), *cert. denied*, 404 U.S. 991 (1971).

16. Phillips v. Martin Marietta Corp., 400 U.S. 542 (1971).

17. Peltier v. City of Fargo, 396 F. Supp. 710 (D.C. N.D. 1975); Meadows v. Ford Motor Co., 510 F.2d 939 (6th Cir. 1975).

18. Andrews v. Drew Municipal School District, 371 F. Supp. 27 (N.D. Miss. 1973), *aff'd.*, 507 F.2d 611 (5th Cir.), *cert. granted*, 44 U.S.L.W. 3200 (1975).

19. 21 *Cath. U.L. Rev.* 103 (1971).

20. Gates v. Georgia-Pacific Corp., 492 F.2d 292 (9th Cir. 1974).

21. Nance v. Union Carbide Corp., 397 F. Supp. 436, 455 (W.D.N.C. 1975).

22. Ibid., at 456.

23. Diaz v. Pan American World Airways, 442 F.2d 385 (5th Cir.), *cert. denied*, 404 U.S. 950 (1971).

24. See 29 C.F.R. 1604.2 (a)(1)(ii), Sex Discrimination Guidelines.

25. Sanbonmatsu v. Boyer, 357 N.Y.S. 2d 245 (4th App. Div. 1974).

26. Harper v. Trans World Airlines, 385 F. Supp. 1001 (E.D. Mo. 1974), *aff'd.* 10 EPD Paragraph 10,498 (8th Cir. 1975).

27. Albemarle Paper Co. v. Moody, 422 U.S. 405 (1975).

28. Lyon v. Pirkle Refrigerated Freight Lines, Inc., 2 CCH *Employ. Prac. Guide* Paragraph 5197 (Wisc. Dept. of Indust., Labor & Hum. Rel. 1973). Cf. Com. Dec. 72-0644, CCH *E.E.O.C. Decisions 1973* Paragraph 6315.

29. Com. Dec. 71-2678, CCH *E.E.O.C. Decisions 1973* Paragraph 6287.

30. Pyzik v. Hoerner-Waldorf Corp., 2 CCH *Employ. Prac. Guide* Paragraph 5251 (Ill. F.E.P.C. 1974).

31. 2 CCH *Employ. Prac. Guide* Paragraph 5132 at p. 3266.

32. See, for example, the consent decree entered in United States v. Household Finance Corp., 4 EPD Paragraph 7680 (N.D. Ill. 1972).

33. Schaefer v. Tannian, 8 EPD Paragraph 9605 (E.D. Mich. 1974).

34. United States v. Allegheny-Ludlum Indus., Inc., 8 Lab. Rel. Rep. 431:125, at 150 (N.D. Ala. 1974).

Editors' Note: At the editors' request Mr. Stacy has outlined the significant issues relating to maternity leave and layoffs. We felt the readers should have the benefit of his comments. Since these issues are still being defined in the courts, his comments must be taken as tentative in nature.

The Maternity Issue

THOSE PORTIONS of the Equal Employment Opportunity Commission's *Guidelines on Sex Discrimination*, 29 Code of Federal Regulations Section 1604, touching upon the treatment of pregnancy and disability incident thereto have enjoyed almost universal endorsement by the courts. That is in keeping with the well-settled principle that the interpretation of the agency entrusted with the administration and enforcement of a federal statute, while not binding on a court, is nevertheless entitled to "great deference." *Griggs* v. *Duke Power Co.*, 401 U.S. 424 (1971). An agency interpretation ought be disregarded only in such peculiar circumstances as where the legislative history indicates a Congressional intent to the contrary. *Espinosa* v. *Farah Mfg. Co.*, 414 U.S. 86 (1973).

For ease in referring to these cases for guidance I have grouped them under the following topics: refusal to hire, discharge, involuntary leave, waiting period for coverage, sick leave or annual leave, health benefits and income maintenance.

1. *Refusal to Hire.* The Sex Discrimination Guidelines, 29 C.F.R. Section 1604, state at Section 1604.10(a): "A written or unwritten employment policy or practice which excludes from employment applicants or employees because of pregnancy is in *prima facie* violation of Title VII."

2. *Discharge.* For clarity in analysis we will treat in turn (a) licit, but nondisabling, pregnancy; (b) disabling pregnancy; and, lastly, (c) pregnancy out of wedlock.

a. To discharge any employee who simply becomes pregnant violates Title VII of the 1964 Civil Rights Act. *Holthaus* v. *Compton & Sons, Inc.*, 514 F.2d 651 (8th Cir. 1975).

b. If the pregnancy should become disabling, Section 1604.10(b) of the guidelines requires that the disability be treated as are other temporary disabilities. Thus discharge would be impermissible unless all other temporary disabilities occasion discharge. *Caveat*: Even facially evenhanded discharge policy may have adverse impact. See 29 C.F.R. Section 1604.10(c) & 2 Employ. Prac. Guide Paragraph 6422.

c. To discharge or fail to hire a female for existing or past pregnancy out of wedlock, or abortion thereof, is impermissible sex discrimination. *Doe* v. *Osteopathic Hospital*, 334 F. Supp. 1357 (D. Kan. 1971); *Cirino* v. *Walsh*, 66 Misc. 2d 250, 321 N.Y.S. 2d 493 (Sup. Ct. 1971) 3 EPD Paragraph 8206; *Andrews* v. *Drew Municipal School District*, 507 F.2d 611 (5th Cir.) *cert. granted*, 44 USLW 3200 (1975); *Drake* v. *Covington County Board of Education*, 371 F. Supp. 974 (M.D. Ala. 1974); *Reinhardt* v. *Board of Education of Alton*, 311 N.E. 2d 710 (Ill. Cir. Ct. 1973), 7 EPD Paragraph 9057.

3. *Involuntary Leave*. The tradition of imposing compulsory maternity leave at the fifth or sixth month rather than leaving it as a matter for the woman and a physician to decide has been condemned in cases arising under both the 14th Amendment and Title VII. *Cleveland Board of Education* v. *LaFleur*, 414 U.S. 632 (1974); *Green* v. *Waterford Board of Education*, 473 F.2d 629 (2nd Cir. 1973); *Buckley* v. *Coyle Public School System*, 476 F.2d 92 (10th Cir. 1973); *Newmon* v. *Delta Air Lines*, 374 F. Supp. 238 (N.D. Ga. 1973). The employer, of course, is as entitled to rely on the judgment of the plant physician in individual cases of disability incident to pregnancy as the employer would be in other types of disability. See Commission Decision No. 72-0372, *CCH Employment Practices Guide Para. 6412*.

4. *Waiting Period for Coverage*. To impose a waiting period for maternity coverage that would not be similarly required, for instance, for a broken leg is to violate Section 1604.10(b) of the Guidelines in failing to treat disability incident to pregnancy like other temporary disabilities. Although as yet there is no reported federal court decision reiterating this teaching, the teaching is underscored in Florida Attorney General's Opinion 74-153, CCH *Employment Practices Guide* Paragraph 5250. See also *Cedar Rapids Community School District* v. *Parr*, 227 N.W. 2d 486, (Iowa Sup. Ct. 1974) 9 EPD Para. 10,016 and Comm. Dec. 72-1919, CCH *EEOC Decisions* Para. 6370.

5. *Sick Leave or Annual Leave*. To require annual leave to be taken rather than sick leave for a period of disability incident to pregnancy is to fail to accord the same treatment afforded other

temporary disabilities as is required by Section 1604.10(b) of the Guidelines. That is the clear holding of *Hutchison* v. *Lake Oswego School District*, 519 F.2d 961 (9th Cir. 1975); *Lillo* v. *Plymouth Board of Education*, 8 EPD Para. 9510, 8 FEP Cases 21 (N.D. Ohio 1973); *Farkas* v. *South Western City School District*, 506 F.2d 1400 (6th Cir. 1974); *Dessenberg* v. *American Metal Forming Co.*, 8 EPD Para. 9575, 8 FEP Cas.290 (N.D. Ohio 1973); *Zichy* v. *Philadelphia*, 392 F. Supp. 338 (E.D. Pa. 1975).

6. *Health Benefits*. To exclude pregnancy from disabilities covered by a group health insurance policy violates Title VII. *Gilbert* v. *General Electric*, 519 F.2d 661, (4th Cir.) *cert. granted*, 96 S.Ct. 36 (1975) and *Wetzel* v. *Liberty Mutual Ins. Co.*, 511 F.2d 199 (3rd Cir.) *cert. granted* 95 S.Ct. 2415 (1975); *CWA* v. *A.T.T.*, 513 F.2d 1024 (2nd Cir. 1975). Contra: *Newmon* v. *Delta Air Lines*, 374 F. Supp. 238 (N.D. Ga. 1973). The *Gilbert-Wetzel-C.W.A.* line of decisions does not appear to be affected by the Supreme Court's June 1974 decision in *Geduldig* v. *Aiello*, 417 U.S. 484 (1974), that under the Equal Protection Clause of the Fourteenth Amendment, the State of California could constitutionally exclude normal pregnancy disability from coverage under its state-operated disability insurance program. *Geduldig* raised Constitutional question and the Supreme Court did not decide whether a similar exclusion of benefits to female workers by an employer covered by Title VII would also be justified. Title VII, a statute enacted pursuant to Congress' power to regulate interstate commerce, imposes a different and more stringent standard upon the conduct of employers than does the Equal Protection Clause of the Fourteenth Amendment. The six federal appellate courts which have considered the guidelines since *Geduldig* have accepted the Commission's view that Title VII imposes a more stringent standard in maternity benefit cases than is imposed under the Fourteenth Amendment. *C.W.A.* v. *A.T.T.*, 513 F.2d 1024 (2nd Cir. 1975); *Wetzel* v. *Liberty Mutual*, 511 F.2d 199 (3rd Cir. 1975); *Gilbert* v. *G.E.*, 519 F.2d 661 (4th Cir. 1975); *Satty* v. *Nashville Gas*, 522 F.2d 850 (6th Cir. 1975); *Holthaus* v. *Compton & Sons*, 514 F.2d 651 (8th Cir. 1975); *Hutchison* v. *School Dist.*, 519 F.2d 961 (9th Cir. 1975).

7. *Income Maintenance*. The same provisions of 1604.10(b) that forbid the exclusion of disability incident to pregnancy

from disabilities under group health insurance policies also forbid the exclusion of disability incident to pregnancy from salary continuation policies. *Wetzel* v. *Liberty Mutual Insurance Co.*, 372 F. Supp. 1146 (W.D. Pa. 1974), aff'd. 511 F.2d 199 (3rd Cir.) *cert. granted*, 95 S.Ct. 2415 (1975).

The *Gilbert* and *Wetzel* cases mentioned in paragraphs 6 and 7 were argued to the Supreme Court on January 19-20, 1976 and are now under deliberation.

Natalie Lang *is Vice President of Corporate Social Policy for Booz, Allen & Hamilton Inc., New York.* Dr. Donald O. Jewell *is Professor of Management, School of Business Administration, Georgia State University, Atlanta.*

This article is reprinted with permission from Atlanta Economic Review, *March-April 1976, pp. 25-31.*

7

The Female Corporate Jock: What Price Equality?

An Interview With Natalie Lang

Donald O. Jewell

Why did you want this interview titled "The Female Corporate Jock"?

I tend to think of the really successful young male in an organization as a "jock." It's the image of the athlete. Competitive, assertive, resourceful, hard working, and respected for his competence by others in the organization. He is a corporate man's man—the role model for others aspiring to succeed.

Young women as yet don't have a corporate role model. There are no female corporate jocks at present. We've had to use the male model and adapt it to our own feminine style.

I guess I would like to see myself as a kind of female jock. By no means am I typical or an ideal role model for other women, but I have been reasonably successful in a male-oriented, rapidly changing company and industry, and hopefully this interview will give other women some insights into what it means to be in a high-level, highly visible position in a large, highly competitive, predominately male organization and with a company top in its profession.

How did you decide to seek a career in business?

As far back as I can remember it was clear to me that I wanted to be in the business world. I can't remember trying to decide between nursing, academics, or other fields. I was always focused on a career in business. I was not clear, however, as to what field in business or what organization would best suit my needs and provide me with the opportunities for growth and success that I desired. One of the basic questions I had to answer was whether or not I wanted to be my own boss. Did I want to run my own company? The question was should women who had the ambition, motivation, and guts try to run their own show and attempt to advance the state of the art, or should they try to get through the corporate ladder in an already established organization? In this decision I was, for the most part, influenced by men and not women. Probably the only identifiable role models known to me at that time were men. I did not, however, take the decision as to a selection of field and organization lightly. I pondered the alternatives for some time and began to search about to determine what other women have done, given similar kinds of backgrounds. In other words, who were my peers and what and whom was I competing against? Throughout my career I have talked with many women in quite dissimilar positions who seemed to have made decisions and who were successful in ways I wanted to be successful—and with whom I counseled. Interestingly enough, and somewhat reassuringly, many successful women are often reassessing their priorities . . .that old question still popping up, "What do I want to be when I grow up?" In spite of their success they, too, still have very basic and serious questions concerning themselves, their careers, personal lives, children, their direction, and the way in which goals are to be achieved. As a group, however, they were convinced that I should seek my career within an already established organization that could afford me the opportunities for impact, growth, and success.

So your choice of accepting a position in Booz, Allen & Hamilton was well thought out, and your entry into the business world was a very clear and conscious decision?

That is definitely true.

What is your current role in your organization?

My title is Vice President of Corporate Social Policy. As part of my responsibility I often act as the bridge between the management and the staff. I help management think through a whole range of questions concerning women, minorities, social policy, and so on. These questions relate to such issues as corporate contributions and community service, as well as personal issues dealing with compensation, upward mobility programs, training, development, and recruiting. I often find myself on internal and external issues defending or explaining management positions, and at the same time trying to bring about and influence change. As you might suspect, this responsibility can often create conflicts. I really have to ask the question as to what kind of credibility do I have when I go to management to discuss issues relative to our professional women. I worry that they will look at me and consider what I am proposing or championing to be self-serving. I often wonder if they are able to look at me as a partner who is genuinely concerned with organizational issues, or feel that I am pushing changes from which I too may receive residual benefit. For this and many other factors, I have on occasion asked myself whether or not I should get out of the social policy area. While social policy can be an extremely meaningful career, and one which I find continually challenging and exciting, I have considered other career alternatives in the firm and my boss and I talk often on this subject. I have been with Booz, Allen & Hamilton for almost ten years, and I'm quite certain the consulting business is a good fit, and I'd like to continue my career here.

Did you begin your career at Booz Allen in social policy?

No. In 1966 I was the first woman recruiter that the firm had ever hired. Recruiting is a critical aspect of our business, and a recruiter's success in the firm is dependent upon the competence and quality of the people he or she may recommend. It is a difficult and demanding job, and one that many of my associates thought I was crazy to accept. You see, at that point in my career I was the President of an executive search company based in Chicago. I felt very strongly that my experience with Booz Allen would broaden me and help develop skills that would be necessary for me to be truly effective and successful in business. They used to say that to be successful in business you needed a B.S., an M.B.A., and a B.A.H. That's how attractive the consulting business, and our firm in particular, was.

When they hired me I was often reminded by many partners that I was going to be somewhat of a pacesetter. They had never hired a woman for a recruitment position. Naturally that put an incredible pressure on me. I had the feeling that I could never do anything wrong because I might ruin it for any other woman trying to get into or through this system. There were other women in the firm at the time, but they were not in recruiting. Interestingly enough, they chose to use my recruiting skills in the areas where I lacked previous experience. They said to me, "We know what you know and that's why we hired you, but we think you can learn and broaden and grow." They said, "We think this assignment will broaden your base," and I replied, "That's the last thing I want to do." I found that challenge frustrating because I didn't think I could score fast enough to be a success. For example, I didn't know anything about the public sector. I didn't know anything about hospitals. Hell, I'd never even been sick. But they felt that they would do better in the long run if they were to build on my base of strengths, expertise, and capabilities. They were right, and I was wrong. I now understand the rationale of building on a base of strengths, because I have since done many things in many areas, including the job I currently hold, that I would never have been able to do if, in fact, the firm had not pushed me into developing a broader base of expertise and skill. Good thing they didn't listen to me in this case.

What effect do you feel your presence in the organization has had relative to the opportunities of other women?

Well, I was the first, and now there are many women and they are in many areas and in many units of our business. One could fantasize that had I broken my pick, which is our expression for failing, that top management might have decided that women might not, for example, make good recruiters and therefore be hesitant to give an opportunity to another woman in the future. I guess the issue would have been whether top management would have seen my failure as a result of my own lack of competence or whether management would have generalized my failures to include all women. In any event, I was successful, and since that time many women have been hired and are very successful in this firm. I also was the first woman to do executive search work in our firm. And in 1969 I was promoted to associate level (middle management level in our firm). We have since hired other women into executive search, and they also have been very successful in this area. It has become a whole new arena for women to consider, and women are very much considered for positions in that function and in many public accounting, management, and consulting firms as well as executive search firms. Could these opportunities be attributed to me? It doesn't have to be perceived as such, but a senior officer said to me when I was promoted into the position, "If you don't do well in this function, you'll make it very hard for other women to aspire to do executive search in this firm. You have a responsibility to show our management and our clients that women can do search work for the top management in our client organizations," which is where our executive search work is concentrated, at the top management level.

What were they looking for when they hired you? What about you do you think they valued? What did you have to be to win in the system?

What made me palatable? My style, I suppose.

Could you expand on that a bit?

They knew I was aggressive. They knew I was well motivated. Not that they were clairvoyant. I told them I was interested in committing myself to a career and to Booz Allen, and that I was willing to work extremely hard to succeed in both.

They found out that they didn't have to say "sorry, Natalie" when they made reference to "you guys" in a meeting. They didn't have to worry about offending me in the everydayness of the firm. The fact is, they offended me all the time—if you're offended by the fact that without the woman's movement there were no guys and gals, hes and shes; the jargon hadn't switched yet. It was a *male* business. There was no way I wasn't offended.

But you did not react to these offenses as being personal?

I did not. When they felt the need to swear to make their point in a meeting they didn't have to apologize or say "oops sorry, Natalie." These were partners in an unliberated world. Women weren't liberated then. They weren't coming into the movement in masses. They hadn't yet dealt with the Pill, the married woman reentering the business world, government pressures, and so on. These were men who at that point had probably never considered that women might someday play a major part in the business world.

Did you ever question that position?

Certainly not at the beginning, and not in any dramatic way. When I was appraised and given my compensation, I didn't view it in terms of my gender. My concern was with my satisfaction, not the implication with respect to women.

Once my boss said to me, "Do you realize you're the highest paid female in the firm?" I told him it sounded to me like the rest of our women were underpaid.

But I really didn't push the system. I had elected to move ahead, but I really wasn't all that threatening. I wasn't a lily pushover, but the spectrum of acceptable behaviors is very wide at Booz Allen. I didn't have the advantage of knowing what was coming for women. I wasn't that perceptive. I really knew only one thing in cement—I wanted to be very successful at Booz Allen. There was no question what my goal was, but I can't remember saying, "Is it possible to get through as a woman?" That's a different question, and maybe I should have asked it. But I wasn't that sophisticated, and very frankly at that time I didn't view that as a problem if I could deliver the goods.

Nobody dealt with that issue at Booz, Allen & Hamilton. And I didn't discuss it with other women in the firm because there weren't any in positions comparable to mine with whom I would have been comfortable discussing this.

Okay, but your being a woman must have been an issue to some extent.

I suspect they said, "Natalie is a woman or a girl—I suspect girl in that case—what are we going to do with her?" I don't think they worried about being able to satisfy my appetite for work, but I don't believe they thought I would come in one day and say "I want to be a Partner." I don't think they were any more sophisticated than I.

Did you see yourself as a jock then?

No. I was just a woman who wanted to succeed in a tough and highly male-oriented industry. I didn't see myself as doing it for women, nor did I see myself as a role model for other women. I was too concerned with my own career. I didn't see myself as a pacesetter in any movement, but there is no question I was visible, and I believe the firm enjoyed having a woman out front. In some respects, Booz Allen was a pacesetter by letting me be out front. The company was willing to take a risk. And in those days it didn't really need the public relations and had no government pressures to respond to.

Did being the visible woman create any special problems?

Yes. Suddenly I found myself wrestling with issues such as what do I do when a guy on the staff asks me out. I was young, single, why not? But I was reluctant to do that. I was traveling from time to time with members of the staff, and I felt the need to develop a platform or a set of guidelines that I could live with forever. One decision was, and I had often heard this one, that you don't play where you work. This was tough. How do you say *no* gracefully, and not injure the male ego and not build future barriers in a working relationship? How do you say *no* to dinner, but *yes* to lunch? As a result of the rules of my game, I've eaten a lot of cottage cheese at my desk. I also decided to give up smoking in the office. I found out that ten minutes was wasted every time I decided to light a cigarette. Whether the guy was a smoker or nonsmoker, he would feel the need to hustle for a match. Today that wouldn't be an issue, but then it consumed a considerable amount of time and it was a total waste. Frankly, as a recruiter you don't have time to waste. So I made it easy and gave up smoking during the interview. Now I smoke only when I am alone in the office. I think I really lucked out on that one.

One of the major adjustments for me was that I had to learn how to travel. The guys that I traveled with always put their luggage under the seat because they didn't want to waste time waiting for their bags. This was a totally new experience for me. I don't think women tend to be compact in packing. Up until this point, when I vacationed I would take three pieces of luggage for one week in the islands. Twenty bathing suits. That was where I was coming from, that was the woman I was. Four pairs of white slacks to go to California for three days. In business when you're traveling constantly, you have neither the time to wait for the luggage nor the strength to carry it. Up until then I would have taken everything but the ironing board and the washer. My whole technique had to change. Today's women already know that. But I was yesterday's woman. I was the 60s woman, not the 70s woman. I don't feel I am over the hill, but I am definitely of another generation. I didn't know what women did when they packed their clothes to be in New York one day and California the next. How did they set their hair? How did they keep their blouses clean? I don't mean to imply that I was totally Mary Poppins. As President of my own company I had traveled considerably, but as the boss I could do it any way I wanted and at my convenience. Now I was in a system where the identifiable role models were men. There weren't many women on the road, so I had to look to the men and adapt my behavior to theirs. That's one reason I started wearing pants suits, because it is often much easier to travel in slacks. You get more mileage with fewer clothes and a few accessories.

I want to get back to the issue of What Price Equality. *Some people may view adapting to the male role model as giving up a lot of things that would be valued by women. I heard you saying some of that.*

Obviously, I'm looking back a lot. There is a difference when I look ahead and talk about today and the future. Did I think then that I was giving up anything? No, because the caveat was to get through the system. I assessed what was palatable for me to give up and what was absolutely out of the question. Take the issue of travel, for example. They don't give you a manual when you join, but you soon learn that you don't travel during working hours. You get up at 5:00 in the morning for the first flight and take the last flight back at night. I immediately changed my life to accommodate that. I felt that was not hard for me to trade off, because the system was the same for everybody. On the other hand, there were some things that might not have been palatable for me. One of those was to go through side entrances of clubs where the firm often held staff meetings. That annoyed me. I didn't do anything about it until I reached my present position, but I objected very strongly at having to walk through the side door of the Union League Club. During meetings I was never asked to take notes or to go get coffee, but I did object when references were made to the fact that I was the only woman present and that reference was somehow a demeaning one. All in all, however, I do not feel that I was compromising my femininity in adapting to the system. I wanted to get through, and I adapted my behavior to fit the demands of the system. May I relate a story at this point that had some important implications for me?

Of course.

I had been involved in an executive search assignment to find the president of a subsidiary company. The day of the presentation to the client the senior officer read the report and said he would take the lead in the presentation because he wasn't particularly impressed with what we had done. I was amazed because I thought we had done well, but I did not, nor did my boss, object. The presentation was made by the senior officer to the chairman of the board of the client and a whole host of his top management. I remained totally silent during the first part of the meeting. I was uncomfortable, and my discomfort was enhanced by the fact that I desperately needed to go to the bathroom. I had been drinking coffee continuously since 8:00 in the morning, and by 11:00 was in serious trouble. Unfortunately, I didn't at that time feel secure enough to excuse myself and walk out of the office nor did I know where to find what I needed. During the lunch break, the senior officer called me over and said, "There are three reasons why you could be here today. The first one is that you are a secretary, and if you are, I haven't seen you take one damn note. The second is that you're here to amuse me, and, as I think about that, the thought has appeal, but since it's also not true, let's talk about the third reason you're here. You're the associate on the job and you've done most of the work and you understand the assignment as well as, if not better than, anybody else here. Now, Natalie, I'll give you one piece of advice that should hold you well as you move through Booz, Allen & Hamilton. A young male associate can be silent at a client meeting and be respected for the fact that he knows when to shut up and let his bosses take the lead. There's a marvelous respect for a young man knowing when not to be visible. When that young man's female peer is brought into a client meeting, however, the client often asks the question, albeit silently, 'Why is she here, what makes her presence here worthwhile?' Natalie, you must make a contribution." At the end of the afternoon, I found one thing to say by asserting myself, but it was very awkward. Since then, in similar situations I am no longer silent if I think I have a contribution to make. To me it's a very interesting point. That senior officer felt strongly that I had to say something in order to establish my credibility. Since that time I'm sure there have been other officers who have wished that I had kept my mouth shut. And other officers who felt I had made an excellent contribution. Evidently, since I have continued to advance, I haven't blown it too many times. I do feel, however, that that advice has served me well. Knowing what to say and when to say it, is a delicate balance that women must constantly contend with.

So there definitely was more pressure on you, being a female, than there was on your male counterparts.

Yes, apparently there was.

You said earlier that you were not, at least initially, attempting to become a role model for other women attempting to succeed in the organization. Obviously you have become one. Do you, as a result of being the woman in the organization that other women look to as a model for their own behaviors, feel any particular pressures?

Quite frankly, the pressure on the visible woman today is enormous, particularly in business. I feel that because I am successful I have to counsel many women for many reasons—some of which I could and should not take time to do. I feel I have to take the time to be thoughtful and helpful to anyone who comes to me with questions concerning their careers. As a result, I am besieged with requests for help. People are constantly wanting me to talk to their wives, their nieces, or their daughters about their careers. Unfortunately, I haven't established my own priorities well enough, nor am I secure enough in my various relationships internally or externally to say I'm sorry, my dance card is filled and I simply don't have the time. I am incredibly care- and feeding-oriented, which may be a function of my gender or it may be just Natalie Lang. How I do my thing in some respects is an incredible pain because it means I can't shortchange anybody. I don't by nature shortchange anything. I am intense by style, and I don't do sloppy work. If you come to me and say, "Please help Carolyn," I can't just help her for five minutes. I have to call her back or say, "Carolyn feel free to call me next Tuesday and tell me how you did"; and then I always seem to stay involved with the Carolyns of the world. My little black book is comparable to the yellow pages. Just look under helping and counseling.

Do you see this as uniquely a female problem?

I'm not really sure. There are guys who take time with people but they seem to understand how to give 5 cents worth instead of $1.00. I'm afraid I'm not mature enough or sophisticated enough. Everything seems to get a priority one tag. I don't know how to give a nickel's worth of quality. I always feel I have to give a dollar. I guess I feel it is just terribly important that women help other women. I believe that very much. I think women should be visibly supportive, so that men can see that women care about other women. We need to break down the misconception that women are afraid to share mantle with other women because they are insecure. I really do not feel that my success will be impaired because other women come to us at Booz Allen. It will not take away from Natalie Lang's future to have many women as partners in the firm. My success will be determined only by my ability to perform. Therefore, having several hundred successful women in Booz Allen will not in any way take away from me or others presently in the system.

So their success can really only help you.

Yes. I see no way that it could hurt. Unfortunately, having achieved considerable success within this organization, I still do not know how to balance my commitment to other women. I have often asked men that I'm close to, how do you give less but still have it be meaningful and worthwhile? How do you give 1% and still have it seem like 100%? This is a dilemma I wrestle with all the time—the demands and the time pressures to meet demands. One never seems to have enough time.

So you feel a pressure not only to perform and be successful, but to be available to help other women.

That's true. I'm good at career counseling, and I feel a strong need to help others. Unfortunately, I also feel tremendous pressure to continue to perform in my job. I feel that it is implicit in my position in social policy to be out front, to continue to maintain the Booz, Allen & Hamilton posture as a leader in social policy. I have to continue to move and shape our firm, the influence we can have on our clients, and others in the consulting industry.

You feel you can't afford to fail.

Correct. I simply can't and don't relax very much. I still act like I'm trying to get through the system. I haven't yet enjoyed one of the degrees of being a partner. I can't decide if that's because of me and my personality or if it's because I'm a woman. Maybe men don't relax either. Maybe it's just a constant "heat in the kitchen" world. I've been a partner only since 1974. Give me 15 years, and I'll tell you. I hope I get interviewed by you in 15 years so I'll know if the whole 15 years was a constant heat in the kitchen. I'm well aware that if one can't stand the heat in the kitchen, they should get the heck out. I can stand it, I have proven that, but is that the way it always is? Isn't there a day when you can move from the kitchen to the living room? How do you know you can go to the living room without jeopardizing your career? At what point can I say, hey, I'm going to give 100% and not give 110%? I'm going to just give 100% and see if anybody notices. I guess I feel that women are the Avis of the industry. We keep trying harder. When do we become the Hertz? I've thought a lot about this. This isn't a glib comment off the top of my head, as you can see. I think about it quite regularly. What caveat could possibly be attractive enough to justify the price? There's only so much money a company can pay you, there's only so much stock it can give you, there's only so much office I can have and so many travel cards. At what point is the trade-off no longer worth it?

Don't you think men have the same questions?

I know they do. But I'm still interested in one important question. Are men and women really putting forth the same amount of effort? Are the men working a little less and getting a little more? Are women having the same results but having to work harder to get them? I don't know that answer. Personally, I think women have to work harder than men. I believe there's less room for errors and they have to work harder to maintain the image of success. I think I probably have to give just a little more to offset being a woman. Is this because of me or the system? I think both.

You just hate to risk it.

Yes. I'm not going to risk it. My career is much too important to me. It isn't worth finding out, so I'll give the extra 10%. I don't want to imply that I'm working harder than men at Booz Allen. I don't want to imply that at all, because I don't know that. I think men or anyone else in our firm work incredibly hard all the time. But I do know that I'm constantly pushing myself beyond the 100% level.

Isn't that going to affect you in the long run?

Yes, I'll probably drop dead of a heart attack. Seriously, I wonder if I have the physical strength to maintain this pace, given the fact I'd like to spend my career at Booz, Allen & Hamilton. I often joke about not living to retirement age—maybe in consulting, retirement should be at 45.

Let me add another dimension to this conversation. Since you feel you are currently 110% committed, do you ever anticipate having the time or the energy for marriage?

Obviously, if I were to marry I'd have to change my life style dramatically. Not because there aren't women who are married and work and are balancing these two worlds, but given the way I approach my job it would take a dramatic turn-about to balance a personal and professional life. I wouldn't see myself as working less, but I would definitely have to reassess my priorities. I guess the fact is that the men who currently turn me on and the men that I would see as potential husbands are ones who would force me to reassess my priorities. The man who would permit me to continue behaving the way I do now is not the guy I would ultimately be attracted to. I can't say that's a totally logical position, but it is true. I know what works for me—personally and professionally—now all I have to do is find some guy who's willing to break down, argue, discard all that I think I know or believe I know and together we will reshape the Natalie Lang "priority totem pole."

Yes. I guess if you're having difficulty balancing your activities and interests while you're single, you really wonder how you could handle your priorities in a marriage.

Exactly. When I was just starting out, my priorities had to do with work, and I said I would put aside my other interests for a while until I achieved reasonable success. The problem is, I have never come back to them. I keep putting other interests aside every day, every year, and only on occasion am I aware of how much I miss them—sometimes when I go on a holiday to La Costa and play tennis, or go to the theatre or a concert, or go to a dinner party and get there at a reasonable hour instead of waltzing in when they're having appetizers or during the second act. When I get there in time for cocktails like a normal human being, it's then that I realize how much I miss these other things in life to enjoy. So when I'm heading home I decide that I'm not going to stay away so long. I really have missed leisure time to visit with friends, shop, and so on. I miss spontaneous fun and the spontaneity of life. It's an incredible ping-pong game that I play with myself, which I believe everyone plays. For example, when I finish reading a book which has nothing to do with business, I say to myself, I really enjoyed that book, why don't I do it more? I'm forever wrestling with my feelings. Why don't I . . . ? Why, because I don't have enough time, and more often I'm too tired.

Well, if these things mean so much, why don't you do them more?

I don't have time. But if I force myself to take the time, it's total enjoyment and pleasure. Instead of going to bed at 12:00, I'm going to stay up until 2:00 because I'm going to read this damn book even if it doesn't enhance my job one bit. I love it, and at 2:00 in the morning when I turn out the light I say, "Boy, that was worth it, I'm going to do it more." But then at 7:00 in the morning, I'm dragging. I'm exhausted. How in the hell will I get to the plane on time? But I do it anyway, it was worth it. I mean I've already done it; I've never missed a plane in my life. As you can see, I have my own conflicts of interests. When I go to the theatre, I sit there thinking I should be home writing that memo or reading tomorrow's work. I'm constantly hassled, frenetic. I eat very fast because I'm always in a hurry. I'm always running. Even when I start at 7:00 I'm always behind. Always saying I've gotta go, I can't stay. I have no extra time because I have a full agenda every day. My dinner plate is always filled. For me to unwind and relax, I have to be absolutely removed from my office and home. I have to go away and I have to be gone for more than a day or two, and then I still have a hard time not calling the office every day. Those are the truths that many women haven't shared with the public but I know they feel.

Would you do it again?

Would I do it all over again? Yes, because I'm nuts. Is Booz
Allen worth it? Absolutely. On balance, and for most of my
years in this firm I wouldn't have missed it for the world. I have
great affection and loyalty for this firm and the people in it.
That's one of the turn-ons in this firm—the people and the
different kinds of people who run it. It's a "people" business
and I'm a "people" person.

So right now, the trade-offs are acceptable?

Yes. Maybe I'm playing my own game with myself, but should I
elect to marry, should I elect to change my direction, I will then
be able to say I have had it or a pretty good taste of it. Not that
I've had it and I'm sick of it, but I've had a taste of what I
wanted and I have had a good taste of it. I've been at the
bottom and I've been at the top; and if I suddenly decide to
stop working, I won't have wondered what it would have been
like. I also won't be feeling that I went away too soon. This has
been in some ways an incredible trip. One can get a lot of bang
for their bucks. Maybe it's just a game I'm playing, or we're all
playing, but I don't think so. I think I am aware of what the
cost is for that ticket, and even at the price it continues to make
great sense for me, Natalie. Currently this is absolutely the place
I want to be. If something comes along that is
unexpected—which is the way I like to live my life, the world of
the unexpected, the unknown, the mystery—I would like to
think I have the intellectual ability and flexibility to change
directions and styles and careers. There are many people who
would probably say, "Natalie is locked in forever." There are
also many who may know me better and would say that Natalie
is bright, responsive, and quick-witted and can rise to her own
occasion and give up what she has to and do whatever she
wants. I want to tell you something. No one ever really knows
you. Generally, I give my constituency what they want. One of
the reasons I've made it is because I believe in giving people
what they want. But deep down no one but me knows whether
I could give it up, and maybe I don't totally know. I know what
my capacities are. I know where my breaking point will be, and
I'll know when I've had too much. I'm playing the game, but I

would like to think I'm playing it my way. Right now I don't feel that I have begun to achieve all that I would like. That's the main reason I stay at Booz Allen. There's no reason why there couldn't be 200 female and male partners at Booz Allen. That's what makes this firm so terrific and exciting. It isn't a corporate structure that is structured or influenced by numbers. I'm incredibly turned on by this environment, and I don't know whether I could give it up. I don't feel I have to have that question answered today. Maybe I'll confront it in the future, and maybe I won't. Maybe everyone in the firm asks that question at times. This is a very exciting company and business, and I'm glad to be part of it.

What you're expressing is very interesting because most of the people we work with are successful men who are just your age, and they are confronted with the very same issues. Perhaps the difference is that this is the first era in which women are having to cope with the same problems. One of the things you said was that you played the game but that you played it your way. I heard you saying that you have found the behaviors that let you be successful in the organization, but you did not lose yourself in the process.

Well, I'm definitely not one of the boys, and I really don't want to be one. I'm not offended if a guy helps me put on my coat or opens the cab door for me. But I don't want him to be uncomfortable when I pick up the check, and I don't want him to feel the need to apologize for his language. At the same time, I really don't care what he thinks of my style, personal taste, and way of life. If a man feels gentlemanly toward me, let him act gentlemanly. I'm not offended and I'm not threatened by somebody helping me in any regard.

When I'm on a date, I often will let others wait on me. On a date I'm often, or at least can be, deliberate in my actions. The rules are very clearly defined. But in my business life they are not clearly defined. As a matter of fact, they are very muddy. So, as I am attempting to get through that system, I often behave as I feel my constituency allows or prefers, or what in my best judgment makes sense. I do believe, however, that there needs to be an allowance for differences. Different strokes for different folks. I don't use Ms., because I'm not caught up in the Ms. movement. I'm yesterday's woman and that was Miss. I don't feel it's reflective of where I am in my head to be called Ms. I don't think that says I'm not a modern woman. Why should I become Ms.? The fact is that it's easier to write to a Ms., and that's *your* problem. If you want to write me and you want to use Ms., then perhaps you don't want to take the time to find out if I'm married or single. The title Ms. doesn't mean anything to me, and I refuse to change simply because it's in vogue or the style. I'm very supportive of women on things that I think are the important issues, and I don't feel Ms. is one. I want respect for my competence and my contribution, and most women feel as I do. And then there's equality. If I'm not respected for that, then nothing else really matters. I'd like to think I'm an up-front, out-spoken, credible, hard-working, disciplined, conscientious, and aggressive person who has sacrificed a considerable amount for success. There are many women in the firm who say they would never work as hard as I do. That may be, but obviously it's what I wanted and want to continue doing.

I guess you'd say that that's their choice.

I should say that, but I don't. Many times when I'm asked by women why I work so hard, I say it's not Booz, Allen & Hamilton's fault or the guy I work for. It may be a reflection of my style or the fact that maybe women just do have to work harder. I don't say if you don't work as I do you won't make it. Each person must work out what works for them. *This* works for me. I don't insist that someone adopt my style, but I will point out if I'm asked why it may be working for me.

Well, evidently then it does upset you that you work so hard.

Yes, it really does because I too want to develop the other sides of myself. I do believe that all work and no play makes a dull girl. I don't want the system to make that happen. I want to play. I want to play with the same concentration, energy, style, and commitment that I give to my professional life.

But obviously you don't take the time to play, you spread yourself too thin.

That's certainly true. For example, the guys in my life have often forced their presence. They call me and tell me that I must leave work *on time* to meet social commitments. They all know better than to call and tell me to leave early. I have found, however, that one can only break dates so long without risking losing relationships, and I know the guys that will wait and the ones who won't—I hope.

You sound as if you want to be recognized and be treated as a professional in your work, but you still prefer men who play the male role.

Yes. It's very complicated, and it's this complexity and attendant confusion that I'm trying to express. I think these are some of the feelings and confusion that career women would love to talk about openly but they don't have the guts. I know a young woman who hasn't been able to decide if she wants a career or a marriage. You see, I want both. I think I'm good enough to have my cake and eat it too. I am, according to many who influenced my life, now at the threshold and another stage of development. That really is the reason for the "What Price Equality" in the title. I don't know that I can't have my cake and eat it too. The question is, how will I go about deciding and making that happen. Hell, I don't even know what my cake is. My cake is not to be domestic. I'm not interested in going shopping all day Saturday, even though I do love clothes and fashion and give considerable attention to the way I dress. I'm not particularly interested in spending my entire Saturday doing that. There are things I don't like about the feminine world. They're not things for me and never were. I'd like to be that contemporary woman who does things on her own and, in addition, does things with someone else.

There are still a lot of things to conquer in my career. There is a personal life to be pursued, developed, and nurtured. There is a pressure incumbent in me to do it well by virtue of other women, and I take that responsibility as seriously as I take my own development. When someone says to me, "How is it all working?" I can say sometimes it works well and sometimes it doesn't work so well. I continue to amaze myself at how many times I go back to the drawing board on the most basic of questions. How did I get here, why am I here, where am I going? I have attained the trappings of success, and I thought that when you had the trappings these kinds of questions would be resolved. Interestingly enough, the questions are more difficult to answer now than they were when I was aspiring to get the damn trappings. I thought when I got to the top things would be clear. I feel I am just now beginning to address myself as to what life is really like. And I'm being influenced more now, but in different ways. My friends have similar problems. Some, of course, are different, but fundamentally many "quality of life" questions are still dangling for them. This makes the load easier for me to carry. People I care for, respect, deal with professionally and personally are likely to provide some help to me on this subject, and I in turn hope to help them. Boy, when you find that others, particularly people you love and admire, are also confronting problems, you sure feel good. Whoever said "misery loves company" was absolutely right! It's really been interesting. In 1974 my top concern was what would I do if I didn't make partner at Booz, Allen & Hamilton. I thought that once that question had been resolved either way I could concentrate more on a balanced professional and personal life. I had this fantasy that if I got to the top things were going to be great. I thought that somehow all of my basic questions would be resolved. Now I'm dealing with some of the same heavy questions. The trappings haven't resolved my dilemmas, they've increased the complexity. I continue to amaze myself, because every time I have some time for myself, or am doing something particularly challenging, or am counseling someone, I, in retrospect, find myself going back to the drawing board of what does it all mean (generally prompted by something someone else says to me).

Well, where are we in this interview? How do we end this?

Why don't we go back to the concept of the female corporate jock?

Okay, but first I would like to say that I don't see myself as strictly a woman's woman or as a man's woman. I think I am able to respond to both. I like and need women as close friends, and I enjoy and need men in my life. I really don't want to be cast in one role or the other.

Sounds like you want to be all things to all people.

Yes, but in my own way and in my own style and dictated, of course, by the needs of the men and women in my personal and professional life.

I guess I see the female corporate jock as the woman whom management sees as its fast-track woman in the same way it views its fast-track guys. Personally, I would hope to continue to be seen as on a fast track at Booz, Allen & Hamilton. That's what I want, that's what seems to be giving meaning to my professional career—it's where I want to be—it's what I want to do—please forgive me, mother, and let's just blame it all on dad!

Mary Bralove *is a Staff Reporter for* The Wall Street Journal.

This article appeared in The Wall Street Journal, *February 5, 1976 and is reprinted with permission of the Wall Street Journal © 1976 Dow Jones & Co. All Rights Reserved.*

8

A Cold Shoulder

Mary Bralove

THE 40-YEAR-OLD bank executive faced a business problem for which no graduate course in management had prepared her. No sooner had she settled into her new job as the first woman vice president of a Midwestern bank than the trouble started. "I was hit from all directions at once with several important bank clients offering me their business on the condition that I go out with them," she recalls, asking that her name not be used. "I was responsible for keeping and building up these large accounts. If they pulled out, my career was finished."

At first she made light of the offers. Then she ignored them. When these tactics failed to stop the persistent phone calls at home and the suggestive remarks at business meetings, she lashed out.

"I sat down with each client and told them that I make it a firm rule to keep business separate from my social life," she says. "I told them that they could take their business to another loan officer if they wanted to."

137

Breaking the Silence

It was a stratagem that worked. Though taken aback, the clients seemed to accept her terms. Not one has taken his business elsewhere. Still, the experience left her shaken. "Nobody ever talks about sexual harassment on the job," she says. "But when it happens to you that first time, it's frightening."

These days, the wall of silence surrounding the issue of sexual harassment is gradually crumbling. Across the country, small pockets of working women are boldly speaking out and seeking protection against unwanted sexual advances by bosses or clients. The incidents they describe are sometimes as blatant as a proposition coupled with the promise of advancement if accepted and the threat of dismissal if rejected. Or the harassment may take the form of a physical overture disguised as a friendly pat, squeeze or pinch.

Men, too, can be the unwilling objects of such advances, but it happens less frequently. Eli Ginzberg, professor of economics at Columbia University's Graduate School of Business, explains: "Since men are in most of the positions of power, (sexual harassment) most often goes the other way."

Casting-Couch Careers

Some women, of course, welcome these unexpected attentions and turn them to their advantage. Corporate and Hollywood lore is spiced with stories of the "casting couch" launching women on to stardom or a successful career. But many women react instead with fear, humiliation or anger. "To every woman who has had it happen, the initial feeling is that there is something wrong with me," says Karen DeCrow, president of the National Organization for Women. "Slowly people are becoming aware that it is a problem that is happening to other people."

Armed with this realization, a group of female employes at the United Nations in New York publicly aired charges of sexual pressure exerted by bosses and diplomats. In Los Angeles, the Screen Actors Guild last October set up a morals complaint bureau designed to arbitrate harassment charges. In Boston, the highly regarded Simmons College Graduate Program in Management bowed to students' requests and recently incorporated the issue into its curriculum. And the City of New York Commission on Human Rights has routinely begun to pencil into corporate affirmative-action programs protection against "unfair abuse of sexual privacy."

No one knows for sure just how many women encounter harassment at work. Many women say that it hasn't touched their careers. Others say that they've faced it repeatedly. Last May, a group of women at Cornell University sponsored a rally on the subject that drew 250 participants, many with stories to tell of their own experiences with the problem. Working Women United, the women's group that sponsored the rally, later conducted an informal survey of 155 working women and found that of those interviewed, 70 had experienced some form of sexual harassment in the office. An overwhelming 92% of those surveyed felt that it was a serious problem.

"Bug Off, Creep"

Unlike unwanted sexual advances by co-workers that can be brushed off with a crisp "Bug off, creep," attentions from bosses or important clients involve an element of coercion and require delicate handling. "It isn't a relationship where people have equal power or equal say," says a 30-year-old Pittsburgh health worker who was the object of amorous advances by a previous boss. "Implicit is the threat that a refusal will hurt your career or salary."

In Jan Crawford's case, the threat was explicit. In 1965, she was a secretary in a California real-estate firm and working hard to get ahead. The hard work was rewarded, and she was promoted to property-managing duties.

Things went well, she says, until her immediate boss, a 45-year-old married man, asked her for a date. She was polite, but she refused. Later, at a business lunch, he told her: "You'll be sorry."

"It really shocked me because he said it in very quiet tones," she recalls. Two months later when she was fired for "inefficiency," her boss reminded her: "I told you that you'd be sorry."

"I was really devastated," says Miss Crawford, now a

32-year-old writer. "For years I was frightened to pour myself into a job again. It was so easy to lose everything."

Psychological damage can manifest itself in other ways. After she was promoted to the post of administrative assistant at one of the laboratories of a prestigious Eastern university, a 44-year-old mother of five discovered that the job included fending off one of her supervisors, a married professor who pawed her at every opportunity. Rather than risk dismissal by telling him off, the woman, who is the sole support of her family, kept quiet. ("I was taught not to hurt other people and to be polite," she says ruefully.) Finally she complained to another supervisor. "He told me that any mature woman should be able to handle it," she recalls.

So she avoided the professor whenever possible. She began to dress dowdily. She took to walking downstairs rather than risk meeting him in an elevator. She asked for a transfer to another department with no success. The pressures finally took their toll. She developed severe neck pains. Nine months after her promotion and in terrible pain, she quit her job. Shortly thereafter, the neck pains ceased. When she tried to collect unemployment compensation, she says that state unemployment officials told her that sexual harassment is not an intolerable job condition.

Corporate Apathy

Despite the apparent extent of the problem, sexual harassment isn't an issue that many corporations treat seriously. "With any other business problem they would have had people hard at work researching and planning," says Margaret Henning, co-director of Simmons' graduate management program. "But as far as we can tell, nobody is doing anything."

Businesswomen concur, noting that employe counselors tend to chalk up charges of misbehavior in high places to back-office gossip. Co-workers, while outwardly sympathetic, often harbor suspicions that the woman encouraged such actions.

Some women admit that they may unconsciously invite improper advances. A former analyst for Arthur D. Little Inc.

recalls one incident not too long ago that led her to examine her own behavior. While on a business trip to New York, she and four vice presidents of a client firm went out for a business dinner. Returning to her hotel, she found that all four men had telephoned her for a late-night date.

"I couldn't stand what was happening to me," she says after a year of psychological counseling. "Clearly my behavior was way out of line."

Thrashing It Out in Court

Women's groups argue that anyone should feel free to rebuff advances without fear of reprisal. To win their point, women are thrashing out the issue in court, within their unions and among themselves.

The legal arena is the toughest to crack. Unlike a more demonstrable job complaint such as low pay, sexual harassment is difficult to prove in court. Women's groups, aided by the U.S. Equal Employment Opportunity Commission (EEOC), are pressing for legal recognition that sexual harassment constitutes unlawful sex discrimination.

Early last year, the EEOC filed a "friend of the court" brief on behalf of two former employes of Bausch & Lomb Inc. who had filed suit in U.S. District Court charging a former supervisor with subjecting them to repeated verbal and physical sexual advances. As a result of these alleged advances, the women claimed, they were forced to quit their jobs. The court, however, said that they hadn't shown their harassment to be related to their unemployment, and the women lost the case.

Washington, D.C., attorney Linda Singer is currently representing a government worker who claims to have suffered the wrath of an embittered boss. According to Mrs. Singer, when the woman rebuffed his advances, the boss proceeded to take away all of her duties and to abolish her position. ("That is the way you fire people in the government," the attorney explains.) Mrs. Singer's client lost the first round in U.S. District Court, but she has appealed. Although she feels the case is strong, Mrs. Singer concedes that it won't be easy to win.

Fear of Blackmail?

"I'm afraid that the judges' reluctance to recognize this as sex discrimination stems from their fears that it could become a cause of action to blackmail men," she says.

By pressing their unions to set down guidelines on harassment, some women hope to forestall incidents before they occur. Besides creating the morals complaint bureau, the Screen Actors Guild has written into its contract a prohibition against conducting job interviews outside the office. "We are more than ever finding out that the casting couch still exists," Guild president Kathleen Nolan says, noting that the bureau receives complaints from both men and women.

As the issue of sexual harassment increasingly comes out into the open, women are turning to one another for mutual support and are sharing tactics to defend themselves against future incidents. Some single women have taken to wearing wedding rings, or to inventing fictional boyfriends, husbands and children to signal their unavailability. Barbara Rogers, head of an ad hoc group of women employes at the UN, says that until women there began talking to one another about harassment, each thought her experience unique. Their discussions also uncovered a common opening gambit used by executives on the prowl: "It starts very subtly when your boss calls you in for a business discussion and then shifts the topic around to his wife," Miss Rogers says.

Indeed, working women subjected to sexual harassment aren't the only ones hurt by it. After an article about the Cornell rally appeared in the press, Lin Farley, one of the organizers, received a letter from a corporate president's wife. The letter described her feelings upon discovering that her husband was forcing his attentions on an employe. "Please excuse me for not signing my name," she wrote. "But I feel highly insulted by my husband's actions, just as much as the woman who feels humiliated by the sexual harassment."

Kay S. White *and* Stewart H. Rowberry *are with Executive Development Systems, Atlanta, Georgia.*

9
Work Is a Family Affair

Kay S. White and Stewart H. Rowberry

THE GROWING NUMBER of women in the work force is increasing the necessity for managers to give more attention to the physical and psychological concerns women introduce on the job. The ways in which males and females relate to one another at work is cause for special concern because "the behavior of each is constantly influenced by the sex of the other."[1] Further complicating the situation are popular generalizations perpetuated by society as to a woman's competency and reliability in the work force. Top managers in business, industry, government, and academic institutions have become concerned enough to sponsor seminar sessions dealing with the topic.

The statements of physical and psychological difficulties discussed in this article were collected during six management seminars attended primarily by men. A seventh seminar was attended by women only. These statements of concern represent the thinking of approximately 180 men and 40 women from government, academic, industrial, and business organizations. Each seminar was conducted in the southeastern portion of the United States, the first in June 1975 and the last in August 1976. Four of the seminars were held in small industrial towns and were attended by people living and working in these respective localities. The other three were held in a large metropolitan city and were attended by people living and working in that area. The concerns identified in the seminars were not limited to the nine discussed here. Those selected for this discussion are the ones that were listed as major concerns primarily by the groups of male managers. Whether fact or fiction, these statements of concern are symptoms of real problems which must be effectively handled.

Physical Difficulties

Examples of statements concerning physical difficulties are:
1. Women just can't perform some jobs.
2. Women lack mechanical aptitude.
3. Women need more and different training.
4. Women get pregnant.

The focus of this discussion is not to elaborate on the causes of the problems at the expense of examining solutions but to achieve a balance between the two. Recent literature indicates that most concerns about physical difficulties women bring to the job can be solved by carefully examining responses to the following:[2]

1. Is the job designed in a manner that makes it possible for any employee to perform it in the most effective and efficient manner?
2. Are the hiring and selection criteria directly related to the requirements of the job and does the employee fit the job?
3. Is the employee adequately trained for the job?
4. Is organizational policy appropriately flexible and up to date?

If the answer to these four questions is yes, the manager should consider a job reassignment or termination for the employee.

Modern technology can be coupled with elements of job analysis and redesign to increase performance effectiveness.[3]

With the rapid technological advancements in industry, it is probable that many jobs have evolved with little or no thought as to how they can be performed most efficiently. If this is the case, men as well as women within the organization can benefit from job restructuring.

Where job redesign is not feasible, the second possible solution may involve aspects of employee recruitment and selection.[4] A critical and documented analysis of the job as performed can lead to a more precise determination of knowledge, skills, and physical attributes actually required to effectively carry out the job. Using this analysis as a guide, recruitment and selection of the most qualified person to fill the position is facilitated.

A third possible solution relates to employee training and development.[5] This analysis also serves as a guide in developing appropriate training which may even be broad enough to include physical development as well as educational experiences.

Concerns related to maternity absenteeism are real but not insurmountable. The management of many organizations is examining and revising leave policy.[6] Indeed, recent court decisions are making review of maternity-leave policy mandatory.[7]

When job requirements and the results of the managerial policy review are such that management still legitimately questions the feasibility of hiring women, statistics should be collected over several years to either substantiate or disprove management's opinion. This evidence can then be used in establishing and enforcing hiring policy or in justifying job reassignments or terminations.

In summary, management concerns about the physical difficulties women may bring to the job can be solved. Solutions are found in time-tested techniques of job analysis and redesign, careful and more effective recruitment and selection, appropriate training, policy reformulation, or job reassignment. None of these solutions are easy and some may be expensive. In order to protect the organization from becoming involved in litigation, even the expensive alternatives must be thoroughly investigated and associated costs carefully documented. This is becoming necessary as problems of this nature are being resolved with increasing frequency in the courts.[8]

Psychological Difficulties

While solutions do exist for concerns of physical difficulties, managerial experience with concerns of a psychological nature is much more limited. Rowe's discussion of the male drive for success as an attempt to submerge feelings of inadequacy where females are concerned implies that the supervisor skilled at handling problems of male employees may be totally inept at dealing with females.[9] Efforts at providing praise for a task well done are frequently just as ineffective as are efforts at discipline for a job incorrectly completed. There are no time-tested techniques that can be applied to solving complex role problems and problems of subtle discomfort associated with frequent and sometimes intense male-female interactions on the job.[10] Yet the 220 managers who attended the seminars mentioned earlier indicated that the effective solution to this group of problems was probably more critical in establishing a healthy work environment for men and women than finding solutions to those problems related to physical difficulties.

Examples of statements concerning psychological concerns are:
1. Women expect special treatment.
2. Male co-workers resent women.
3. Women don't communicate openly.
4. Women often cry at work.
5. Women are seductive.

"Psychology is the study of human behavior ... social psychology deals with behavior as it relates to other individuals."[11] Psychological difficulties as discussed here refer to the perceptions men and women have toward each other that may create problems on the job. These perceptions may be either real or imagined. The statements listed previously are so interrelated that it is difficult to discuss each one separately. Therefore, this discussion will focus on the general causes as well as possible solutions for the problems that may occur. Whatever the case, the difficulties that arise center around the issue of control—how women exert it and how men resist; how men exert it and how women resist.

People Are Controlled

Control is something each person is called on to cope with during his or her lifetime. Children are controlled by parents.[12] As students, they are controlled by teachers and as employees, by supervisors. Gillespie found that problems are minimized when the control mechanism coincides with the individual's personal needs and desires.[13] Feelings of frustration arise, however, when these needs and desires are not met.[14] This can create organizational problems.

Young children throw temper tantrums when they cannot have a particular toy they want.[15] Adolescents cheat, rebel, or cut class when their needs conflict with parental or faculty demands. Employees may express dissatisfaction with control by tardiness, procrastination, forgetfulness, or by otherwise obstructing normal administrative processes.[16]

Within an organizational setting, control is one of the defined functions of management and consists of activities involving budgets, schedules, and reports.[17] In general, management texts and training courses seem to dwell on helping managers develop skills in budgeting, scheduling, and reporting at the expense of helping them develop skills in the psychological aspects of control that occur in interpersonal relationships on the job. Lack of skills in the latter area can lead to problems.

The authors' experiences with seminar participants from many disciplines (business and industrial managers, physicians, dentists, and educational managers) reflect a real need to focus on examining alternatives for solving problems with a psychological basis. These difficulties have existed in the traditionally male-dominated work world, and supervisors have been uncomfortable when confronted with problems related to psychological control. While a literature search does not reveal this, it seems reasonable to suggest that supervisors are probably even more uncomfortable with these situations when they involve women. The discomfort the supervisor may be feeling is often communicated nonverbally to the employee resulting in a counterproductive work relationship.[18]

This combination of circumstances seems to point toward a need to more clearly understand the basic psychological and emotional differences that exist between men and women. Psychotherapists tell us that awareness of our own personal emotional needs is the first step that must be taken in order to understand the dynamics of interpersonal relationships.[19] Each individual structures his or her behavior so that personal emotional needs are met. Emotionally healthy people have learned how to express their needs directly and, therefore, seek gratification directly. Other people have not learned how to satisfy their needs directly and therefore resort to an indirect approach. In the early family life an individual learns how to get his or her needs met and forms attitudes about achievement, socializing,[20] anger, threats to the group, sharing work, economics, morality, dependability, sex, and many other intangible characteristics.

Psychological Difficulties Originate in the Family

Sociologists have found that "despite all alleged 'loss of function in modernized contexts,' the family remains the unit in terms of which virtually all individuals acquire the basic learning on which all else rests."[21] Therefore, it is probably within the primal family unit that each individual first experiences the consequences associated with struggling for and acquiring power. It is within this unit that the person first tests his or her abilities. Those skills are then tested outside the family unit. Skinner maintains that positive reinforcement will increase the probability of behavior repetition or recurrence.[22] That is, if the child's temper tantrum which is an indirect expression of anger puts him in control and he enjoys that position of power, he is likely to repeat the behavior. Likewise, the repetition of certain behavior will occur in adults when the consequences are positive.

While these ideas have been tested in the experimental laboratory and generalized for the population as a whole, the conclusions appear to be valid for interactions involving any man and woman and, more specifically, a man and woman working together on the job. Each brings to the job some successful and some unsuccessful behavior patterns. The behaviors that have brought the greatest pleasure through the years will probably be the ones that recur. Further, Fromm asserts that individuals behave in the manner necessary to "overcome the horror of separateness, of powerlessness, and of lostness"[23] in order to feel at home. These needs, he says, are shared by all people but can be satisfied in different ways. Both men and women bring certain behaviors to the job. Some of these are the same; others are different. That is, a smile may be characteristically successful for both, while telling a colorful joke may be more successful for one than the other.

As was noted by Athanassiades, "neither ancient mythology nor history assigns women to an inferior status; that in early societies women flourished and achieved power, independence, and recognition."[24] In fact, society has created a matriarchal environment that has a patriarchal facade. This facade has been undergirded by traditional rules of etiquette that place women on the proverbial pedestal and at the same time insist that she is the weaker sex. The men who insist on perpetuating this situation often fail to see that placement of the woman on the pedestal gives her a position of power and puts her in psychological control. Those men have, almost inevitably, placed themselves in a double bind. That is, a male supervisor may feel guilty if he does not show the female employee special attention; but if he does, the male co-workers are resentful. This seems to have worked to the advantage of many female employees who use their tools of psychological control skillfully. Understandably, men resent this nebulous form of control.

The statistical reality stands to remind working women that men still dominate management positions.[25] Men still make most decisions about hiring, firing, and promoting. If a man is uncomfortable around a woman at work and cannot identify exactly why, his discomfort may be related to the woman's use of and his reaction to psychological control. For while women have virtually been trained in the use of psychological control techniques over the years, many men have never learned how to cope with this form of control. In fact, some men may not even realize that they are being manipulated.[26] Solutions to unraveling this situation must be worked out by women as well as men. It is a cop-out— indeed, self-destructive—for the woman to view the situation solely as "the man's problem." If men and women are ever to learn to work together effectively, patient cooperation is especially needed so that man's discomfort with woman's use of psychological control can be brought into his conscious awareness and both can learn to deal with it effectively.

The absence of conscious awareness on the part of many men probably stems in general from the high regard in which the mother figure is held. Freud has said that in choosing a sexual partner, "a man, especially, looks for someone who can represent his picture of his mother as it has dominated his mind from his earliest childhood."[27] This early influence that governs a man's choice of a sexual partner may carry over to his preferences for friendships with other women.[28] Because of this unconscious and strong influence of his mother, the man may be especially vulnerable to female control that may be exerted directly or indirectly through the use of tears, nagging, or sex. Her use of and his reaction to these types of control are learned in the family environment. For example, his reaction to his mother's direct control may be compliance or rebellion. His reaction to tears from his daughter, mother, wife, or sister may be sympathy and compassion. His reaction to his wife's use of nagging or sex as control may be submission to her wishes. He appears to be totally controlled in these ways and unable to break out.

Interpersonal Relationships Can Be Controlling

Interpersonal problems between men and women are not caused by the job but are superimposed on the job. Sociologists report that "the family in all known societies is so strategic in the socialization process as to influence the behavior of the individual in or out of the family context forever afterwards."[29] While attitudes and behaviors are influenced and may change somewhat when the individual leaves the family, men and women are each products of their respective upbringings and are forced to relate to each other on the basis of those early relationships. Most problems between any two people at work, especially between a man and woman, occur because one or the other is unable to express his or her needs and desires openly and directly. That is, interpersonal problems at work are caused by people who bring to the job behavior patterns that cause them to seek need gratification indirectly.

Not only does the family mold individual behavior, but "the

general functional problems facing the family are analogous to those facing society as a whole."[30] Bell and Vogel identify four broad areas where functional problems occur in families: (1) task performance, (2) leadership, (3) integration and solidarity, and (4) group maintenance.[31] Problems hindering the effective functioning of nonfamily groups revolve around these same four areas. It, therefore, seems reasonable to study the male-female relationships within the family in order to understand interpersonal problems that occur in the work situation.

Consider the psychological difficulties identified in the survey mentioned earlier. Recently, the management of a paper mill was required to hire women at the worker level. Many of the other employees and most supervisors resented the presence of the women. Basically, the men felt that the dirty, hot paper mill was no place for a woman to work. The new women employees, on the other hand, took jobs in the mill because the pay was better than that associated with their other options. These women, however, brought to the job some problems with a psychological basis. For example, some of the women did not want to get dirty. They expressed this nonverbally. Co-workers and supervisors noticed their nicely-groomed hair, freshly-polished nails, and clean, pastel clothing. The women, not wishing to openly disturb, quietly stood by as their male co-workers performed the unpleasant and dirty tasks. Then some of the men began to complain. They were heard to say, "When you have a woman in the group, you're one man short; women don't carry their load." One woman openly complained about the unpleasantness of several tasks and asked her supervisor for a reassignment. The supervisor, a man in his middle fifties, was concerned. He, too, resented her demand for special treatment but felt he had to accommodate her wishes since top management said she had to stay. When queried about his need to comply with her demands, he recounted his feeling about the "ladylikeness" of women, their fragility, and his need to protect them.

As with other work groups, the paper mill work group resembles the family group. The relationships that occur in families recur at work. The supervisor's position of authority will allow him to react to the problem as he might in the family role of father, son, brother, or husband. Two of the role behaviors (father and son) are almost entirely emotional as the man unconsciously resists the woman's psychological control so familiar to him from his family life. To become successful in managing women, the male supervisor should become conscious of the controlling nature of the daughter and mother roles played by women in the family and aware of how this tends to lure him into playing roles at work that are emotionally loaded.

The male supervisor must also realize that he can initiate the role playing with female employees, thereby setting up unhealthy work relationships himself. That is, in reality, the manipulation that occurs can be managed by either the man or woman, whichever of them is seeking need gratification indirectly rather than directly.

Since few supervisors are psychologically trained, it would be unrealistic to expect an in-depth problem analysis and diagnosis in psychological language. It is not unrealistic to expect lay people with some training in interpersonal relations to be able to identify general behavioral patterns as familiar as those initially learned in the family.

In dealing with any personnel problem, the supervisor may, as one option, choose to ignore it. In some instances, the problem will solve itself. If, in this example, the mill supervisor ignores the problem, he will retain control only as long as neither the woman nor her co-workers determine to take aggressive action. This is a passive form of control and is usually counterproductive since problems involving struggles for power infrequently solve themselves.

Father-Daughter. The woman who is requesting special treatment is attempting to gain control in the work group. Since her techniques for gaining control were primarily learned in the family, those behaviors may recur on the job. If she is somewhat younger than her supervisor, it would not be unnatural for her to unconsciously begin to act as a daughter might toward her father. She may present herself as helpless; to be pitied and cared for. This set of behaviors may tend to lure the supervisor into the role of father. That is, he may make excuses for her or otherwise shield her from criticisms of co-workers. If this occurs, he will relinquish his control to her in much the same manner that many fathers do with their daughters. When a daughter does not get her way, she often sulks until the intensity of her anger subsides or the f notices her. On the job, the woman may resort to sii behaviors—still seeking control of the work group. In order to deal with the problem effectively, the supervisor should be able to analyze what is happening so that he can guard against being lured into playing the role of father-protector. Gordon and Strober recognize the presence of these role performances and problems associated with them.[32] However, they do not mention the perhaps inadvertent, but at the same time real, psychological control the daughter or, in Gordon's words, "pet" has over her father.

Mother-Son. If the woman involved in the situation at work is older than her male supervisor (as are many administrative assistants, secretaries, receptionists, nurses, and dental hygienists), it would be easy for her to unconsciously begin to act toward her supervisor as a mother might toward her son. The mother is often seen as either indulging or using her son. At work she typically serves as the "confidante to whom others can bring their problems and seek support."[33] Gordon and Strober note that carrying out this role may accrue three costs to the woman:

1. She is seen only as a trusted confidante, not competent to take initiative or carry on other tasks.

2. She is seen only as the accepting, praising, indulging mother devoid of skills in critiquing and analyzing.

3. She is seen as specializing in emotional issues rather than as competent in handling issues of a rational and logical nature.[34]

A fourth cost that often accrues to the woman performing the role of mother is that she is viewed as the power behind the throne and therefore resented by other employees. In performing this aspect of the mother role, she may offer suggestions that will be "good for everyone" or make decisions for her supervisor on the premise that her tenure in the job gives her unusual wisdom. Her set of behaviors may lure the supervisor into performing the role of son. That is, he may feel that he must agree with her—because she must know what is best. If this occurs, he will have no control at all—in the same manner that the young son is powerless in the family. When a mother senses that her wishes are not being obeyed, she often becomes cold and reserved and appears to be self-reliant. This may be a mechanism she uses to regain control. For when someone notices her behavior and responds to make her happy, she is once again in control. The woman who performs the mother role is generally seen as emotionally independent of her son. Moment and Zaleznik define the independent person as one who is concerned primarily with task performance rather than with socializing, process, or power.[35] If the woman playing the mother role is really an emotionally dependent person who cannot reveal this to her co-workers or supervisor, her independence may be an act and her decisions may not be based on sound reasoning. This could easily lead to organizational problems. Because of the costs to the woman and because it is difficult, without professional assistance, for the male supervisor to determine whether or not the woman's independence is an act, it is advisable for both man and woman to avoid becoming involved in a relationship of this nature. In addition, performance effectiveness will be hindered if the other employees resist the "mother's" control, or if the supervisor grows weary of the game and attempts to regain his power.

Brother-Sister. Another relationship that has an origin in the family but recurs at work is that of brother-sister. This relationship is a useful model since the manipulative techniques that generally govern behaviors in the father-daughter and mother-son relationships are less effective. That is, a male supervisor would not be as affected by a female subordinate's sulking, outbursts of anger, or other attempts at control. In the paper mill example, the supervisor could react to the woman as a brother might toward a sister, by calling her in, clearly explaining the job requirements, frankly discussing her resistance to performing some of the tasks, and directly seeking to involve her in finding an appropriate solution. While she may respond by sulking, being angry, or crying, he will not be severely affected by her attempts to psychologically control him. By approaching the problem in this manner, he can be more objective with her and fair to all employees. He will also help her learn to communicate openly about her concerns with regard to the job.

Husband-Wife. Another family relationship that may recur on the job is that of husband-wife. This relationship is even more complicated than the previous three since each person may bring to marriage certain tendencies to behave as mother, daughter, father, or son. Each may also bring certain expectations for the roles of the marriage partners that may not be realistic. Bott notes that role relationships between husband and wife can be jointly organized, totally segregated, or one that is somewhere between the two—called intermediate.[36] In regard to that, consider three possible marriage-like arrangements that can occur on an emotional level: (1) strong man-weak woman; (2) strong woman-weak man; or (3) strong man-strong woman.

The strong man-weak woman relationship closely resembles the father-daughter relationship. Because of this, the role behaviors and associated problems on the job are the same as previously discussed. In a marriage this relationship sometimes is seen as master-slave, where the man is totally dominant and the woman is totally submissive.[37] On the job, if a woman plays the totally submissive role, it may appear that she is happy when, indeed, her productivity might be even greater if a more equitable relationship existed.

The strong woman-weak man relationship resembles the mother-son relationship, and the role behaviors and associated problems on the job are similar to those previously discussed.

The strong man-strong woman relationship either may present problems or may be ideal. Problems occur when the people involved are unable to communicate or when neither person is willing to subjugate his own vested interest for the overall good of the family or work unit. This type of relationship is ideal if both individuals are mature, able to talk out their difficulties, and able to work together for the common good of the family or work group on a rational, unemotional basis. Such a close, open, and mutually negotiable relationship is difficult to achieve either at home or on the job.

The husband-wife relationship involving a strong man and strong woman is similar to a brother-sister relationship. The major difference between the two is that there is a deeper level of emotional involvement and commitment in the husband-wife relationship than in the brother-sister relationship. This may be due to the fact that the behavior of those individuals involved in a husband-wife relationship is governed by their perceptions regarding the threat of rejection.

"Ironically, the reason men often feel so uncertain about how to relate to women is that they are trapped in traditional sex roles themselves."[3 8] A male supervisor may find himself shifting quickly from one of these roles to another during a short time span while carrying out managerial tasks involving many different women. He may encourage, verbally or nonverbally, certain reactions from the women with whom he works. That is, to some he may project a fatherly image, causing them to respond as daughters. Likewise, he may project the image of a son, evoking the mother role from other women. Or, on the other hand, he may project the "healthy" husband or brother images. However, while increasing the likelihood of a complementary role response, his projection of these images will not guarantee the woman's response in a "healthy" wife or sister role. She may, in fact, respond as a daughter or mother. The male supervisor should learn, therefore, to identify which roles are being played so that he can begin to build patterns of behavior that are not psychologically controlling[3 9] —especially on him, since he needs to maintain as much psychological autonomy as possible to effectively carry out his managerial duties.[4 0]

The manager interested in developing these skills should look for a consultant who can help or a course on human dynamics designed to teach recognition of personal and relational problems in the work setting.

Emotional Behaviors Can Be Controlling

While a knowledge of interpersonal relationships can reduce the level of control many managers may feel, the presence of women in the work setting brings controlling behaviors with which managers must also cope.

Tears. Perceptions of men and women differ in regard to tears. Traditionally, in the American society, a man seldom cries except when he is overwhelmed by grief or extreme physical pain. The male supervisor may interpret a woman's tears on the basis of his own feelings. That is, he may think she is physically hurt or feeling a great loss, and sometimes she is. This tends to evoke his compassion and sympathy. But it rarely occurs to him that she may be anxious, deeply hurt emotionally, frustrated, angry, or, at times, happy.

Again, reflection on the family environment may be revealing. A woman growing up is taught that, unlike a man, she cannot curse, scream, pound the table, or physically fight it out if she is angry. Such actions are not thought to be ladylike. But she can *cry*. That is, she has been taught to deal with her feelings of anger indirectly. Within the same family her brother is taught that it is unmanly to cry, so he develops his muscles, fights physically, or does anything necessary to relieve his anger—*except* cry. He is taught to deal with his anger directly, but with his feelings of hurt indirectly.

The apparent lack of comprehension by men that tears, in actuality, could be termed liquid anger may be the reason that so many of them are uncomfortable around crying women. Women attending a management seminar revealed experiences with male supervisors who frequently shrugged their tears off as indications of female cycling. This, they said, significantly increased their anger.

Consider the female worker who bursts into tears when her supervisor assigns her a task. She may actually be crying for any one of a variety of reasons—she had planned to take the afternoon off for personal business and this sudden, short-deadline work assignment cannot be completed within the remaining time; her workload is already heavier than that of her co-workers, but she is dependable, and her supervisor often gives her high-priority work since he knows her work to be on time and of a high quality; the work assignment is really boring, uninteresting, and she feels "put down" by having been given the task; she feels that by giving her the assignment, her supervisor is placing her in the middle of a powerfully subtle office feud, and she feels used.

The male supervisor may interpret her behavior in a number of ways and react accordingly. That is, he may ignore or otherwise shrug off her tears and verbally or nonverbally attribute her tears to female cycling. He may, out of bewilderment, organize a quick retreat by attempting to cheer her or otherwise stop her tears, or he may attempt to cover his confusion by shouting angrily for her to stop crying. He may think she needs sympathy and react by putting his arm around her shoulder or in some other way attempt to console her. If she is really angry and he does any of these, it is likely that he will increase her frustration and anger. If he never discusses her frustration and deals only superficially with her tears, but holds firm to his decision, she may conclude that he does not really understand her needs or that he understands but is incapable of handling her feelings of anger. This may increase her feelings of resentment. If the supervisor deals only superficially with her tears and concedes his position, the woman may conclude that she can win through use of her tears and he will, inadvertently, have fortified her ability to control him.

If, however, the supervisor recalls that women may also cry when they are frustrated and angry, he might say: "I know that my decision on this must make you angry. As soon as you are able to pull yourself together, we'll talk about it." In most cases, the woman, feeling that the supervisor understands and cares about her feelings, will regain her composure quickly and may even say, "It surely does make me mad!"

By recognizing that her tears are an expression of anger and by reacting in this manner, the supervisor has freed the woman to express anger in a way that can be constructively handled in a work situation. Also, when the supervisor poses the question regarding anger, an opening is made for the employee to provide explanation if she so desires. When the tears have subsided, the supervisor will be better able to deal with her resistance to his decision and take whatever managerial action is necessary to get the job done.

As a general rule, managers can safely assume that a working woman's tears are an expression of anger. Recognizing this, the first reaction in response to her crying should be a question to verify that. The word *anger* or *frustration* should be used in the question—do not simply ask her why she is crying, as she may not realize her tears are indicative of anger until the supervisor mentions it. In fact, "most people are never aware of all their needs; many . . . needs are at the subconscious level; therefore, in managing people, it is useless to ask of one, why do you behave in such a manner; few could give an accurate answer."[4][1]

Sexuality. Consider the events which may lead to sexual control by either individual over the other as it relates to the work situation. From childhood, boys and girls notice that they are physically different. Mothers teach girls to care for their hair, nails, clothing, and general appearance. Fathers compliment their daughters—tell them that they are pretty. From this, girls learn that it is pleasing to be attractive to men. In a similar manner, young men take pride in developing their muscles and athletic prowess. Football games with their cheerleading squads illustrate how the football hero is sought after by the attractive young cheerleader. Boys and girls grow up depending on the opposite sex for ego building.

Adult men and women are bound by their pasts, and still need to have the opposite sex affirm them as attractive, sexual beings. On the job, this need for affirmation is frequently fed by flirtation, joking, compliments, and invitations to coffee or lunch. This sexual by-play is fun and is one aspect of the workday that cannot exist without women and men being together.

Members of some advocacy groups attempt to make a case for treating their members as "persons" or "human beings."[42] This is not possible in the purest sense, because individuals have no concept of a "person" or "human being" divorced from that person's manliness, womanliness, or childlikeness. That is, when one enters a room and sees someone seated behind a desk, the mind's eye sees a man, woman, or child—not a "person." Further, a man or woman must realize that his or her competence is, of necessity, seen by the opposite sex only after he or she is seen as a sexual being—masculine or feminine. This tends to set up situations in which subtle forms of sexual control can occur.

Gordon and Strober describe alterations in male behavior when a woman enters the scene: subtle changes in posture (such as standing straighter or pulling in stomachs) and in conversation (if discussing business, each man attempting to sound more astute than the other). They may engage in mild flirtation[43]—which really is a subtle invitation.

Many women also behave differently when relating to men. When women are around men rather than only women, they may wear shorter skirts, lower their eyes at appropriate times, assume seductive postures, or, if discussing business, couch their remarks in low-key, easy-to-take language. They, too, may engage in mild flirtation—again, a subtle invitation.

These sex-stereotyped behaviors are not necessarily dysfunctional in the work setting. They may, in fact, contribute to helping men and women achieve the sexual affirmation they each need. There is a danger, however, when the sexual by-play becomes a force that controls the behavior of either the man or the woman and the primary reason for being together—work—is ignored. This danger is realized if either party takes seriously the teasing in the relationship and presents an invitation to further involvement. The invitation may be open or it may be subtle—depending on the people involved and on the intensity of the relationship. Similarly, the acceptance or rejection of the invitation may be open or subtle.

In either case, when the teasing is taken seriously by either the man or woman working together, there is potential for damage to the interpersonal and work relationships.

Consider how easily this controlling mechanism may be activated. At first, both the man and woman innocently flirt with each other. They begin spending more and more of their free minutes together chatting. There develops a closeness and a biological attraction. Eventually they begin seeing each other after working hours. There then develops an open agreement that the relationship is only physical and will last only as long as they each enjoy it. After a time, one or the other may begin to lose interest—not only after working hours but during the day. The rejected individual, desiring the closeness found in the relationship, grows more aggressive—going to the other person's work area more frequently; calling more often; suggesting that they meet outside work; and, in general, attempting to take control by demanding more and more of the other's time. If the individual finally gives in and agrees to the more aggressive person's demands, the relationship becomes increasingly controlled by the aggressor, it is more difficult to terminate, and, consequently, the working compatibility that initially facilitated the job performance is seriously damaged.

Sometimes, the rejected individual will, out of desperation, resort to overt use of power in an attempt to reactivate the relationship. This is seen when one person threatens to damage the other's job or career future.

The use of sexuality as a control mechanism, like the others that have been discussed, is learned and practiced in the family. Husbands and wives frequently attempt to control one another by withholding sex. Its use in this manner is as destructive to the relationship as its use in the work environment.

These remarks do not relate only to affairs involving physical contact. While the argument presented does include those situations, it is not limited to them. Frequently more damage is done to individuals, personally, as well as to the interpersonal relationship, when the affair is a deep, emotional one that is not characterized by physical involvement.

Conceptions—Real or Imagined. Related forms of controlling pressure are exerted by outside groups, family members, and organizational peers whose imaginations govern their conceptions concerning men and women working together. Supervisors should be aware of these conceptions when assigning a man and a woman to a job requiring overtime or travel. While these conceptions are probably imagined, they may constitute real problems for the individuals involved and must not be ignored by the supervisor.

Those working with members of the opposite sex on a day-to-day basis should become consciously aware of the potentially controlling nature of man-woman relationships and should take whatever precautions are necessary to avoid doing harm to either individual directly, to family, to other social relationships, or to the organization itself.[44]

Summary

The psychological implications of control within the interpersonal relationships between the supervisor and employee are much more complicated than this discussion indicates. The primary purpose of this discussion is to simplify the analysis of work relationships by drawing comparisons between on-the-job problems and their counterparts in the family unit. The job problems have been discussed within the context of the following relationships: (1) father-daughter, (2) mother-son, (3) brother-sister, and (4) husband-wife.

It has been suggested that the supervisor should become consciously aware of:

1. The type of role that is performed in relation to female employees.

2. The type of reaction that may best reduce the controlling mechanisms primarily employed by females.

Some managers, after reading this discussion and being made aware of the potential problems and possible solutions, may have sufficient knowledge and skill to begin applying the concepts. Others may wish to obtain further information and training.

"It is neither possible nor even desirable for people to ignore the sex of one another. At this point in our cultural development, it is more desirable to increase awareness so that one can understand how the sex of another is affecting one's behavior."[4][5]

Footnotes

1. Francine E. Gordon and Myra H. Strober, *Bringing Women into Management* (New York: McGraw-Hill Book Co., Inc., 1975), p. 45.

2. Weeks v. Southern Bell Telephone and Telegraph Co., 408 F. 2d 228 (5th Cir., 1969); and Leo Kanowitz, *Women and the Law: The Unfinished Revolution* (Albuquerque, University of New Mexico Press, 1969), p. 182.

3. Wendell L. French and Cecil H. Bell, Jr., *Organization Development* (Englewood Cliffs, New Jersey: Prentice-Hall, Inc., 1973), pp. 162-164.

4. Douglas Bray, "Identifying Managerial Talent in Women," *Atlanta Economic Review*, March-April 1976, pp. 38-43; and Frances Lear, "EEO Compliance: Behind the Corporate Mask," *Harvard Business Review*, July-August 1975, pp. 138-146.

5. Bray, "Identifying Managerial Talent in Women"; and Judith Hennessee, "What Progress Women at CBS?" *Personnel*, July-August 1975, pp. 34, 38-39.

6. Hennessee, "What Progress Women at CBS?"; and Sandra Ekberg-Jordan, "Preparing for the Future—Commitment and Action," *Atlanta Economic Review*, March-April 1976, p. 48.

7. Donald R. Stacy, "The Intrepid Executive's Guide to Avoiding Sex Discrimination," *Atlanta Economic Review*, March-April 1976, pp. 9-14.

8. Ibid.

9. M. Rowe, "Why Women Take and Keep Low Paying Jobs," *Business and Society/Innovation*, Spring 1973, pp. 55-60.

10. John C. Athanassiades, "Myths of Women in Management," *Atlanta Economic Review*, May-June 1975, p. 8.

11. James L. Gibson, John M. Ivancevich, and James H. Donnelly, Jr., *Organizations: Structures, Processes, Behavior* (Dallas, Texas: Business Publications, Inc., 1973), p. 6.

12. Eric Berne, *A Layman's Guide to Psychiatry and Psychoanalysis* (New York: Ballantine Books, 1957), pp. 60-62.

13. James J. Gillespie, *Free Expression in Industry* (London: Pilot Press, 1948), pp. 94-96.

14. Chris Argyris, *Integrating the Individual and the Organization* (New York: John Wiley & Sons, Inc., 1964), pp. 40-42.

15. Berne, *A Layman's Guide*, p. 60.

16. George R. Bach and Herb Goldberg, *Creative Aggression* (New York: Avon Publishers, 1975), pp. 100-124.

17. Leonard J. Kazmier, *Principles of Management* (New York: McGraw-Hill Book Co., 1969), p. 33.

18. Edward T. Hall, *The Silent Language* (Greenwich, Connecticut: Fawcett Books, 1967), p. 10.

19. Rollo May, *Love and Will* (New York: Dell Publishers, 1969), p. 245.

20. David C. McClelland, *The Achieving Society* (Princeton, D. Van Nostrand Co. Inc., 1961), pp. 336-390.

21. Norman W. Bell and Ezra F. Vogel, *A Modern Introduction to the Family* (New York: Free Press, 1960), p. 19.

22. B.R. Bugelski, "The Systematic Views of Skinner," in *The Psychology of Learning Applied to Teaching*, 2nd ed. (Indianapolis: Bobbs-Merrill Co., Inc., 1971), p. 91.

23. Erich Fromm, *The Anatomy of Human Destructiveness* (Greenwich, Connecticut: Fawcett-Crest Books, 1975), p. 255.

24. Athanassiades, "Myths of Women in Management," p. 7.

25. "Up The Ladder, Finally," *Business Week*, November 24, 1975, p. 58.

26. Julius Fast, *The Incompatability of Men and Women* (New York: Avon Publishers, 1971), p. 51.

27. James Strachey, *Sigmund Freud: Three Essays on the Theory of Sexuality* (New York: Basic Books, Inc., 1962), p. 94.

28. Sigmund Freud, *An Outline of Psychoanalysis* (New York: W.W. Norton & Co., 1949), p. 90.

29. Ansley J. Coale et al., *Aspects of the Analysis of Family Structure* (Princeton: Princeton University Press, 1965), pp. 31-35.

30. Bell and Vogel, *A Modern Introduction to the Family.*

31. Ibid.

32. Gordon and Strober, *Bringing Women into Management*, p. 49.

33. Ibid., p. 50.

34. Ibid.

35. David Moment and Abraham Zaleznik, *Role Development and Interpersonal Competence* (Boston: Harvard University, Division of Research, Graduate School of Business Administration, 1963), p. 161.

36. Elizabeth Bott, *Family and Social Network* (London: Tavistock Publications, 1957).

37. Fast, *The Incompatability of Men and Women*, p. 17.

38. Gordon and Strober, *Bringing Women into Management*, p. 51.

39. Mary F. Sargent, *The Psychology of Managing People* (Springdale, Connecticut: Motivation, Inc., 1963), p. 30.

40. Ari Kiev, *A Strategy for Handling Executive Stress* (Chicago: Nelson-Hall, 1974), p. 159.

41. Sargent, *The Psychology of Managing People*, p. 10.

42. Caroline Bird, *Born Female* (New York: David McKay Co., Inc., 1973), pp. 215-238.

43. Gordon and Strober, *Bringing Women into Management*, pp. 45-46.

44. May, *Love and Will*, p. 109.

45. Gordon and Strober, *Bringing Women into Management*, p. 56.

References

Mintzberg, Henry. "The Manager's Job: Fact and Folklore," *Harvard Business Review*. July-August 1975, p. 61.

Twedt, Dik. "Management Handbooks for Continuing Education," *Harvard Business Review*. July-August 1975, pp. 36-46, 161.

White, Kay S. "Evaluation of Laboratory Management Training," *Health Laboratory Science*. October 1975, pp. 347-350.

II
Women
and Management

THEIR NUMBERS ARE small, but there have been women in management roles for many years. Women can be effective managers, we know that for a fact. Still as evidenced in the last section, for most people the role "Woman Manager" is a new and unfamiliar one—both to be in, and to deal with. The carry over of stereotypes of other female roles—mother, wife, etc.—is persistent. Women have the talent, but an accepted, widely-understood role mode is sorely lacking.

Bette Ann Stead *is a faculty member of the College of Business Administration at the University of Houston.*
This article appeared in Business Horizons, *February 1974, pp. 32-36. Copyright, 1974 by the Foundation for the School of Business at Indiana University. Reprinted by permission.*

10
Women's Contributions to Management Thought

Bette Ann Stead

THE EVOLUTIONARY process through which the field of management has come since the turn of the century can be briefly described in three eras: 1910 to late 1920s—scientific management (work-measurement approach); late 1920s to 1959—human relations (contented-cow approach); and 1960 to the present—behavioral management science (interdisciplinary approach using psychology, sociology, and anthropology). To each of these areas, women have made significant—but largely unrecognized—contributions. These contributions may be termed highly unusual since women traditionally have been barred from management careers.

Why have women been moved to contribute to an area in which neither they nor their contemporaries could find a future? We may see the answer in the nature of woman herself. Women have always been interested in the betterment of life for all people. Women have worked in fields devoted to improving the human condition, such as nursing, teaching, and social work. It follows as a natural progression that women would be interested in bettering the human condition in the vast area of the work environment. This article reviews some of the past and present contributions made by women to the field of management.

The Scientific Management Era

The scientific management era began about 1910 and is credited to Frederick W. Taylor. Much of the thinking during this era was characterized by the notion that people work for only one reason—money. Much of the work was organized as piecework, and workers were paid by the number of items they produced. Therefore, much of the research was aimed toward influencing workers to produce more pieces. The notion was that, since people worked only for money, they could be treated as machines and trained to produce more and more. No one contributed more to this era of management than Lillian Gilbreth (1878-1972).

Probably more is known of the personal life of Gilbreth than any of the other women discussed in this article. The Gilbreth family has been immortalized in books; *Cheaper by the Dozen*, *Bells on Their Toes*, and *Frank and Lillian Gilbreth: Partners for Life* all portray the events and characters that made up her life. In addition, Myrna Loy's touching portrayal of Gilbreth in the popular 1950 movie *Cheaper by the Dozen* is still run occasionally on television.

We know that Gilbreth felt the burden of discrimination in her life. Her Phi Beta Kappa key was delayed. She coauthored with her husband a significant work, *Primer of Scientific Management*, yet only her husband's name appears on the work. The publisher did not want a woman's name to appear as collaborator. Her thesis "The Psychology of Management" was refused by several publishers, who explained that they could not accept a book on such a subject by a woman author. Finally, in a series of articles appearing from May 1912-May 1913, the magazine *Industrial Engineering* published it, and in 1914 a book publisher accepted it. However, in both instances her name appeared as L.M. Gilbreth, and no publicity could be given to the fact that the author was a woman.

Even in later years, after she had been honored with awards, honorary degrees, and memberships on prestigious committees, she was denied entrance to two clubs. The University Club in New York refused to let her in, even though her name was printed on a program as a participant in an event being held inside. The Engineering Club denied her entrance, although she was a member of an American Society of Mechanical Engineers committee which was meeting within. The committee members told her to eat alone at a nearby restaurant, and that they would meet with her later for a few moments. However, her record of continuing honors showed that she would not allow these slights to deter her work.

Frank Gilbreth died in 1924, and Lillian Gilbreth remained a major figure in management for more than forty years after his death. Together, they began the field of motion study, which combined the fields of management and mechanical engineering. But it was Lillian who quickly recognized that the key to managerial success is the individual and his feelings. Her thesis dealing with the psychology of management presents the underlying theme of all her work. As early as 1911, she was recognized for her work, which was absolutely different from that being followed by any other researcher in the scientific management field. She stressed that the emphasis in good management must be more on the man than on the work, and that effective teaching would enable the man to make better use of his abilities.

She never put quantitative results over the consideration of the quality of the worker's life while he was on the job. She genuinely believed in political democracy, and was convinced that its preservation depended on industrial democracy.

The Human Relations Era

A new management era dawned in the early twenties when the famous Hawthorne studies began. These studies brought with them a significant breakthrough in management thinking—people's feelings must be considered. We can look back at Gilbreth's work to see that she had been heralding this approach for a long time. Mary Parker Follett (1868-1933), another woman who had been calling for the consideration of the worker as a person, had made her mark in the field of management. Ironically, she died near the beginning of the era she had worked to bring about.

Follett's philosophy and approach came fifty years ahead of their time. She stressed that intelligent organization and the administration of government and industry should work toward an honest integration of all points of view, to the end that every individual's efforts are mobilized so that he counts both as a person and as an effective part of the group and of society. These ideas ring of today's management theme of encouraging the individual to meet his own needs as well as the needs of the organization.

As a noted political scientist, her work with the Boston Placement Bureau, Vocational Guidance Bureau, and Massachusetts Minimum Wage Board, as well as her books, brought her into contact with the thinking of many businessmen. She made the natural transition to social administration, then to industrial organization and administration.

Her thinking can be clearly seen in the current behavioral approach to management science. She applied her knowledge of psychology and sociology to industrial problems. Today colleges of business administration are removing the word "business" from their titles as they realize that the principles of administration can be applied to many areas of activity other than business. Follett saw too that the principles that are discovered in the social sciences are applicable in many areas. Her viewpoint that every human activity is merely a moment in a process can be seen in today's systems approach. Her notion of reciprocal reaction in solving differences through conference and cooperation is indeed a forerunner of today's conflict resolution techniques. Follett's approach involved having the parties evoke each other's latent ideas based upon the facts of the situation, come to see and understand each other's points of view, and integrate those viewpoints by uniting toward a common goal.

She was already searching for how business management might become a profession—a problem which still needs a solution. Among her writings are more than twenty-five papers presented here and in England about business organization and administration. Her wide acceptance by businessmen would be enviable today but may be considered a phenomenon of the time in which she lived and worked.

The Behavioral Science Era

The human relations era had brought about a rash of extrinsic solutions for improving employee morale and increasing production. The years between 1930 and 1959 introduced coffee breaks, plush carpets, fine office furniture and equipment, and piped-in music. All of these accoutrements were intended to treat the worker as a human being or make him into a "contented cow." But they only worked up to a point.

By 1960 the "affluent society" had become a reality for many people. Management discovered that not only had all the coffee breaks, plush carpets, and so on, not been completely effective, but labor problems were becoming more prominent. The era of behavioral management science began about 1960. During this era came the realization that our understanding of the worker had to be much broader than it was in the superficial human relations era. To get this deeper understanding, management turned to the disciplines of psychology, sociology, and anthropology, and considered these within the context of the work environment. This era is relatively new, but it was encouraged by Gilbreth through her work in psychology and by Follett through her efforts in sociology. Today women in increasing numbers are active in behavioral management science.

Truly a "superstar" in management today is Jane Mouton. Her research and writing with Robert R. Blake are known throughout both academia and industry. Blake and Mouton began as teachers, but now they are president and vice-president, respectively, of Scientific Methods, Inc., Austin, Texas. Their company is actively involved in management consulting all over the world. They have been prolific writers, and their work has appeared in scholarly journals, business journals, and books.

Their most well-known work is probably *The Managerial Grid*, a finely researched volume that presents an instrument for identifying leadership style. The authors show how a manager can simultaneously maximize two leadership styles—production- and people-oriented—thus achieving the benefits of both. By using the model in the book, a manager can study and change his own leadership style.

Beginning managers may have scientific, engineering, or business service skills and yet there may be a missing ingredient. That ingredient is the ability to create the environment in which people will willingly work toward company objectives. Blake and Mouton, along with some other coauthors, have researched and written several books about this topic, including *Corporate Excellence Through Grid Organization*, *The Grid for Sales Excellence*, and *Corporate Darwinism*. Another work, *Corporate Excellence Diagnosis*, describes a means of total corporation health assessment through a 72-window rubric.

The Blake-Mouton writing style is clear and readable. Behavioral management science is new compared to other recognized disciplines, but these two authors have successfully analyzed and synthesized the research that has been done, and they have presented it in a form that industry can easily apply. This feature of applicability is a major breakthrough—a bridge between academia's research and industry's needs.

Joan Woodward, a faculty member in industrial sociology at the Imperial College of Science and Technology, is a social scientist of the first rank. Her works, *Industrial Organization: Theory and Practice* (1965) and *Industrial Organization: Behavior and Control* (1970) are considered "musts" for every graduate student in business who is studying organizational behavior. She is outstanding in her ability to conceptualize and hypothesize, and to do research that is aimed at building a strong body of knowledge for organization theory.

Her first book was a study of 100 firms in South Essex. By relating the firms' organization characteristics to three simple categories of technology, she found that specific organizational patterns were associated with each category. In the past, technology had been ignored and the predominant view was that there is one best way to run any manufacturing business.

Her second book looks at medium to large batch production firms and firms with a component assembly production system. She points out that variations in structure and behavior found in these firms depend more on the nature of the control system than on the technology.

Her studies in the field are all made within the same conceptual framework; in this way she identifies common threads that can be related to theoretical considerations. She stresses that patient and detailed exploration of what actually happens inside industrial firms is a prerequisite to developing an organization theory comprehensive enough to provide managers with a reliable basis for their decisions and actions. She asks that managers use her work as an explanatory framework to compare their own firm with the firms she describes to understand how and why theirs are different.

Riva Poor is known as a leading advocate for the four-day, forty-hour work week. As author, lecturer, and management consultant, her first book *4 Days, 40 Hours* was a collection of thirteen articles and five appendixes that assembled the writings and research of fifteen authors. She also pursued the topic of decision making.

She majored in social sciences at Bennington College and in organizational development at the Sloan School of Management, MIT. She holds a master's degree in city planning from MIT. Edward C. Bursk, editor of *The Harvard Business Review*, is her partner in Bursk and Poor Publishing. She has owned and operated several small businesses, edited several business reports and newsletters, and started a successful minority business program.

The "Acknowledgements" section of Poor's book gives some insight into her personal life. She credits her parents with rearing her to be a businesswoman and her husband for being a true helpmeet. We know that cultural biases from the family environment have done much to discourage or thwart the educational and professional development of many women. We have all seen girls who were brought up to believe that having a husband and children should be their only goal in life. We have all seen husbands who, insecure in their own right, have stood in the way of their wives' chances for any sort of development.

Christel Kammerer is known for her concept "gleitende arbeitzeit" or "gliding time." She is a West German management consultant who was hired by Messerschmitt-Bolkow to work on problems of absenteeism and punctuality. In 1967, the gliding time system was launched, and since then about 3,500 West German firms have adopted it. Some people are biologically programmed to be "day" or "early" people and are eager to get started in the morning. "Night" people do their most productive work late in the day.

Companies using gliding time keep their doors open from 7 a.m. to 7 p.m.; employees schedule themselves to fill a forty-hour week.

In one West German company, one-day absenteeism dropped 60 percent under gliding time, while production went up 5 percent and morale soared. In this country gliding time has been successfully used by the American Optometric Association since February 1973. Of their seventy employees, forty are now on gliding time and, according to J. Harold Bailey, executive director, they seem to like it. Bailey states that the amount of work performed has increased while the amount of overtime has dropped considerably.

Gliding time may prove to be a real breakthrough. Not only can it solve problems of absenteeism and morale, but there may be some possible interesting and useful spin-offs. For example, how much traffic congestion could be relieved in downtown and office park areas if all employees could come and go at different times?

April 2, 1972, brought a new era for women. On that date Revised Order 4, issued under Executive Order 11246, went into effect. Within 120 days from the commencement of a federal contract, each prime contractor or subcontractor with fifty or more employees and a contract of $50,000 or more must develop a written affirmative action compliance program setting forth goals and time tables for the employment and promotion of women. If women have made significant contributions in the past to a field that has been closed to them, we can only speculate on what contributions they will make in the future to a field that is beginning to open to them.

Dr. John C. Athanassiades *is Professor of Management, School of Business Administration, Georgia State University, Atlanta.*
This article is reprinted with permission from Atlanta Economic Review, *May-June 1975, pp. 4-9.*

11

Myths of Women in Management: What Every Businessman Ought to Know But May Be Afraid to Ask

John C. Athanassiades

"IT JUST doesn't seem natural for women to be in executive jobs," says a business executive.[1] "Women are not suited to play at men's games," exclaims another.[2] "There are sex differences in the mind, too," heralds a well-known business publication.[3] A chorus of other voices responds with shouts of "sexism" and "male chauvinism."

This crescendo of dissonance has now reached levels that cannot be ignored, even by those hard of hearing. It then behooves all concerned to face up to the problem, in the hope of finding appropriate solutions.

Obviously, in their quest for a redefined role, women today are focusing attention and demands on areas and activities traditionally thought to be exclusively male preserves. There are several reasons for this. First, those male preserves constitute highly visible elites—managerial, administrative, military, hierarchical. Second, these elites are associated with high prestige, status, and/or economic rewards. Third, they are thought by some to be the stepping stones to woman's full independence. Finally, they seem to be viewed, rightly or wrongly, by some as the bastions of *machismo* and, as a result, viewed also as festerings of sex discrimination.

Indeed, business, government, the military, and the church are the major institutions today that, for all practical purposes, exclude women from their upper echelons. Yet, whether from machismo, inertia, or other reasons, these institutions are burying their heads in the sand of sex discrimination. By denying women full participation, they not only help perpetuate the second-class status of women, but also forgo the opportunity to tap the talents, creativity, and energy of one half of society's human resources.

The purpose of this article is not to argue whether or not discrimination exists. There is already ample evidence that it does.[4] Rather, the purpose is to discuss some whys and hows of sex discrimination in the hope of gaining a better understanding of it and its effect on both sexes. The approach, an examination of the mythology of sex discrimination, is based on the view that mythologies—a body of related myths—reflect past cultural or societal norms. At the peak of their acceptance, myths seldom are recognized as such. They are taken as facts and reality by their contemporaries. Only when new realities replace the old ones are old "realities" recognized as myths. Thus myths simply reflect past beliefs, attitudes, and, in general, standards of behavior. A study of relevant myths over time, then, will reveal, it is hoped, changes in beliefs, attitudes, and social norms regarding the status of women, as well as norms of behavior for both sexes.

Sex Discrimination Mythology

Before embarking on the analysis of myths, it is necessary to discuss briefly the important question of cause and effect.

The view that sex discrimination is caused by unfounded myths has an increasing popular appeal. This view probably draws on Argyris' approach which, in a different context, posits that (a) generation of valid information, (b) assurance of free choice, and (c) internal commitment are the sine qua non of effective organizational change.[5] It assumes a myth-discrimination syndrome that can be broken by disproving such myths; i.e., certain myths are the cause of sex discrimination, and by disproving such myths (by generating valid information) sex discrimination can be eradicated.

However, an examination of the myth-discrimination syndrome from a broad perspective reveals that, despite numerous past successes in disproving individual myths thought to be the roots of discrimination, new myths consistently seem to spring up, Hydra-style, for every myth stricken down. This suggests the reverse of the myth-discrimination relationship as a more plausible explanation of this phenomenon—i.e., myths are the products, rather than the cause, of discrimination. Thus although individual myths can be, and have been, disproved, discrimination—the generating force—does survive. For example, the old myth of male cosmogony reappears over and over as the new "reality" of the male genius: man—the father of art and science, the shaper of society, the creator and architect of civilization. It must be noted that, as in many other cases, it is difficult to determine cause and effect, and causation should not be taken for granted.

Another oversight of the myth-discrimination school is that it ignores Argyris' two other requirements: free choice and internal commitment. One may well ask how free men are *not* to discriminate against women? What kind of pressures exist to block internal commitment? We shall return to these questions later.

Past, Present, and Future Realities

Following the approach outlined earlier, we shall examine some myths representing past "realities." We shall look at present reality, asking what aspects of it may become the myths of tomorrow, and speculate about future realities regarding sex discrimination and the status of women.

Realities of the Past

Even a cursory look at various mythologies of the past reveals that the older the mythology, the stronger the references to a great Female Goddess, possibly reflecting the relative importance of women at those times.

Some Great Fertility Goddesses. The oldest archaeological evidence (c. 25,000 B.C.) is a statuette known as the Venus of Willendorf, thought to be related to the fertility rites of that period.[6] The earliest written references to a great goddess are found in Sumerian mythology (c. 3500 B.C.). They speak of the goddess Nammu, the primeval mother of the Universe.[7] Early Egyptian mythology (c. 3000 B.C.) tells of a fertility goddess, Hathor.[8] Hesiod (c. 700 B.C.), recording the Greek version of the cosmogony myth, describes how, out of Chaos, the wide-bosomed Gaia was born,[9] whom Homer calls the great Mother of us all.[10] Is it unreasonable to suggest that all such myths simply reflect the reality that we are all born of women?

Myths Beyond Fertility and Reproduction. Old mythologies do not restrict the female to the realm of fertility and reproduction. Rather, ancient mythologies tend to confirm the view of modern anthropology that the female pioneered the development of civilization. The ancient Egyptians thought that the goddess Isis was the discoverer of wheat and barley.[11] Virgil referred to the goddess Pallas Athena as the "founder of the plow" and spoke of woman as "oleae inventrix" (discoverer of the olive).[12] The Greek myth of the contest between Athena and Poseidon for the patronage of the city of Cecrops is a most interesting allegory of the roles of woman and man in two contrasting ways of organizing society: she, through agriculture and commerce; he, through force and war.[13] There are two versions of this myth; in both, Athena wins the contest—and the city of Cecrops is named in her honor: Athens.

Other myths strongly suggest the important role of women in what may have been significant events of their time. The myth of Ariadne, whose legendary thread guided Theseus out of the Labyrinth after the slaying of the Minotaur; and the myth of Medea, whose magic potions enabled Jason to harness Aietes' fire-breathing bulls—an otherwise impossible task—are just two examples.

But even stories that on the surface may seem to reflect negatively on woman, on close examination provide some interesting insights into woman's character. To illustrate:

Pandora's opening of the forbidden box or Eve's tasting the forbidden fruit may well allude to woman's intellectual curiosity, to her initiative, and to her spirit of independence—to say nothing of her willingness to take risks. Indeed, it is not surprising that in both Egyptian and Greek mythologies, two goddesses, Isis and Athena, were perceived also as the embodiments of wisdom and of intellectuality.

Similarly, although the origin of fire is generally attributed to man, Frazer in his collection of myths about the origin of fire—ranging from the story of Prometheus to the Kakadu women of Australia—finds such myths to be about equally divided between the sexes in crediting the discovery.[14]

Chinese myths identify China (which means "Goddess of Silk") as the discoverer of silk. And Indian legend associates a woman, Princess Nur Mehal, with the development of cloth and perfumes.[15]

The plethora of such references has convinced historian Peake,[16] among others, that it is the collective woman—the developer of agriculture, the founder of civilization—who has been immortalized by all ancients. The people of Asia Minor called her Nammu or Didymene; the Egyptians, Hathor and Isis; the Greeks, Demetra and Athena; the Romans, Ceres and Minerva; the Chinese, China; the Indians, Nur Mehal.

It should not be surprising, then, to note, along with John Stuart Mill, that myths and doctrines of free and independent women are associated with societies in which women actually enjoyed independence.[17] Therefore, it should not be surprising to note that both Plato and Socrates propounded doctrines supporting the social and political equality of the sexes. Socrates observed that he knew of no indication of intellectual differences between the sexes.[18] Plato attested that "the gifts of nature are alike diffused in both" and that all the pursuits of men are also the pursuits of women.[19] Even antifeminist Aristotle saw men and women in the household as equals but with different roles.[20]

By contrast, in the more recent past new myths and new doctrines reflect new realities. St. Paul, it is reported, reasoned the subordination of woman to man on the basis of the "Eve from the rib of Adam" story of cosmogony. Since woman was made from a part of man, she was created for man.[21] St. Ambrose, also drawing from that story, proclaimed that woman's subjugation to man is her atonement for leading him to sin. And St. John Chrysostom viewed woman as more dangerous than the wildest of animals.[22] The early church fathers and the influential Canon Episcopi also propagated the view of woman as "Janua diaboli"—the gateway of the devil.[23]

Were these great thinkers really woman haters? Or were they simply voicing rationalizations of what existed? Let us not blithely blame the ecclesiasts for such views. They were simply reflecting the new status of women. The doctrines of that and later periods gave impetus to a rising wave of antifeminism. Blackstone, in his *Commentaries on the Laws of England*, reflecting the realities of England, wrote that on marriage "the very being or legal existence of the woman is suspended."[24] Just recently, Supreme Court Justice Mr. William J. Brennan, Jr., noted that through most of the past history of the United States the position of women has been "comparable to that of the blacks under the pre-Civil War slave Codes."[25] Nietzche saw in woman's struggle for independence the "uglification of Europe,"[26] and Weininger proclaimed that "women have no existence and no essence."[27] To such depths, alas, had the status of women fallen. Is it a wonder, then, that Freud[28] formulated his doctrines to reflect all the so-called feminine traits (submissiveness, passivity, emotional instability, and so on) with which the new reality had saddled women?

Some Myths Masquerading as History. Present mythology (not generally recognized as such) reflecting the inferior status of women in modern society asserts that "historically" woman occupied a secondary status and played an insignificant role in all societies. Contrary to this popular misconception, history records that women in many societies did attain and did hold positions of importance and prominence—as rulers, intellectuals, and persons of property, wealth, and commerce. A very brief review will illustrate, as follows:

1. *Babylon*—There, women, according to the laws of Hammurabi, enjoyed many important rights, including the right to own and inherit property,[29] rights which have been denied to women in more recent times.

2. *Egypt*—Historians and archaeologists tell us that in Egypt all land belonged to the queen; that accession to the throne was

only through marriage to her.[30] We also know that Egypt produced many great queens: Aahkotep, known for her military prowess; Ti, for her political astuteness; Hatshepput, who changed the whole Egyptian sacred order.[31] And not only great queens—Egypt also produced women who engaged successfully in trade.[32] Women in Egypt had the same rights as men: the right to inherit and own property; to appear in court; to marry of their own choice; to transact business and engage in commerce.[33] As a result, women in Egyptian society occupied a very important position, to the extent that some historians have concluded that in Egypt women were the dominant sex.[34]

3. *Greece*—In light of the foregoing, some treat Egypt as an exception, suggesting that women in Greece and elsewhere were suppressed. One of the most famous but unfortunate references fortifying that view is Thucydides' "women should neither be seen nor heard." One must remember, however, that at that time Thucydides was recording a war between Athens and Sparta, the Peloponnesian War of 30 years, and his opinion was probably colored by the public mourning of dead soldiers by their womenfolk, whose emotional outbursts and wailings he may have viewed as demoralizing at a time of war. Viewed in this context, his statement significantly changes one's views of ancient Greek women in their society. Although Aristotle's antifeminism had great impact on Western thinkers such as St. Thomas Aquinas, Freud, and many others, historians suggest that Aristotle's views had little impact on his contemporary Athens.[35] The stereotype of ancient Greek women living a listless, isolated life does not stand close scrutiny.[36]

Rather, the picture that emerges from a multitude of historical evidence is one of women living a free life, often doing precisely as they pleased.[37] The long list of famous Grecian women recorded in history paints a picture other than that of women subjugated to male domination. Themista, thought of as a "female Solon"; Gnathena, famous for her wit; Theano, Callisto, Poteme, Axiothea, all of whom led philosophical schools and achieved recognition in their own rights as philosophers; Sappho, one of the great poets of all time—these were not timid little hausfraus by any stretch of the imagination. Aristocratic Aspasia is remembered for her intellect and the influence she wielded in Athens as well as for her attachment to Pericles. And Phryne amassed so much wealth (and arrogance) that, it is said, after Alexander the Great had demolished the walls of Thebes, she offered to rebuild the walls, provided the Thebans would inscribe the words: "Alexander destroyed them, but Phryne the hetaera rebuilt them."[38] Her offer was rejected, probably by male chauvinist Thebans!

Although Athenian women of wealth did not usually work, poorer women did engage in trade and held a dominant position in the marketplace.[39] In ancient Sparta, women enjoyed even greater independence, Plutarch reports. Sophocles is said to have been horrified at the sight of Spartan men and women exercising in public—naked; even wrestling each other at the gymnasium.[40]

4. *Rome*—In their time, Roman women too had a heyday. They enjoyed a high degree of equality and independence; had the right to inherit property; children were heirs of their mothers also; wives had equality with husbands; daughters had equal rights with brothers. In general, the Roman family was based on "conjuctio sanguinis."[41]

Beyond that, there is ample evidence suggesting that during the Roman Empire era, Roman women enjoyed great freedoms. During that period, in fact, many Roman women were able to pursue openly activities previously reserved for men.[42]

5. *Etruria*—Undoubtedly, the status and customs of Etruscan women which, one reads, "shocked and scandalized" the rest of the world must also have exerted great influence on their less-advanced Greek and Roman sisters. For example, Etruscan women had their own names and identities; that is, Etruscans of both sexes were identified by their matronym as well as by their patronym. The mother's name and rank were transmitted to her children, and there was no stigma of illegitimacy assigned to children whose father was not known. In addition, Etruscan women were highly educated, participated in public life to a great degree, and shared completely in the wealth, leisure, and pleasures of their society.[43]

The Present Realities

Nowadays, sin and sex having somewhat parted company, and Freud's female sexual inadequacy theories and the associated "feminine" traits having been put to pasture by findings on female sexuality,[44] one would expect new myths (initially confused with reality, or valid information) to spring up. They have begun. Selective animal studies purporting to prove the "natural" domination of the male over the female;[45] the "biology is destiny" view, purporting to show, by way of hormones, that differences in behaviors of the sexes have a biological basis;[46] sex stereotyping and internalization of different values by the two sexes through the process of socialization—these are just a few examples of these new realities. My guess is that all these will soon become the myths of the future.

Myths of the Future

Animal studies, hormone differences, internalization of sex stereotypes; ergo, the old chestnut of male superiority and male domination now are being presented as new realities.

But, already, recent findings have raised serious doubts. In many species of animals no male domination has been observed;[47] hormone differences alone may not be satisfactory explanations of all behavior differences.[48] Findings of more similarities than differences in the behaviors of children and young adults of both sexes,[49] and findings that feelings of inadequacy and role strains are not limited to females[50] suggest that the internalization hypothesis may be just that.

Consider a recent study of business executives by this author.[51] Among other things, considerable differences were found between men and women in their perceptions of autonomy and their need for independence at work. Approximately 87% of the women perceived that they were supervised too closely, and 93% expressed the need for more independence at work. On the other hand, only 36% of the males thought themselves too closely supervised, and only 54% expressed a need for greater independence. One may ask, then: if women have, indeed, "internalized" dependence, submissiveness, and so on, why are they so much aware of their lack of autonomy? And why do they express the need for greater independence? Is the "internalization of sex stereotypes" another phallocentric myth in a new guise?

Indeed, the myths may be changing, but the mythsters are not. The theme remains the same: male superiority. *Le plus ça change, le plus c'est la même chose.*

And how does the marketplace respond? The median salary of women with college degrees is only 67% of that of their male counterparts,[52] and women generally are either completely excluded from, or present in insignificant numbers in, upper- and middle-level executive positions. Of about 5 million business establishments in the United States, only 100 chief executives are women.[53] Of 3,068 members of the Producers Guild, only 8 are women. Of the 2,466 members of the Director's Guild, there are 23 women.[54] In the military and the church, how many women are in high echelons? How many women are in the President's Cabinet? How many are governors of states? How many are senators?

Some Pertinent Questions

We have seen that neither ancient mythology nor history assigns women to an inferior status; that in early societies women flourished and achieved power, independence, and recognition. Today, however, women are reduced to an inferior status on the basis of spurious rationalizations.

Why? Engels[55] and Steinem,[56] in examining contemporary and exploitative man-woman relationship, think that the economic and social gains that men derive from this relationship are at the root of the problem. But there may be other reasons.

Let us take a quick look at some primarily male institutions—the church, the military, or some business organizations, for example. First, observe their formal structures. One must note the existence of two parallel hierarchies: the highly visible hierarchy of authority, for one, and then an invisible but ever present hierarchy of fear and insecurity. It does not take great insight to recognize that organizational man is more dominat*ed* than dominat*ing*; more aggress*ed* than aggress*ive*; more scared than brave; more mouse than lion. Could it be, then, that the "weaker" and "delicate" sex, the "dizzy blondes" or "dumb broads" who "can't play at men's own games" and therefore "it does not seem natural for them to be in executive jobs" because "there are sex differences in the mind, too"—*could it be* that all these are taboos and rationalizations designed to conceal the fears and insecurities of the male? To protect his ego? Could it be that present sex mythology reflects these realities?

Rowe[57] suggests that men's drive for success may be no more than an attempt to cover for deep feelings of inadequacy vis-à-vis the female. Komarovsky[58] detects considerable male role strains among male adults; and Sears[59] reports high "anti-social" scores among young males—all clinical symptoms of insecure, threatened personalities.

On looking at organizational behavior, one is again aware that hierarchical organizations require stability and orderly subordination for effective functioning. Obviously, the male—an insecure, timid, and docile individual—makes an ideal member of such organizations. But let us assume that this insecure and docile creature, in the presence of the female, becomes stimulated to compete with other males. Under such circumstances, it stands to reason that organizations, which thrive on stability and orderly subordination rather than on the unruly competition of their members, will take steps to remove the unwanted stimulus from their milieu. Could it be that the taboos and exorcisms of the female by such organizations are intended to maintain the docility of the male by excluding the female stimulus from the organization? Could it be that present sex mythology reflects these realities also?

It is of significance that the more autocratic organizations and those which put high premium on stability have also the strongest taboos against women and offer the strongest resistance to women's admission into their hierarchies. Military, religious, and many business organizations clearly fit this pattern. One may speculate, then, that the subjugation of women is a by-product of the rise of the hierarchical form of organization.

Indeed, prior to the predominance of this form of organization, the extended family was the most prevalent form of organizing human activity. Such organization was based more on the cooperative natural symbiosis of the sexes than on an arbitrary positioning of its members. Stability was achieved and maintained, not by hierarchies of authority and fear, but rather by family bonds. And the competitiveness among members of one sex for members of the opposite sex within such an organization was minimized through taboos of incest.

Given present conditions, the nature of hierarchical organizations, the psychological pressures that such organizations exert on their members, and the insecurities and fears they generate, one well may ask whether under such conditions men can be free enough and secure enough *not* to engage in sex discrimination and, for that matter, in any form of discrimination.

Conclusion

In light of the preceding, given existing conditions and existing organizations, one may draw the following tentative but pessimistic conclusions:

1. New myths reflecting the existing inferior status of women will continue to spring up to replace the disproved ones.

2. These new myths will be offered as new arguments against the admission of women in managerial and other hierarchies.

3. Aspiring women will continue to meet resistance in their efforts to gain access to organizational hierarchies as long as organizations require stability and expect docility from their members.

4. Under such circumstances, aspiring women executives—if they hope to succeed—must shed or camouflage their femininity and avoid, at any cost, stimulating competitiveness among the males in the organization.

5. Women must defeminize themselves not only in appearance (pants, lipstickless lips, and so on), but also in thought. They must learn to "think like a man" so as not to upset established male patterns and thus accentuate male insecurity.

6. Such aspiring women must themselves become as docile and uninspired as the typical "organization man," lest any spark of creativity, originality, initiative, or independence ignite fears and insecurities of the male and/or explode his competitiveness—which may damage the stability of the organization.

7. These conditions will continue as long as men remain insecure, locked in the organizational hierarchies of fear.

Footnotes

1. M. Bender, "More Women Advancing Into Key Business Posts," *The New York Times*, January 20, 1974, p. 1.

2. T. Alexander, "There are Sex Differences in the Mind, Too," *Fortune*, February 1972.

3. Ibid.

4. Special Subcommittee on Education of the House Committee on Education and Labor, 1970 hearings, *Discrimination Against Women, Parts I and II.*

5. C. Argyris, *Intervention Theory and Method* (Reading, Massachusetts, Addison-Wesley Publishing Co., Inc., 1970).

6. M. Pallottino, *The Meaning of Archaeology* (New York, Harry N. Abrams, Inc., 1968), pp. 207-208.

7. S.N. Kramer, *The Sumerians* (Chicago, University of Chicago Press, 1963).

8. S.N. Kramer, *Mythologies of the Ancient World* (Garden City, New York, Doubleday & Co., Inc., 1961).

9. W. Auden, editor, *Greek Reader* (New York, Viking Press, 1967), p. 52.

10. Ibid., p. 66.

11. H. Peake, *Origins of Agriculture* (London, E. Benn, Ltd., 1928).

12. Virgil, *Georgics*, English translation by P.B. Smith (Chicago, University of Chicago Press, 1956).

13. E. Hamilton, *Mythology* (New York, Mentor Books, 1942), p. 269.

14. J. Frazer, *Myths of the Origin of Fire* (London, MacMillan & Co., Ltd., 1950).

15. M. Beard, *On Understanding Women* (New York, Greenwood Press, 1968), p. 54.

16. Peake, *Origins of Agriculture*; also, J. Hill, *Highways to Progress* (New York, Doubleday & Co., Inc., 1910).

17. John Stuart Mill, "The Dull and Hopeless Life," *The New York Times*, August 18, 1973, p. 21.

18. Beard, *On Understanding Women*, p. 126.

19. Plato, *The Republic*, in *Great Dialogues of Plato*, translation by W.H.D. Rouse (New York, Mentor, 1956), pp. 249-255.

20. Aristotle, *Politics*, in R. McKeon, *The Basic Works of Aristotle* (New York, Random House, 1941).

21. St. Paul, I Corinthians, xi, 7-9.

22. S. De Beauvoir, *The Second Sex* (New York, Bantam Books, 1961), pp. 78-79.

23. H. Cox, "Of Witches and Pagans Female," *The New York Times*, October 1, 1973, p. C-35.

24. W. Blackstone, *Commentaries on the Laws of England*, quoted in M. Beard, *Woman as a Force in History* (New York, MacMillan, 1946), p. 78.

25. Supreme Court Decision No. 71-1964, May 14, 1973. Frontiero et vir vs. Richardson, Secretary of Defense, et al.

26. F. Nietzche, *Beyond Good and Evil*, translation by W. Kaufman (New York, Random House, 1966), p. 231-239.

27. O. Weininger, *Sex and Character* (London, Heinemann, 1906), pp. 273-286.

28. S. Freud, "Femininity," in J. Strachey (ed.) *New Introductory Lectures on Psychoanalysis* (New York, W.W. Norton & Co., Inc., 1965).

29. De Beauvoir, *The Second Sex*, pp. 78-79.

30. B. Mertz, *Temples, Tombs and Hieroglyphs* (New York, Coward-McCann, 1964), p. 221.

31. Ibid., p. 167.

32. E.B. Schwartz, *The Sex Barrier in Business* (Atlanta, Publishing Services Division, School of Business Administration, Georgia State University, 1971), p. 7.

33. De Beauvoir, *The Second Sex*, pp. 79-80.

34. Vaerting, Matthilde, and Mathias, *The Dominant Sex* (London, Allen and Urwin, 1923).

35. Aristotle (see *Generation of Animals*) describes the female as sexually defective, passive, and therefore inferior to the male. St. Thomas Aquinas, perhaps echoing Aristotle, views woman as defective, misbegotten, and lacking the active power of the male (see Summa Theologica). Freud, too, through his postulates of female deficiency, views women as passive, submissive, and therefore inferior (see *Femininity*).

36. Beard, *On Understanding Women*, pp. 121-122.

37. S. Bell, *Women: From the Greeks to the French Revolution* (Belmont, California, Wadsworth Publishing Co., Inc., 1973).

38. Beard, *On Understanding Women*, p. 126.

39. W.K. Lacey, *The Family in Classical Greece* (Ithaca, New York, Cornell University Press, 1968).

40. Bell, *Women: From the Greeks to the French Revolution*.

41. De Beauvoir, *The Second Sex*, p. 87.

42. Bell, *Women: From the Greeks to the French Revolution*, pp. 48-69.

43. L. Warren, "Etruscan Women: A Question of Interpretation," *Archaeology*, October 1973.

44. M. Sherfrey, "The Evolution and Nature of Female Sexuality in Relation to Psychoanalytic Theory," *Journal American Psychoanalytic Association*, vol. 14, no. 1, 1966; also, J. Bardwick, *Psychology of Women* (New York, Harper & Row, Publishers, 1971); also, W. Masters and V. Johnson, *Human Sexual Response* (Boston, Little, Brown & Co., 1966); also, C. Thompson, "Penis Envy in Women," *Psychiatry*, 1943.

45. L. Tiger, *Men in Groups* (New York, Random House, 1969).

46. Bardwick, *Psychology of Women*, pp. 123-127.

47. N. Weisstein, "Psychology Constructs the Female," *Roles Women Play*, edited by M. Garskof (Belmont, California, Brooks/Cole Division, Wadsworth Publishing Co., 1971).

48. S. Schachter, "Some Extraordinary Facts about Obese Humans and Rats," *American Psychologist*, 1971, pp. 129-144; also, Weisstein, "Psychology Constructs the Female."

49. Bardwick, *Psychology of Women*, pp. 123-127.

50. M. Komarovsky, "Some Problems in Role Analysis," *American Sociological Review*, December 1973, pp. 649-662.

51. J.C. Athanassiades, "An Investigation of Some Communication Patterns of Female Subordinates," *Human Relations*, March 1974.

52. P. Gabrine, "Women with New Consciousness, Strive to Advance," *The New York Times*, January 7, 1973, p. 52F.

53. P. Gabrine, "Women in the Work Force," *Management Review*, vol. 59, 1970, pp. 20-23; also, "Small Cold Room at the Top," *Spokeswoman*, vol. 1, 1971.

54. P. Gabrine, "How To Succeed: Fail, Lose, Die," *Newsweek*, March 4, 1974, p. 51.

55. De Beauvoir, *The Second Sex*.

56. G. Steinem, quoted in "For the Liberated Female," *Time*, December 20, 1971, p. 52.

57. M. Rowe, "Why Women Take and Keep Low Paying Jobs," *Business and Society/Innovation*, Spring 1973, pp. 55-60.

58. Komarovsky, "Some Problems in Role Analysis."

59. R. Sears, "Relation of early socialization experiences to aggression in middle childhood," *Journal of Abnormal and Social Psychology*, 1961, vol. 63, pp. 466-492.

Dr. Christine L. Hobart *is Associate Professor of Management and* Karen L. Harries *is an M.B.A. candidate and Graduate Assistant, Northeastern University, Boston, Massachusetts. The senior author is indebted to the researchers in the course "Women Managers" who gathered and assessed the findings. They are R. Galen, J. LeCheminant, S. Lawler, B. Davis, S. Bradbury, M. Leahy, R. Saniipour, and D. Wilson.*

12
Sex-Role Stereotyping Among Future Managers

Christine L. Hobart and Karen L. Harries

IT IS GENERALLY accepted that the existence of sex-role stereotypes affects the advancement of women in management. Our society has created and perpetuated beliefs about the differing characteristics of women and men. The perceptions that men and women have of each other and of themselves become evident in their decision-making behavior.

That sex-role stereotypes exist is recognized and documented.[1] In a recent study by Rosenkrantz et al., it was found that among male and female college students men were perceived as more aggressive and independent than women.[2] Women, in contrast, were perceived as being gentler, quieter, and more tactful than men. Moreover, the study also revealed that the self-concepts of these students corresponded to their respective stereotypes. In addition, both sexes frequently put a higher value on stereotypically masculine characteristics than on feminine characteristics.

Similar results were obtained in the research conducted by Sherriffs and McKee.[3] They found that college students of both sexes considered men more rational and competent intellectually, franker and more straightforward in social relations, and more effective in dealing with their environment. They further found that women were considered to be more socially inclined and to have greater emotional warmth. When characterizing themselves, the students chose qualities stereotypical to their sex role.

Schein states that the managerial job can be classified as masculine, because there are more men than women in management.[4] Due to this classification, stereotyping occurs and male attributes are considered more appropriate; thus the male is perceived to be better qualified for high-level management positions. Because of sex-role stereotyping, not only male attitudes[5] but also women's self-concepts[6] deter women from advancing into higher professional and managerial levels. The evidence seems overwhelming that women do encounter negative responses toward aspirations for managerial status.

To determine the effects of sex-role stereotyping and its influence on managerial decisions, Rosen and Jerdee conducted several important studies on the decision-making behavior of undergraduate business students and bank supervisors.[7] These studies were conducted on an entirely male population to determine whether sex-role stereotyping affected such personnel decisions as promotion, career development, and supervision. The researchers also wished to examine how commonly held beliefs and attitudes of males toward male and female capabilities influenced their decision-making process. These studies were designed in such a way that only the sex variable in each of the personnel problems was manipulated. The results confirmed the presence of discriminatory attitudes against women by male managers. Usually the basis for discrimination was general suitability and potential for long-term service. Further, women were considered less capable than men of handling demanding managerial positions. The results also indicated that when role conflicts occurred between the job and family circumstances, the respondents thought it was more appropriate for women to be involved with family obligations than it was for men.

Rosen and Jerdee next surveyed readers of the *Harvard Business Review* (*HBR*) to determine how sex-role stereotyping affects a large population of managers in a similar array of personnel problems.[8] The same approach was employed as in the previous studies. Each reader was asked to respond to a series of incidents—i.e., to assume a managerial role in a hypothetical organization. Each participant received one of two versions of several incidents in which only the sex variable in each incident was manipulated while all other factors were held constant. The exercises were presented in such a way that half of the incidents in the first version involved each sex, with the sex reversed in the second version (i.e., Mary Brady in the first version and Mark Brady in the second). Comparison of the responses to each version yielded conclusions about the influence of sex-role stereotyping on managerial decisions. A return rate of 30 percent was obtained from the survey. Of the respondents, 94.7 percent were male and 5.3 percent were female, possibly reflecting the *Harvard Business Review* readership. Because females comprised only a small percentage of the sample, the results were combined. When there were differences in response behavior, the differences were given but caution was advised in the interpretation. It was concluded that male employees received greater organizational concern and support than did female employees. In terms of career demands and family obligations, the male was expected to give a higher priority to his job whereas the female was expected to put family obligations first. It was concluded further that managers displayed more discriminatory behavior against females in terms of selection, promotion, and advancement. In the exercises involving personal conduct, greater effort was' made to retain the valuable male employee than an equally valuable female employee. The Rosen and Jerdee studies seemed particularly suitable for futher exploration by the research group in a "Women Managers" seminar in the Graduate School of Business Administration at Northeastern University.

Northeastern University Survey

A survey was consequently conducted at Northeastern University (NU) in the Graduate School of Business Administration, using 283 students in the Organizational Behavior courses as the population. Because the Rosen and

Jerdee study[9] consisted of an almost entirely male management population of which 65 percent were between the ages of 30 and 50, the authors questioned whether the same results would be obtained from the NU population.

It was hypothesized that the findings obtained would not be as discriminatory against females and that different patterns of attitudes and behavior would be evident from the future decision makers in management because of a younger population with a higher incidence of female students. It was further hypothesized that not only would different attitudes and behavior be manifested from increased exposure of faculty and male students to women but also that there would be a difference in the perceptions and expectations that the students have of each other and of themselves. The subsequent higher incidence of female students in management training perhaps would increase the acceptance of their capabilities in handling various aspects of business.

Of the 62 percent who responded, 77 percent were male and 23 percent were female students.[10] An equal number of each version of the exercises were returned which facilitated analysis and gave additional credence to interpretation of the data. Whereas the Rosen and Jerdee survey contained a population of which 65 percent were between the ages of 30 and 50, this survey contained a population of 64 percent below the age of 30. (See Exhibit 1.) Of these student respondents, 89 percent were in the part-time program, and on the average they had taken six courses at the time of the study. Average length of employment was six years, with the male students coming predominately from positions associated with various aspects of engineering and the female students from a wider variety of jobs—research, finance, administration, and education.

Methodology

Each of the students was given one of two versions of an "in-basket" exercise that contained several incidents. Only the sex variable in each incident was manipulated between the versions, in the same manner as in the Rosen and Jerdee study. As in the original survey, each student assumed a role as an important manager in a hypothetical organization and had to

Exhibit 1: Characteristics and Comparisons of Participating Respondents

Age	Harvard Business Review	Northeastern University
Under 30	18%	64%
30-34	20	21
35-39	17	6
40-44	15	6
45-49	13	2
50-54	9	0
55-59	5	1
60-65	2	0
Over 65	1	0

Marital Status	Harvard Business Review	Northeastern University
Married	85.0%	68%
Single	11.3	32
Other	3.7	0

Sex	Harvard Business Review	Northeastern University
Male	94.7%	77%
Female	5.3	23

respond to various communications requesting appropriate action. The versions were compared to determine whether sex affected the decision-making process. Since the original study combined results of both the male and female respondents, our results are also combined and differences, if any, between the male and female students are compared.

Rosen and Jerdee analyzed results in three areas: (1) career demands and family obligations; (2) personal conduct; and (3) selection, promotion, and career development. The same organization, observation, and reporting of results were incorporated in the present study. Overall conclusions drawn from these separate incidents appear at the end of this article.

Career Demands and Family Obligations

Three of the incidents examined conflicts that can occur between career demands and family obligations. These incidents showed how executives might maintain different expectations from male and female employees regarding resolution of such conflicts.

The first incident involved a job-related social decision that created family tensions. It portrayed a junior executive and spouse discussing whether they should continue to attend business-related cocktail parties that the junior executive believed were important for his/her advancement in the organization and that the spouse found boring. The students were asked to choose one of three alternative approaches for resolving the problem: (1) the spouse should stop making an issue of the cocktail parties and continue to go; (2) the junior executive should attend the parties alone; or (3) the junior executive should stop attending the cocktail parties. Exhibit 2 shows that the *HBR* respondents believed that it was important

Exhibit 2: The Cocktail Party (Career Demands and Family Obligations)

Percent Approving	Spouse should go to parties and stop making it an issue	Junior executive should attend parties alone	Junior executive should stop attending parties

Female Junior Executive: Harvard Business Review

Female Junior Executive: Northeastern University

Male Junior Executive: Harvard Business Review

Male Junior Executive: Northeastern University

for the male junior executive's wife to continue to attend the parties, but in the case of a female junior executive, the husband should either continue to attend or the female junior executive should go alone. These respondents, therefore, believed that it was more important for a woman to participate in her husband's career than it was for a man to participate in his wife's career. On the other hand, the NU students believed that both sexes had an obligation to attend social activities associated with their spouses' careers. However, the female students felt less strongly than the male students that the spouse of either sex should continue to attend the parties. They felt that if a family conflict arose the junior executive should go alone, most especially if the junior executive were female.

The next exercise portrayed a situation in which a valuable accountant requested a month's leave of absence in order to take care of the children due to failure of day-care arrangements. The spouse, a school principal, is unable to take a month off. The respondents were asked to evaluate the appropriateness of the leave-of-absence request on a six-point scale ranging from highly inappropriate to highly appropriate. They were then asked to decide whether the leave should be granted with or without pay, using the same six-point scale. The respondents to both the current and *HBR* surveys felt it was more appropriate for the female accountant to take a leave of absence without pay than for the male accountant (see Exhibit 3). The female students considered the request entirely appropriate. In this instance, the NU and *HBR* respondents believed that the female has a legitimate reason for preferential treatment when conflicts arise between her role as a working woman and her role in the family. A great majority of the respondents felt the request was inappropriate for the male employee.

The third incident in this area involved a conflict between the professional careers of a husband and wife. This is a situation in which the spouse of an important computer operator has been offered an attractive managerial position on the West Coast. The respondents were asked to evaluate four alternative courses of action on the six-point scale: (1) offer the computer operator a sizable raise as an incentive to stay; (2) try to convince the computer operator that too much has been

Exhibit 3: Request for Leave of Absence (Career Demands and Family Obligations)

Percent Approving	Appropriateness of leave request	Grant leave without pay	Grant leave with pay

| 100 |
| 90 |
| 80 |
| 70 |
| 60 |
| 50 |
| 40 |
| 30 |
| 20 |
| 10 |
| 0 |

Female Accountant: Harvard Business Review

Female Accountant: Northeastern University

Male Accountant: Harvard Business Review

Male Accountant: Northeastern University

invested in his/her career to leave; (3) try to find an attractive position in the organization for the spouse; or (4) do not try to influence the computer operator. Exhibit 4 shows that *HBR* respondents felt it was more important to convince a male employee to stay than to try to influence a female employee. The NU respondents felt that it was important to try to convince the valuable computer operator to stay regardless of the sex of the operator. A higher percentage of male student respondents favored finding a position in the organization for the male employee's wife. The female students felt it was definitely more important to try to find a position in the organization for the employee's wife than for the employee's husband. Thus the male employee was considered more valuable by both the *HBR* and the NU respondents, with the implication that he be encouraged to remain with the organization. This

Percent Approving	Try to convince operator to remain with organization	Don't try to influence computer operator	Offer raise as an incentive to stay	Find attractive position in organization for spouse

Female Computer Operator: Harvard Business Review
Female Computer Operator: Northeastern University
Male Computer Operator: Harvard Business Review
Male Computer Operator: Northeastern University

suggests that the wife should follow the husband and consider her career secondary.

Thus, in the area of career demands and family responsibilities, it was indicated that the male employee was perceived by both the NU and *HBR* respondents to be more career-oriented, with the assumption that he was more valuable to the organization.

Personal Conduct

The next area examined was employee personal conduct and how the manager resolved various disciplinary problems.

The first incident involved a design engineer whose tardiness had become chronic, despite frequent reprimands from his/her supervisor. Respondents were requested to evaluate three alternative courses of action on the six-point scale: (1) threaten to fire and follow through with the threat if necessary; (2) warn of one-week's suspension without pay if it continues; or (3) do not make an issue of the tardiness. Exhibit 5 indicates that both sets of respondents felt it was more appropriate to reprimand the female employee with either suspension or firing. The female students in our survey were harsher on the female in terms of suspension, and they also felt that it was more appropriate not to make an issue of the tardiness of the male employee.

The second situation involved an issue in which the personal activities of a junior executive might interfere with job performance. The employee was having an affair, and the

---

Exhibit 5: Chronically Late Design Engineer (Personal Conduct)

Percent Approving	Suspend for one week for continued tardiness	Threaten to fire and follow through if necessary	Don't make an issue of tardiness

Female Design Engineer: Harvard Business Review

Female Design Engineer: Northeastern University

Male Design Engineer: Harvard Business Review

Male Design Engineer: Northeastern University

Exhibit 6: Philandering Junior Executive (Personal Conduct)

Percent Approving	Do nothing unless junior executive raises the issue	Advise junior executive to see a marriage counselor	Confront employee and threaten termination unless affair stops

100
90
80
70
60
50
40
30
20
10
0

Female Junior Executive: Harvard Business Review

Female Junior Executive: Northeastern University

Male Junior Executive: Harvard Business Review

Male Junior Executive: Northeastern University

spouse was threatening to make it public. Since it might affect the employee's work, different strategies were suggested for resolving the problem. The respondents were asked to evaluate each strategy on the six-point scale. The alternatives were: (1) the employee should be confronted and told to terminate the affair or be fired; (2) advise the employee to see a marriage counselor; or (3) do nothing unless the employee brings it up. Exhibit 6 shows that the *HBR* respondents believed the male employee should be encouraged to see a marriage counselor, and in the case of the female employee, they preferred to do nothing unless she brought it up. The NU respondents felt it was more appropriate to do nothing unless the employee, whether male or female, brought the matter up.

Therefore, with respect to employee personal conduct, the

on-the-job behavior of the female employee was more closely watched and less tolerated than that of the male employee. Disciplinary action was recommended for inappropriate off-the-job behavior by the *HBR* respondents in order to retain the valuable male employee, and inappropriate on-the-job behavior was overlooked. The NU students believed that off-the-job behavior of an employee of either sex was not the concern of the organization. The younger respondents in the NU survey may be reacting as incumbents in lower status positions, the observed rather than the observer, as well as reflecting the mores of the time.

Selection, Promotion, and Career Development

Although new personnel policies and goals have been established by organizations due to recent legislation and social pressures to provide women with equal employment opportunities,[11] discriminatory behavior still appears in selection, promotion, and career development. Three incidents in this area reflect how such behavior might be manifested in various types of personnel decisions.

The first incident portrayed the disadvantage that can occur when women compete with men in the selection process for career development. Two candidates were equally qualified to attend an important conference on production supervision, and only one could be sent. One version of this exercise was a choice between an older, unpromotable male and a younger, highly qualified female. The opposite choice was available in the other version. The respondents were asked to choose one of the candidates. It is clearly evident in Exhibit 7 that the *HBR* respondents chose the older, loyal employee regardless of sex. A majority of the NU students chose the younger candidate regardless of sex, with the male students indicating a higher preference for the male. The female students indicated a higher preference for the female candidate regardless of age. These results indicate that the *HBR* respondents preferred an older, more established person, preferably a male, for career development. The male student future managers would send a younger, potentially valuable person, preferably male, to the conference; the female student future managers would

Exhibit 7: Training Conference (Promotion and Career Development)

Percent recommending

100	
90	
80	
70	
60	
50	
40	
30	
20	
10	
0	

Young Female Representative: Harvard Business Review
Young Female Representative: Northeastern University
Young Male Representative: Harvard Business Review
Young Male Representative: Northeastern University

discriminate against the male in any circumstance. The greatest divergence between the two surveys emerges out of this incident. Both age and sex seem to be important factors. This may be an indication of a reverse form of discrimination.

The next incident examined the effects of travel on the decision-making process in the selection of a new purchasing manager. The person selected must travel extensively to purchase clothing accessories. A thorough knowledge of raw materials and pricing was expected. A resume was received from a person who has had extensive experience at several retail clothing stores. The applicant was married with four young children. The respondents were asked to accept or reject the candidate and then to rate the candidate on a six-point scale for suitability and potential for remaining on the job. When the male and female student responses were combined, the results indicated that regardless of sex the candidate was not acceptable. These findings were consistent with the *HBR* respondents as shown in Exhibit 8. A higher percentage of female student respondents expressed acceptance of the candidate than did the male student respondents regardless of the sex of the candidate. A higher preference for the male candidate was subsequently indicated by these female student responses.

The final incident in this area involved a possible conflict between job demands and family obligations in the consideration of promotion. The person being considered for promotion to personnel director was one of the most competent employees in the corporate personnel office.

Exhibit 8: Selection of Purchasing Manager (Promotion and Career Development)

Percent recommend-ing selection and percent rating applicant favorably	Recommend selection	Favorable rating of applicant's suitability for the job	Favorable rating of applicant's potential to remain on the job

Female Applicant: Harvard Business Review

Female Applicant: Northeastern University

Male Applicant: Harvard Business Review

Male Applicant: Northeastern University

Exhibit 9: Promotion to Personnel Director (Promotion and Career Development)

Percent recommending promotion and favorably rating actions	Do not promise	Persuade candidate to make stronger job commitment prior to promotion	Base promotion on past experience

```
100
 90
 80
 70                                                          ╱╲
 60                                              ┌─┐         ╱╱
 50                                              │ │         ╱╱
 40                        ┌─┐                 ┌─┐╱╲         ╱╱
 30  ┌─┐                   │ │╱╲    ┌─┐        │ │╱╱         ╱╱
 20  │ │╱╲    ┌─┐          │ │╱╱    │ │╱╲      │ │╱╱         ╱╱
 10  │ │╱╱    │ │╱╲        │ │╱╱    │ │╱╱      │ │╱╱         ╱╱
  0
```

Female Candidate: Harvard Business Review [▢]
Female Candidate: Northeastern University [╱╱]
Male Candidate: Harvard Business Review [▢]
Male Candidate: Northeastern University [╱╱]

Although this person was fully capable of handling the new position, there was concern that he/she would not be willing to subordinate time with his/her family to his/her career if the new position required it. This person has stated that the family has his/her highest priority, although this has not affected job performance in the past. Respondents were requested to choose one of three alternative courses of action: (1) do not promote; (2) try to persuade him/her to make a stronger commitment before promoting; or (3) promote on the basis of past performance. As shown in Exhibit 9, both sets of respondents preferred to promote the male on past performance. The female students strongly favored promoting the male on past performance and preferred persuading the female candidate to make a stronger job commitment before promoting.

An analysis of the area of selection, promotion, and career development suggests that sex discrimination indeed does continue to exist. When family responsibilities were indirectly involved, the male was promoted without question and was given higher preference for career development. In a situation where a choice had to be made between a man and a woman, the female students discriminated against the male candidate. When the variable of sex was not an obvious factor, the male was preferred by both sets of respondents. Here again, the female students were more pronounced in their stereotyping than their male counterparts.

In three incidents not reported in the original survey by Rosen and Jerdee with *HBR* readers, it was found that when candidates clearly were either not qualified for a certain position or fitted the position perfectly, the candidates were rejected or accepted regardless of sex. The results from the present survey on these three incidents also reflect the same rejection or acceptance pattern. As Rosen and Jerdee suggest, "it may be relatively easy to make unbiased decisions in situations where a candidate's qualifications are clearly unacceptable or clearly acceptable. ... On the other hand, in situations where available information is ambiguous or contradictory, decision makers may fall back on preconceived attitudes (sex-role stereotypes in this instance) to arrive at their ultimate decision."[1][2]

Conclusions

The results from these two surveys seem to indicate the continued presence of forms of sex-role stereotyping which affect the day-to-day decision-making behavior of management. Male and female employees are placed in stereotypical roles, not only by present practitioners in management and future male managers, but also by future female managers.

Expectations of certain appropriate characteristics and behaviors affect decision-making behavior because of the perceptions that males and females have of themselves and others. These perceptions and expectations sometimes stand as barriers to women to advancing into higher levels which still are predominated by men.

In several of the incidents it was noted that the female student respondents were harsh in their appraisal of situations involving female portrayals. In terms of discipline, inappropriate behavior is not tolerated, and, when promotion is considered, the female continually must give evidence of a stronger commitment. Females expect this from other females, and, once they occupy higher levels of management, their behavior can be studied perhaps in the same way as males.

Although both male and female student respondents in our survey were more inclined to hire or promote a well-qualified candidate whose name was masculine rather than feminine, given identical qualifications the percentage of the responses was not as biased as the original survey by Rosen and Jerdee with older *HBR* respondents. In the one exercise in the survey where sex was an obvious factor and a choice had to be made, a greater percentage of discriminatory behavior was evidenced by the female students for the female candidate. This suggests that women may choose a less qualified female candidate over a more qualified male in their decision-making process. Further study with a larger sample of men and women in equal positions of influence is needed to pursue the implication of this form of reverse discrimination.

The impact of sex-role stereotypes affects the perception of women as being less qualified than men for high-level management positions. Therefore, requisite management characteristics are more commonly ascribed to men than to women. This may account in part for the limited number of women in higher levels of management. Yet Wexley and Hunt, in their study of behavior patterns and skills of male and female supervisors, found no significant differences between the performance of male and female supervisors in human relations and administrative skills.[13] They also found that the sex of the subordinates had no effect on the performance of the supervisors. This study implies that the unfavorable attitudes commonly held by male managers toward the supervisory potential and capabilities of females is not warranted.

Our original hypothesis that discriminatory attitudes against women would be less evident in the younger respondents was upheld. There appears to be increasing recognition that the female employee is as valuable and important to the organization as the male, with less discriminatory attitudes appearing in the areas of career demands and family obligations and personnel decisions. Etaugh obtained similar results regarding younger professionals and their attitudes.[14] The younger respondents in the study expressed a more positive attitude toward the female professional, thus indicating a gradual eroding of sex-role stereotyping.

The dual role of married career women has been recognized as a factor in the promotion of women to higher management levels. There are indications that negative attitudes of male faculty regarding married professional women strongly influence career choices by discouraging competent female students from pursuing professional training.[15] In the job market, also, negative male attitudes exist toward the woman's ability to cope adequately with home and career responsibilities.[16] These negative attitudes in education and the professions, added to society's expectations of her role, influence the woman's occupational choice. It is proposed by some scholars that until the socialization process is changed[17] and the education of males and females is redesigned to include curriculums based on principles of individual need and limitless career opportunities[18] few females will choose careers in management and be accepted as equals with males.

The responses from the male and female students in our survey indicate that changes in attitudes and behavior are surfacing. In the area of career demands and family obligations, the male and female students indicated that the professional woman's career should be recognized not only by her family but also by the organization.

In the area of personal conduct, on-the-job behavior of the female employee was not overlooked as was the case for a male employee. The female students indicated a higher percentage for censorship of her behavior. As noted earlier, this could be a reflection of the standards professional women demand of themselves and others of their sex.

Both managers and educators have an important part to play in preparing qualified individuals for the increasingly complex jobs of the future. Awareness of the overt and subtle forms of sex stereotyping that result in unintentional discriminatory decisions is but a first step. More needs to be done as to the causes. On the whole there has been a good faith effort to increase the numbers of women. We are at a point now where we need to learn more about why their numbers have not increased in proportion to their efforts. Experimentation with curriculum dealing with this area of concern and study is one way the educators can help. Further studies such as noted in this article is certainly another. Business organizations should look inwardly on some disciplined basis for similar ways to make their managers aware of how their organizational behavior may be affected by sex stereotyping.

Footnotes

1. L.E. Tyler, *The Psychology of Human Differences* (New York: Appleton-Century-Crofts, 1965); J.P. McKee and A.C. Sherriffs, "Men's and Women's Beliefs, Ideas and Self-Concepts," *American Journal of Sociology*, Vol. 64, 1959; and S.W. Fernberger, "Persistence of Stereotypes Concerning Sex Differences," *Journal of Abnormal and Social Psychology*, Vol. 43, 1948, pp. 97-101.

2. P. Rosenkrantz et al., "Sex-Role Stereotypes and Self-Concepts in College Students," *Journal of Consulting and Clinical Psychology*, June 1968, pp. 287-295.

3. A.C. Sherriffs and J.P. McKee, "Qualitative Aspects of Beliefs About Men and Women," *Journal of Personality*, June 1957, pp. 452-464.

4. V.E. Schein, "The Relationship Between Sex Role Stereotypes and Requisite Management Characteristics," *Journal of Applied Psychology*, Vol. 57, 1973, pp. 95-100.

5. C.D. Orth and F. Jacobs, "Women in Management: Pattern for Change," *Harvard Business Review*, July-August 1971; also G.W. Bowman, N.B. Worthy, and S.A. Greyser, "Are Women Executives People?" *Harvard Business Review*, July-August 1965.

6. A.H. Stein and M.M. Bailey, "The Socialization of Achievement Orientation in Females," *Psychological Bulletin*, November 1973; W.C. House, "Actual and Perceived Differences in Male and Female Expectancies and Minimal Goal Levels as a Function of Competition," *Journal of Personality*, September 1974, pp. 493-509; T.J. Coates and M.L. Southern, "Differential Educational Aspiration Levels of Men and Women Undergraduate Students," *The Journal of Psychology*, Vol. 81, 1972, pp. 125-128; and J.M. Bardwick et al., *Feminine Personality and Conflict* (Belmont, California: Brooks/Cole Publishing Co., 1970).

7. B. Rosen and T.H. Jerdee, "The Influence of Sex Role Stereotypes on Evaluations of Male and Female Supervisory Behavior," *Journal of Applied Psychology*, Vol. 57, 1973, pp. 44-48; B. Rosen and T.H. Jerdee, "Influence of Sex Role Stereotypes on

Personnel Decisions," *Journal of Applied Psychology*, Vol. 59, 1974, pp. 9-14; and B. Rosen and T.H. Jerdee, "Effects of Applicant's Sex and Difficulty of Job on Evaluations of Candidates for Managerial Positions," *Journal of Applied Psychology*, Vol. 59, 1974, pp. 511-512.

8. B. Rosen and T.H. Jerdee, "Sex Stereotyping in the Executive Suite," *Harvard Business Review*, March-April 1974, pp. 45-58.

9. Ibid.

10. This was consistent with the total male/female distribution of the Organizational Behavior class population.

11. C.L. Meacham, "The Law: Where It Is and Where It's Going," in E. Gordon and M.H. Strober (eds.), *Bringing Women into Management* (New York: McGraw-Hill Book Co., 1975); also R. Loring and T. Wells, *Breakthrough: Women into Management* (New York: Van Nostrand Reinhold Co., 1972).

12. Rosen and Jerdee, "Sex Stereotyping in the Executive Suite," p. 56.

13. K.N. Wexley and P.J. Hunt, "Male and Female Leaders: Comparison of Performance and Behavior Patterns," *Psychological Reports*, Vol. 35, 1974.

14. C.F. Etaugh, "Attitudes of Professionals Towards the Married Professional Woman," *Psychological Reports*, Vol. 32, 1973.

15. Ibid.

16. M.M. Kaley, "Attitudes Toward the Dual Role of the Married Professional Woman," *American Psychologist*, March 1971; also Bowman, Worthy, Greyser, "Are Women Executives People?"

17. A.B. Heilbrun, C. Kleemeier, and G. Piccola, "Developmental and Situational Correlates of Achievement Behavior in College Females," *Journal of Personality*, September 1974, pp. 420-436; V.J. Bieliauskas, "Recent Advances in the Psychology of Masculinity and Femininity," *The Journal of Psychology*, July 1965, pp. 255-263; and J. Block, "Conceptions of Sex Role—Some Cross-Cultural and Longitudinal Perspectives," *American Psychologist*, June 1973.

18. H. Taylor, *On Education and Freedom* (New York: Abelard-Schuman, 1954); also Kaley, "Attitudes Toward the Dual Role of the Married Professional Woman."

Dr. Virginia E. Schein *is Associate Professor of Organizational Behavior, School of Management, Case Western Reserve University, Cleveland, Ohio.*
This article is reprinted with permission from Atlanta Economic Review, *March-April 1976, pp. 21-24.*

13

Think Manager–Think Male

Virginia E. Schein

ALTHOUGH THE number of women in the work force has increased markedly over the last 10 years, there has been no noticeable increase in the number of women in middle- and upper-level managerial positions. Despite outside pressures for change from governmental forces and women's groups, and internal organizational efforts to recruit and promote women, there is still a dearth of women in top management positions in most organizations. Although explanations for this outcome, such as the inability to find qualified women and the recency of their entry in lower level managerial jobs, do have some validity, they belie the complexity of the problem. The introduction of women into upper managerial ranks is by no means a simple task. There are psychological and sociological barriers confronting both men and women which make this endeavor difficult. In order to effectively improve the status of women in management, it first is necessary to understand and document the existence of these covert barriers.

One major barrier impeding the progress of women may be the sex-typing of the managerial job. Occupations can be described as sex-typed when a large majority of those in them are of one sex and when there is an associated normative expectation that this is how it should be.[1] Characteristics necessary for success in a sex-typed occupation are usually those associated with either the male or female sex-role stereotype. For example, a female type occupation tends to require characteristics associated with femininity, such as emotionality, nurturing, and empathizing, whereas the male type occupation tends to require characteristics associated with masculinity, such as coolness, detachment, and analytic objectivity. If the managerial job is classified as a male type occupation, then the managerial position would tend to require personal characteristics often thought to be more commonly held by men than by women. This sex-typing of the managerial position, then, would cause a woman, regardless of her ability, to be perceived as less qualified than a man for high-level management positions.

Despite the strong possibility of sex-typing of the managerial position and its resultant negative influence on the recruitment, selection, and promotion of women, there is little or no evidence documenting the existence of this phenomenon. Such empirical evidence is essential. Documentation of the relationship between sex-role stereotypes and perceived requisite personal characteristics for the middle manager's job not only adds to the knowledge regarding barriers to women in management, but also gives both direction and credibility to change efforts designed to alter this situation. The purpose of the present study, therefore, was to determine if, in fact, it is true that when we think "manager" we think "male." Specifically, the investigation sought to determine if successful middle managers are perceived to possess those characteristics, attitudes, and temperaments more commonly ascribed to men in general than to women in general.

A second and equally important purpose of the study was to compare the perceptions of male and female managers with regard to the relationship between sex-role stereotypes and requirements for the managerial job. Thus far, the majority of studies pertaining to women in management have used only males as respondees.[2] As the weight of evidence from these studies indicating discriminatory attitudes toward women in management increases, the use of all-male samples for study implies that it is male managers that are responsible for impeding the advancement of women in management. Although such may be the case, it is important to determine the extent to which female managers hold attitudes toward women which are similar to or different from their male counterparts.

The Study

Respondee Characteristics

The male sample was composed of 300 middle line managers of various departments within nine insurance companies located throughout the United States. Their median age was 43 years, their median years of experience was 10.

The female sample was composed of 167 middle line managers within 12 insurance companies, 8 of which were the same ones from which the male sample was drawn. The female managers' median age was 43.5 and median years of experience was 6.5.

Questionnaire

Three forms of a 92 Item Descriptive Index[3] were used to determine both the perceptions of male and female sex-role stereotypes and the characteristics of successful middle managers. All three forms contained the same descriptive items and instructions, except that one form asked for a description of successful middle managers (Managers), one for a description of women in general (Women), and one for a description of men in general (Men).

The instructions were as follows:

On the following pages you will find a series of descriptive terms commonly used to characterize people in general. Some of these terms are positive in connotation, others are negative, and some are neither very positive nor very negative.

We would like you to use this list to tell us what you think (women in general, men in general, or successful middle managers) are like. In making your judgments, it may be helpful to imagine that you are about to meet a person for the first time and the only thing you know in advance is that the person is (an adult female, an adult male, or a successful middle manager). Please rate each word or phrase in terms of how characteristic it is of (women in general, men in general or successful middle managers).

Within each company, an equal number of the three forms of the Index were distributed to male and female managers with a salary range of approximately $12,000 to $30,000 and a minimum of one year of experience at the managerial level. Each manager received only *one* form of the Index and was not aware of the purpose of the study.

Results

The questionnaire information was analyzed two ways. First, an overall analysis of the responses was performed in order to determine statistically the existence or lack of existence of a relationship between sex-role stereotypes and perceptions of requisite managerial characteristics. Second, the more exact nature of the relationship was explored by analysis of responses to individual items.

The Male = Manager Equation

Within the male sample, the overall analysis revealed a large and statistically significant resemblance between their descriptive ratings of Men and Managers ($r'=.60$) and a near zero, nonsignificant resemblance between their ratings of Women and Managers ($r'=.06$). Similarly, within the female sample, there was a large and significant resemblance between their descriptive ratings of Men and their descriptive ratings of Managers ($r'=.54$). Although within the female sample there was also a significant resemblance between their ratings of Women and Managers ($r'=.30$), this resemblance was significantly less than the resemblance between Men and Managers. Thus, both male and female managers tend to perceive the personal characteristics necessary for success as a middle manager as more likely to be possessed by men in general than by women in general. Sex-role stereotyping does influence our perceptions of requisite management characteristics such that to think "manager" is to think "male."

Such thinking would seem to account, in part, for the limited number of women in managerial positions. The perceived similarity between the characteristics of successful middle managers and men in general increases the likelihood of a male rather than a female being selected for or promoted into a managerial position. Through sex-role stereotyping, the male applicant is viewed as possessing certain masculine characteristics which, based on this research, also are seen as necessary for managerial success. Hence, the male, by virtue of his gender alone, has the competitive edge before the race even begins.

This view of masculine characteristics as being requisite ones for the managerial position may also prevent some women from even entering the race. If a woman's self-image incorporates the feminine sex-role stereotype, she may be reluctant to choose a managerial career since the perceived requisite "masculine" managerial behaviors would be inconsistent with her own feminine self-image.

She Thinks Like a Man

The marked similarity between female and male managers' responses shows that female managers are as likely as male managers to be influenced by sex-role stereotypical thinking so as also to make selection and promotion decisions in favor of men. Hence, contrary to popular thought, simply increasing the number of women managers will not necessarily facilitate the entry of other women into these positions.

More importantly, these findings pertaining to women managers suggest that acceptance of the stereotypical male characteristics as a basis for success in management may be a necessity for women seeking to achieve in the current organizational climate. To "think like a man" may be vital for a woman if she is to be accepted and successful in predominately male organizations. The current investigation also found that the perceived similarity between masculine characteristics and those characteristics necessary for managerial success was strongest among managers with only one to five years of managerial experience. Similarly, an interview study[4] of successful women executives revealed that these women admitted to identifying with the masculine stereotype of what constituted success during their early managerial careers.

Elements of the Male = Female Equation

What are these important masculine characteristics? Are there any managerial characteristics viewed as more "feminine" than "masculine"? Are there any differences between the male and female managers? These and other questions were answered by the analysis of the responses on an individual item basis.

As shown in Exhibit 1, both male and female managers viewed characteristics such as leadership ability, self-confidence, aggressiveness, and desire for responsibility both as important for managerial success and as more likely to be possessed by men than by women. Males went even further than females and also perceived characteristics such as emotional stability and analytical thinking as requisite managerial characteristics more commonly ascribed to men than women. Female managers, on the other hand, tended to view these latter characteristics as important for managerial success, but as likely to be possessed by a woman as a man.

Only with "employee-centered" characteristics does it appear that stereotypical thinking is advantageous to potential women managers. Both male and female managers viewed items such as intuitiveness and helpfulness as more feminine than masculine and important for a successful manager. Although encouragement of stereotypical thinking in selection and promotion decisions is clearly dysfunctional, perhaps some focus on these feminine characteristics that are related to managerial success might foster a climate of greater receptivity to women managers.

Finally, both sexes perceived characteristics such as competency and intelligence as requisite management characteristics which are as likely to be found more or less as easily among women or men. That expertise is not viewed as a sex-linked characteristic explains why most women in middle

Exhibit 1: Representative Items in Three Outcome Categories: Female and Male Samples

A *Female Sample Only*	B *Both Samples*	C *Male Sample Only*
	Manager = Male	
(Not) desire for friendship	Leadership ability Competitive Self-confident Objective Aggressive Forceful Ambitious Desires responsibility	Emotionally stable Steady Analytical ability Logical Consistent Well informed
	Manager = Female	
Modest Creative Cheerful	Intuitive Helpful Humanitarian values Aware of feelings of others	Sophisticated
	Manager = Qualified Person	
Emotionally stable Steady Analytical ability Logical Well informed Consistent	Competent Intelligent Persistent (Not) devious (Not) bitter	Tactful Curious

and upper managerial positions tend to be in or have entered through staff rather than line positions. The finding also suggests that in organizations in which sex-role stereotyping of the managerial position is especially pervasive, placement of women in positions where expertise is an important component of authority can be an acceptable way of facilitating their entry into managerial positions.

Directions for Change

The strong external and internal organizational pressures for improving the status of women in management necessitates serious consideration of ways to eliminate the sex-typing of the managerial job. One way to alter this situation is through the presentation of these research results within management development sessions. Many managers are unaware of their own stereotypical thinking regarding the requirements for a managerial position. A discussion of this empirical demonstration of the phenomenon based on responses from managers similar to themselves can do much to expand their awareness that, in fact, such sex-role stereotyping does exist. The use of the study questionnaire within the training session can also be a way to demonstrate their stereotyping of male, female, and managerial characteristics.

While attitude change is important, of equal importance are changes within the organization designed to minimize the influence of stereotypical thinking on selection and promotion decisions. Such influence can be minimized by increasing the objectivity of the information used in the decision-making process. Here the key is the development of measures of the actual job-related and behaviorally based requirements of managerial positions, the development of complementary objective measures of candidates' skills and abilities, and the use of such a job-person matching system to select qualified managers. Also, based on knowledge of skills, abilities, and expertise required of particular top-level jobs, career pathing programs can be developed to ensure that women acquire the appropriate expertise for these jobs. Career pathing is an especially effective way to qualify women for line management positions. Overall, greater objectivity of the criteria and the candidate evaluation system reduces the negative impact of stereotypical thinking on selection and promotion decisions.

Finally, consideration should be given within the organization to ways in which it reinforces and perpetuates the sex-role stereotyping of the managerial job. Although rarely documented, there are many informal behaviors which treat the female manager as special or different, thereby reserving the traditional managerial role for the male manager. For example, references to a woman's appearance during business meetings, overt and often exaggerated demonstrations of "chivalry" such as chair holding and cigarette lighting, and introductions such as "our woman vice-president" serve to set women managers apart from male managers. Organizations also should examine the extent to which they tend to reward or favor women managers who accept the masculine view of the managerial job. If such acceptance on the woman manager's part also entails inner conflict over "being a woman" and "being a manager," such conflict may be a high and unfair price to pay for success. Also, such a reward system does little to encourage the qualified woman who has a more feminine self-image.

The sex-typing of the managerial job developed in a time when most managers were male. The advancement of women in management makes this view out-of-date and dysfunctional. If women are to gain access to middle- and upper-management positions, it is imperative that individual and organizational changes occur such that the elements of the equation "think manager—think male," become "think manager—think qualified person."

Footnotes

1. B.M. Bass, J. Krusell, and R.A. Alexander, "Male Managers' Attitudes Towards Working Women," *American Behavioral Scientist*, vol. 15, 1971, pp. 221-236.

2. E.A. Cedil, R.J. Paul, and R.A. Olins, "Perceived Importance of Selected Variables for Male and Female Job Applicants," *Personnel Psychology*, vol. 26, 1973, pp. 397-404; C.F. Epstein, *Woman's Place* (Berkeley, University of California Press, 1970), p. 152.

3. M. Hennig, "What Happens on the Way Up," *MBA—Master of Business Administration*, March 1971, pp. 8-10.

4. Virginia Schein, "The Relationship Between Sex Role Stereotypes and Requisite Management Characteristics," *Journal of Applied Psychology*, vol. 57, 1973, pp. 95-100.

Dr. John Smith Herrick *is Professor of Management, Department of Business Administration, Western Kentucky University, Bowling Green.*

14

Female Executives and Their Motives

John Smith Herrick

CONSIDERABLE DISCUSSION, complaint, and legal action centers around the number of women who are employed in business and government with positions in the executive ranks. Information on the capability of women of holding executive positions, which once was sparse, is now appearing at a steadily increasing rate. The subject of this discussion is that of women in executive positions, and it is based on four studies made by the author in different populations.

A limited portion of the study has been discussed previously.[1] Now, however, there is more data at hand, and conclusions can be made from a broader base of data. The first study was conducted within a population of public service executives in the federal government, the second in the Commonwealth of Kentucky, the third in the state of Illinois, and the fourth, exactly five years later, was a replication of the first study. All of these studies sought to determine work motives of executives.

Motives and Motivation

Studies of motivation have habitually encountered problems of naming and classifying needs and motives. This is understandable since needs and motives are but expressions of personalities and value systems. More understanding is required when one realizes that the individual's personality is the totality of the inherited and acquired traits and characteristics. Moreover, each of these factors is another, multi-factor variable.

Where and how the inherited traits and characteristics originate is the subject of widespread theorizing and speculation. Since one of the concepts is needed to help explain a finding from the author's study, it will be introduced briefly. Bardwick points out the effects of hormones on sexuality: "All aspects of reproduction, in all animals, are basically dependent upon the presence of the appropriate sex hormones. Hormones are powerful chemical substances that are produced in the endocrine glands and secreted into the bloodstream to affect all other parts of the body."[2]

It is interesting to note that Freud may have had thoughts along these lines. He is better known for his structures and methodology, but even at that he was alert to the possible presence of chemical effects on sexuality. "Since we cannot dismiss the entire notion that sexual excitation is derived from the operation of certain chemical substances, it would seem that some day biochemistry will reveal two distinct substances, the presence of which produces male and female excitation respectively."[3] Thus it seems that Freud did not close the door to theories other than his own, but left the door open for chemical effects on the operation of the human personality. Later, Bardwick highlighted the medical position that the chemicals are hormones.

Bardwick points out: "In the male, the main hormone involved in developing and maintaining the sex characteristics is testosterone, one of the group known as androgens. This single hormone supplies the chemical basis for male sexual behavior."[4] Bardwick suggests that the hormone, and hence sexual control in the male, is a rather simple, physiological control mechanism.

With the female, however, the process of control is much

more complex. Female control is exercised through a series of switching systems that regulate the quantities of hormones in the bloodstream which, in turn, serve as a control for the female's sexual behavior.

Bardwick also points out that biochemical problems can occur. She says: "For one, androgens may be biotransformed into estrogens in men and gestagens (a pregnancy hormone) may break down later into androgens in women. Second, inside the body the sex hormones are unstable chemical compounds—androgens, estrogens, and progesterone change into related forms."[5] Such transformations occurring within the organism, since they probably affect behavior in the first place, could account for changes in behavior in males and females.

Of course, this discussion is not to negate or neglect the effects of environment on human behavior. Effects of culture and environment are too widely recognized and accepted. One of Mead's comments may be relevant: "To the extent that women are denied the use of their minds, their sons suffer as well as their daughters."[6]

This quick view of personality, according to a limited approach, was taken so that some explanation might be made when the research findings are discussed later in the report. Since the difficulty of classifying motives has already been pointed out, the method used in the study will be discussed next.

Classification

The research being reported was conducted using a classification in a grouping of motives and needs according to a hierarchy of prepotency.[7] Maslow suggests that there are first level—basic—needs for balance of the bloodstream. Part of these, and accompanying them, are needs for food, water, and the like. These needs must be satisfied to some extent first, but neither the needs nor the extent of satisfaction are specified. After the individual satisfies the physiological needs, higher levels of needs begin to make themselves felt. The higher levels of needs are classed as psychological, as opposed to the biological nature of the lower needs. The next level is concerned with safety or security needs and when these are satisfied to some extent, the love and belongingness needs exert themselves. When these are satisfied to some extent, the two-part esteem needs seek satisfaction. First, the individual needs to think well of himself, and second, he needs to have others think well of him also. The needs are best satisfied when both are high and when they correspond. Highest of the needs is self-actualization—the need to accomplish and succeed according to one's capabilities. As each of the lower needs is satisfied to an extent acceptable to the individual, wants and desires emanate which are related to a higher order of needs. It was around this concept of needs, motives, and satisfactions that the studies were developed.

Participants

The next choice was that of participants in the study. Since an analysis of people holding responsible and influential positions was desired, there was a problem of position identification. Considerable difficulty was encountered in finding an acceptable definition of the terms *manager* and *executive*. When the definitions could not be found, the term *manager* was dropped and the term *executive* was defined by the amount of pay or the grade held by the participant.

In the federal study, executives were considered to be those people holding grades GS-11 (and corresponding grades in non-Classification Act positions) up through Executive Level V. In the Commonwealth study, participants started with grade 14 and went up through grade 23, and included Commissioners of executive departments. In the state of Illinois, grades 15 through 28 were included.

Method

The data for all four studies were obtained by means of a questionnaire. The questionnaire contained classification items and sixteen questions. Thirteen of the questions were concerned with items classifiable into a Maslow-type needs hierarchy. The printed instructions said:

Following are listed several characteristics or qualities connected with your own management position. For each such characteristic you will be asked to give three ratings:

a. How much of the characteristic is there now connected with your management position?

b. How much of the characteristic do you think should be connected with your management position?

c. How important is this position characteristic to you?

For all of the questionnaire items the respondents were to answer the foregoing three questions by circling a number on a rating scale extending from 1 to 7, where "Low numbers represent low or minimum amounts, and high numbers represent high or maximum amounts."

A typical item appeared as follows on the questionnaire:

The opportunity for personal growth and development in my management position:
a) How much is there now?   (min) 1 2 3 4 5 6 7 (max)
b) How much should there be?   (min) 1 2 3 4 5 6 7 (max)
c) How important is this to me?   (min) 1 2 3 4 5 6 7 (max)

In the Results section of this article answers to parts (a) and (b) of each item provide data on perceived deficiency in need fulfillment. Answers to part (c) provide the data for evaluating the importance of each type of need to the respondent.

Categories of Needs and Specific Items

Shown here are the categories of needs used in these studies, along with the specific items used to bring out the desired information. The items were listed randomly in the questionnaire but are grouped here according to their respective need category. Shown first is the need category, followed by the items, numbered as they were in the questionnaire:

I. Self-Actualization Needs

3. The opportunity for personal growth and development in my management position.

7. The feeling of self-fulfillment a person gets from being in my management position (that is, the feeling of being able to use one's own unique capabilities, realizing one's potentialities).

10. The feeling of worthwhile accomplishment in my management position.

II. Autonomy Needs

2. The authority connected with my management position.

5. The opportunity for independent thought and action in my management position.

12. The opportunity, in my management position, for participation in the setting of goals.

13. The opportunity, in my management position, for participation in the setting of methods and procedures.

III. Esteem Needs

1. The feeling of self-esteem a person gets from being in my management position.

4. The prestige of my management position inside the agency (that is, the regard received from others in the agency).

8. The prestige of my management position outside the agency (that is, the regard received from others not in the agency).

IV. Social Needs

11. The opportunity, in my management position, to give help to other people.

15. The opportunity to develop close friendships in my management position.

V. Security Needs

6. The feeling of security in my management position.

Procedure and Sample

This report covers four different studies, so there are four different sets of procedures and samples. They are basically the same, however, so only a few of the principal differences will be outlined. In the first federal study, the questionnaires were distributed to 1,620 executives, selected in a random manner from the ten executive departments in the Washington, D.C.-southern Maryland-northern Virginia area. In the Commonwealth of Kentucky study the executive structure was very small and the sampling technique was discarded when the executive population was found to number less than 200 people. Thus the entire population was solicited. In the state of

Illinois study, sampling was again used. Randomization was used to obtain a sample of 508 respondents. Five years after the initial study the federal departments had been increased to twelve and the number of participants to 2,062.

Control lists of addresses were made in all instances, and distribution was mostly through the U.S. mails. Enclosures included the questionnaire, a pre-addressed and stamped envelope, and a separate pre-addressed and stamped post card. The latter card was intended as a control, to be mailed separately by the recipients and to be checked off against the control lists for determination of follow-up mailings. When completed questionnaires stopped coming in, a follow-up card was sent. When responses to the follow-up card ceased, an analysis of non-responses was made. In the first study the response rate was 55.7 percent, in the second study it was 91.9 percent, in the third it was 65.0 percent, and in the five-year replication it was 49.1 percent.

From the classification questions it was possible to classify responses on a number of different variables. For this article, however, only the male vs. female variable is used. (See Exhibit 1.)

Results

Perceived deficiency in fulfillment for each respondent, for each questionnaire item was obtained by subtracting the answer to Part (a) of an item ("How much of the characteristic is now connected with your position?") from Part (b) of the item ("How much of the characteristic do you think should be connected with your position?"). This included an assumption that the larger the difference (a subtracted from b), the larger the degree of dissatisfaction or the smaller the degree of

---

Exhibit 1: Distribution of Respondents

	Male n	Female n	Ratio
First federal study	719	40	18/1
Commonwealth of Kentucky	160	13	12/1
State of Illinois	259	71	4/1
Second federal study	933	79	12/1

satisfaction. In this manner there is an indirect method of measuring satisfaction. That is, a value is obtained from two questions which were answered by the respondent for all of the questions. There are two presumed advantages. The subject is not asked directly concerning his job satisfaction. This reduces tendencies toward response sets and socially acceptable answers. The method is a more conservative measure than would be a single question. It considers, too, that higher level positions should be expected to provide greater satisfactions because it uses differences between obtained and expected satisfactions. In effect, the method asks, "How satisfied are you with your position as compared with what you expected from it?"

For the male vs. female variable the results are shown in Exhibit 2. In this exhibit there are two sets of data. In the upper part are the responses to the questions regarding lack of fulfillment of needs; a larger score indicates a greater lack of fulfillment, or a greater dissatisfaction, or a lesser satisfaction. In the lower part are the responses as to the perception of importance of the needs; a larger score indicates a greater perceived importance of the item. A directional hypothesis was used, and a one-tail t test was used to determine significance. Due to the small numbers in the cells of the Kentucky study, a Mann-Whitney U test was used.

In the first federal study the female executives indicated a greater deficiency in fulfillment of self-actualization needs than did their male counterparts. The significance was at the .05 level. In the love and belongingness needs, they indicated much less dissatisfaction and the difference was significant at the .01 level. In the perceived importance of needs, the greater importance assigned by males to the autonomy needs only approached significance. The females assigned a lesser importance to the esteem needs which was significant at the .05 level.

In the Kentucky study the females perceived self-actualization needs to be more satisfied than did the male executives; and the difference was at .02 level. The females were most satisfied in security needs, but the difference between the two only approached significance. In the importance of needs, at all need levels, there were no significant differences.

In the Illinois study deficiency in fulfillment of self-actualization, autonomy, and security needs was greater for

Exhibit 2: Comparison of Male and Female Perceptions

Perceived Deficiency in Fulfillment of Needs

Need Level	Federal—1			Kentucky			Illinois			Federal—5		
	x_m	x_f	Significance	x_m	x_f	Significance	x_m	x_f	Significance	x_m	x_f	Significance
Self-Actualization	1.22	1.47	.05	.91	.56	.02	1.43	1.69	.08	1.19	1.33	none
Autonomy	.94	.97	none	.68	.67	none	1.24	1.51	.07	.89	1.04	none
Esteem	.67	.77	none	.59	.64	none	.92	1.14	none	.62	.66	none
Love and Belongingness	.42	.10	.01	.36	.27	none	.52	.52	none	.40	.24	none
Security	.22	.40	none	1.35	.62	.07	.58	.96	.07	.08	.17	none

Perceived Importance of Needs

Need Level	Federal—1			Kentucky			Illinois			Federal—5		
	x_m	x_f	Significance	x_m	x_f	Significance	x_m	x_f	Significance	x_m	x_f	Significance
Self-Actualization	6.20	6.28	none	6.30	6.15	none	6.28	6.40	none	6.10	6.07	none
Autonomy	5.74	5.57	.10	5.92	5.64	none	5.86	5.88	none	5.77	5.49	.007
Esteem	5.21	4.92	.05	5.38	5.18	none	5.29	5.40	none	5.17	5.05	none
Love and Belongingness	5.40	5.21	none	5.76	5.27	none	5.58	5.46	none	5.42	5.30	none
Security	5.17	5.25	none	5.53	5.39	none	5.68	6.10	.025	5.19	5.48	.10

females but the differences only approached significance. In importance of needs, the security needs were more important to the females, and the significance was at the .025 level.

In the replication of the federal study, five years later, there was no significant difference in fulfillment of any needs. In importance of needs female executives perceived autonomy needs as less important than did the males to a significant extent. The females assigned more importance to security needs but only to a degree approaching significance.

There was one difference in the Illinois population; it was found that 43 percent of the female position titles were similar to Social Worker, Rehabilitation Counselor, and the like. These could not be factored out, and might cause differences in perceptions. Effects are unknown.

These are the results of four different studies. Each was at least a year apart from the other, and one was a five-year replication of an earlier study. Yet it is clear that no pattern of significant differences emerges.

The first federal study is selected as being representative, and is selected for some other findings. The length of employment of the females ranged from a minimum of 1 year to a maximum of 40 years, and the average for all of them was 14.4 years. There were sixteen of the females who might have possessed a "twenty-year pin" if such an award had been made.

One of the classification questions asked: "Number of people in organization headed by you, in your position." The responses were as follows: 15 or less by 75.6 percent; 30 or less by 9.8 percent; 60 or less by 7.3 percent; 125 or less by 2.4 percent; and 126 or more by 4.9 percent.

Another classification question asked: "Indicate the level of your management position."
a. Manager over full-time staff and line units ...... (14.6%)
b. Manager over other managers (may have staff units) (17.1%)
c. Manager over first-line supervisors .... (22.0%)
d. Supervisor over employees .... (39.0%)
e. Employee .... (7.3%)

Included in parenthesis is the percent of the females who checked the particular level of their management position.

Discussion

Whatever the reasons for neglecting females as a source of executive talent, employers should not claim differences in motivation as a true reason. Females do not seem to be significantly different from males in their perceptions of needs.

Certainly females cannot be considered as short-term employees when they join the executive ranks. They do not take a job for a while only to move on or to leave when some short-term need has been satisfied. Although there were new employees, there were also women who had been in their agency for over twenty years, and one of them had been there forty years.

As far as job level is concerned, the females were fairly distributed over all of the levels provided. Perhaps the classification item failed in providing a description of the very highest jobs. In any case, over half of the females said that they were "managers."

The questions concerning why there is so little difference between the perceptions of the males and females have still not been answered. One can only speculate that the psychological need hierarchy is an accurate representation of all of man's needs, and the difference is in how people go about satisfying the needs.

Another speculation is that Bardwick may have pointed a finger at some internal happenings in the biochemistry of the human being. It may be that the hormone balance may affect the expression of the individual needs, and the successful female executive may have a mix similar to that of the male.

In any case, it appears evident that the four studies provide a solid base for recommendations for the employer. That recommendation would amount to: "Don't overlook the female employee as a potential executive. Her perceptions are enough like those of the male executive that she should be successful wherever he would."

Footnotes

1. John S. Herrick, "Work Motives of Female Executives," *Public Personnel Management*, September-October 1973, pp. 380-387.

2. Judith M. Bardwick, *Psychology of Women* (New York: Harper & Row, 1971), p. 22.

3. Sigmund Freud, "Female Sexuality," in Hendrik M. Ruitenbeek, *Psychoanalysis and Female Sexuality* (New Haven, Connecticut: College & University Press, 1966), p. 102.

4. Bardwick, *Psychology of Women*, p. 22.

5. Ibid., p. 44.

6. Margaret Mead, *Male and Female* (New York: Mentor Books, 1952), p. 272.

7. Abraham H. Maslow, "A Dynamic Theory of Motivation," *Psychological Review*, 50 (1943); and Abraham H. Maslow, *Motivation and Personality* (New York: Harper & Row, 1954).

Dr. John B. Miner *is Professor of Management, School of Business Administration, Georgia State University, Atlanta.*

Reprinted by permission from The Human Constraint, *by Dr. John B. Miner, copyright © 1974 by The Bureau of National Affairs, Inc., Washington, D.C. 20037.*

15
New Sources of Talent

John B. Miner

ONE OBVIOUS NEW source of managerial talent to consider is the female population. While women constitute over 35 percent of the national labor force, they hold only 16 percent of the managerial positions. Although this figure represents a considerable rise above the 12 percent found in 1940, it remains true that women are distinctly underrepresented at the management level.

A survey conducted by Professor Eleanor Schwartz, of Georgia State University, indicates that at least a third of all companies have practically no women in management at all. Banks, insurance companies, and merchandising firms have the most female managers, and the larger firms are more likely to have a sizable female managerial component than the smaller ones. In terms of level, women are most likely to be first-line supervisors or, somewhat less frequently, in middle management; they are almost nonexistent in top management. There is also considerable variation among the different areas of a business, with female managers most prevalent in general administration and production.

A survey by The Bureau of National Affairs, Inc., confirms a number of Professor Schwartz's findings while adding certain additional information. It is evident, for instance, that outside the business sector, in government, hospitals, and the like, where shortages of male managerial talent have long existed, there is a much more extensive use of female managers. Furthermore, within the business world it is the manufacturing companies that have used women least. However, there does appear to have been an increase over the past five years in the number of women in management in all types of organizations. To what extent this has been caused by the pressure of fair employment and equal opportunity laws is not entirely clear.

Reported company experience with women in managerial jobs is definitely favorable. Furthermore, it appears that women succeed as managers for essentially the same reasons that men do—because they possess the will to manage, the intelligence to make decisions, and the necessary knowledge. In my own studies I have repeatedly found that motivation to manage is just as closely related to promotion and successful management-appraisal ratings for women as for men. In a department store, for instance, where over half of the managers are women, the amount of managerial motivation rises steadily as one moves from the lowest level of management, the selling supervisors, to the assistant department managers and finally to the department heads. These female department managers have

Exhibit 1: Motivation to Manage of Female Managers at Different Levels in a Department Store

	Selling Supervisors	Assistant Managers	Department Managers
Motivation to Manage			
High Motivation	9 (33%)	2 (40%)	8 (67%)
Low Motivation	18 (67%)	3 (60%)	4 (33%)
Desire to Exercise Power			
High Motivation	16 (59%)	3 (60%)	10 (83%)
Low Motivation	11 (41%)	2 (40%)	2 (17%)
Desire for a Distinctive Position			
High Motivation	11 (41%)	2 (40%)	7 (58%)
Low Motivation	16 (59%)	3 (60%)	5 (42%)

particularly strong desires to exercise power and to be in distinctive positions.

The Supply of Female Talent

Insofar as the intelligence aspect of management potential is concerned, there is little difference between men and women. Thus, on this particular dimension the female population clearly does offer a major pool of unused managerial talent. On the other hand, women have not been attracted to colleges of business and engineering in anything like the proportions they represent of the overall college student population, and thus, there is a problem in finding women with knowledge relevant to managerial work. In the business student groups that I have been studying since 1960, only about 10 percent are females, and there is some indication that this proportion has been shrinking recently. A number of business schools have discontinued their majors in secretarial science and business education, with the result that the female students who ordinarily selected these majors, and were required to take a broad range of business subjects as a consequence, have shifted to other curricula in the university.

Motivation to manage does not appear to differ to any meaningful extent when male and female managers are studied. In the department store mentioned earlier there was no real difference in overall motivation; the largest difference in a particular aspect was in assertiveness, where the women were clearly lower, a not unexpected finding in view of the association of this measure with masculinity. Other research suggests that in some settings female managers may have less desire for power, but may compensate for this with a more favorable attitude toward authority. In any event, among practicing managers the women can be expected to have just as strong a will to manage as the men, although there may be differences in specific aspects. Thus, from this perspective the talent is there.

A problem is apparent, however, when one looks at the college groups from which future female managers must be drawn. Among business school students the females have considerably lower motivation to manage than the males. This has been a consistent finding in all of the groups that I have studied. The same pattern emerges outside the business school, among liberal arts majors, for example, although it is not

Exhibit 2: Motivation to Manage of Male and Female Managers in a Department Store

	Male Managers	Female Managers
Motivation to Manage		
High Motivation	16 (62%)	27 (61%)
Low Motivation	10 (38%)	17 (39%)
Favorable Attitude Toward Authority		
High Motivation	12 (46%)	28 (64%)
Low Motivation	14 (54%)	16 (36%)
Desire to Compete		
High Motivation	15 (58%)	19 (43%)
Low Motivation	11 (42%)	25 (57%)
Assertive Motivation		
High Motivation	17 (65%)	19 (43%)
Low Motivation	9 (35%)	25 (57%)
Desire to Exercise Power		
High Motivation	11 (42%)	19 (43%)
Low Motivation	15 (58%)	25 (57%)
Desire for a Distinctive Position		
High Motivation	14 (54%)	20 (46%)
Low Motivation	12 (46%)	24 (54%)
Sense of Responsibility		
High Motivation	14 (54%)	26 (59%)
Low Motivation	12 (46%)	18 (41%)

present among students in the field of education, where male and female students have very similar levels of motivation to manage. This results largely from the fact that females with more such motivation appear to be attracted to school teaching. Having chosen this career, however, and invested time and effort in preparing to follow it, it seems unlikely that many female education majors can be diverted into business management. Female education students, then, are not a likely executive talent source, except for those interested in educational administration.

Among the various aspects of motivation to manage, female college students are particularly lacking in assertive motivation, desire to exercise power, and desire to compete. They tend to have more favorable attitudes toward authority than the males. This suggests that women might be most likely to fail as managers, if they do fail, because they do not take charge and push hard for results and their own advancement. Success would most likely stem from their ability to get along well and avoid conflict in a hierarchical system. Research conducted by Marshall Sashkin and Professor Norman Maier, at the University of Michigan, indicates that when women are placed in positions of authority they are less likely than men to take liberties and to act on their own, unless they are specifically instructed to do so. They are distinctly sensitive to the wishes of higher authority, and do not wish to risk offending it.

The survey noted in Chapter 5 [John Miner, *The Human Constraint* (Washington, D.C., BNA Books, 1974)], conducted by Rosalind Barnett and Professor Renato Tagiuri, of the Harvard Business School, indicates that of the young people aged seventeen and below contacted through subscribers to the *Harvard Business Review*, the females are much less likely to be considering managerial careers than the males. In response to the direct question, "Would you like to be a manager?" there were positive responses from 53 percent of the males and 35 percent of the females. But when various alternatives were presented and the question asked for the *most* preferred choices, 40 percent of the males and only 10 percent of the females chose management or business alternatives.

The picture which emerges is that a great many young women continue to reject management and business careers as unsuitable, and that this is why there are so few females in the professional schools that prepare people for occupations in business. Studies conducted by Virginia Schein, of Metropolitan Life Insurance Company, indicate that managing is viewed as largely a masculine occupation. Successful middle managers are considered to possess characteristics, attitudes, and temperaments of a kind more commonly ascribed to men than to women. To the extent that women accept this view, and many clearly do, they simply will not flock into managerial work in large numbers. Presumably the lesser managerial motivation of college women is a factor in this decision.

Based on what is known now it appears that a high proportion of the women with a desire to manage have already

	Male Students	Female Students
Motivation to Manage		
High Motivation	346 (51%)	25 (39%)
Low Motivation	328 (49%)	39 (61%)
Favorable Attitude Toward Authority		
High Motivation	295 (44%)	37 (58%)
Low Motivation	379 (56%)	27 (42%)
Desire to Compete		
High Motivation	376 (56%)	28 (44%)
Low Motivation	298 (44%)	36 (56%)
Assertive Motivation		
High Motivation	207 (31%)	11 (17%)
Low Motivation	467 (69%)	53 (83%)
Desire to Exercise Power		
High Motivation	355 (53%)	21 (33%)
Low Motivation	319 (47%)	43 (67%)
Desire for a Distinctive Position		
High Motivation	473 (70%)	43 (67%)
Low Motivation	201 (30%)	21 (33%)
Sense of Responsibility		
High Motivation	339 (50%)	35 (55%)
Low Motivation	335 (50%)	29 (45%)

found their way into management occupations. Such women certainly should be encouraged to follow managerial careers; they have a good prospect of succeeding. But fewer female college students than males want to manage, and, in spite of women's liberation, many females are not attracted to what they perceive as the masculine occupation of managing. To the extent that men also view the occupation as masculine they will tend to "discriminate" against women who may desire to become managers. All in all it becomes clear that if women are to be a major source of managerial talent, major cultural changes must occur, well beyond those that have already occurred, so that more women develop the motivation to manage and more men view the managerial role as appropriate for women.

This will require something more than the basic input strategy of selecting women with high intelligence, motivation to manage, and the requisite knowledge. Such a strategy at the present time will not come close to filling the needs of the management talent shortage. On the other hand, extension of the basic input strategy into more specific placements and the use of certain of the mediator strategies may yield more favorable results.

At this point I feel that the well-reasoned recommendations advanced by Professor Marshall Brenner, of the University of Southern California, offer the best guidelines for supplementing an initial effort to find and select female managers with true management potential. He makes the following suggestions:

1. Select and/or develop women who have expertise in their field clearly superior to that of the great majority of the people to be supervised.

2. Explain to women candidates for management the organization's role requirements for a manager, and let them consider these requirements carefully before beginning development activity.

3. Select potential managerial positions for development and placement in areas where the occupations are least sex-typed.

4. Select positions where the majority of the subordinate personnel are experienced.

5. Select positions where the superior is exceptionally supportive for development and initial placement.

6. Select positions where expertise is a large and important component of authority.

7. Make role training a basic and continuing segment of management development.

8. Provide husbands of the development candidates with an understanding of the support functions required of them.

9. Establish interacting groups of eight to twelve management development candidates, both male and female, and maintain the consistency of these groups.

10. Provide visibility for a program of "womanagement" development.

At the present time women can provide only a partial solution to the need for effective executive talent. In the future, assuming a continuation of current societal trends and appropriate company action, their contribution can be much greater. The crucial need is to overcome a major deficiency in the will to manage in a society where this motive is already in decline.

Dr. Mildred E. Buzenberg *is Assistant Dean, College of Business Administration, Kansas State University, Manhattan, Kansas.*

16

Women's Careers–
Femininity–Marriage

Mildred E. Buzenberg

THE BUSINESS community, prodded by Affirmative Action and other legislation, is more willing to hire women college graduates for executive training programs and first step administrative jobs than ever before. They complain, however, that too few women apply for such positions. Robert Levy writing in *Dun's* says, "Where, industry wonders, are all the women who want to be executives?"[1] The radical feminists of the 1960s blamed the scarcity of women in executive positions on discrimination. In response to that, legislation was passed and industry is now required to open their doors to women at all levels. The results, however, have been less than spectacular. Current information about the penetration of females into top management positions indicates that women account for less than two percent of the managers in the economy.

From research information gained at Kansas State University, it appears industry alone is not responsible for the very few women in executive ranks. The women themselves are not pursuing management positions. Supporting this theme during a conference in February 1975, Dr. Virginia Trotter, recently appointed Assistant Secretary of Education, said: "If job discrimination should end tomorrow, there wouldn't be very much change in the number of women in positions of authority."

The women who are in the best position to apply for administrative jobs are those graduating with masters or bachelors degrees in business, accounting, engineering, or other applicable disciplines, or those women who have worked in industry. Since about 40 percent of the work force is comprised of women, there are many women with experience who could become executives. This study, however, is limited to university women.

To the extent that Kansas State University is a microcosm reflecting the attitudes of women juniors, seniors, and graduate students in all universities, it throws considerable light on the problem of why pipelines to top positions remain empty of college graduate women. Women students who were enrolled in a course at Kansas State University to develop management skills expressed apprehension about working in a man's world. Their fears were centered in three areas. These were: (1) fear of social pressure against working at man's work; (2) fear of losing femininity if they work in positions of authority; and (3) fear of losing out in marriage if they pursue a career. The mitigation of these fears through educational institutions or in industry workshops could be instrumental in increasing the number of women executives and administrators available to industry. The methods employed at Kansas State University appeared to be successful. Most of the women who had been in the class obtained high-level jobs with industry or government, and some have already moved into positions of responsibility never before held by women in their particular firms.

Why Some Work is Labeled "Women's Work"

The first step in re-education of the young women was to point out why the world of work has for years been divided into "men's work" and "women's work." The second step was to explain why this division no longer makes sense in today's world.

Table 1 lists the occupations in which 70 percent or more of

Table 1: Occupations in Which 70 Percent or More of the Workers Were Women, 1960

Occupation	Percent Female	Percent of Female Labor Force in Occupation
Apparel and accessories operatives	74	1.3
Attendants in physicians' and dentists' offices	98	0.3
Attendants, professional and personal services	70	0.2
Boarding and lodging housekeepers	88	0.1
Bookkeepers and cashiers	82	5.2
Chambermaids and maids	98	0.8
Dancers and dancing teachers	77	0.1
Demonstrators	92	0.1
Dressmakers and seamstresses	97	0.5
File clerks	86	0.5
Fruit, nut, and vegetable graders and packers	71	0.1
Hairdressers and cosmetologists	89	1.2
Hospital attendants, practical nurses, and midwives	81	2.3
Housekeepers and stewards	80	0.6
Knitting mill operatives	78	0.2
Laundry and dry cleaning operatives	72	1.3
Librarians	86	0.3
Library attendants and assistants	77	0.1
Milliners	91	0.0
Nurses	98	2.8
Office machine operators	74	1.1
Private household workers	96	7.9
Receptionists	98	0.6
Sewers and stitchers	94	2.6
Stenographers, typists, and secretaries	96	10.0
Teachers	72	5.4
Telephone operators	96	1.6
Textile spinners	79	0.2
Waitresses, counter and fountain workers	84	4.0
Total		51.4

Source: Valerie Oppenheimer, "The Sex-Labelling of Jobs," *Industrial Relations*, VII (May 1968), p. 220.

the workers were women in 1960. A careful study of these occupations points to two facts. First, a majority of these occupations historically consisted of the kind of work women did in the home before there was a market economy. These are occupations such as hospital attendants, housekeepers, waitresses, maids, laundresses, milliners, and textile workers. When the market economy developed, women who needed to work for a cash income moved into the occupations they had learned at their mother's knee, and as the years passed, tradition kept them locked into these jobs.

The second reason for these being predominately women's work is that none of these jobs require the employer to spend time or money in training the employee. Jobs such as teacher, dietician, and bookkeeper required that the person be trained (educated) for their work before being employed. The others take very little training. Over the years employers have been reluctant to give women on-the-job training because their assumption was that women did not have job continuity. They were expected to quit in a few years to get married, have babies, or move to another city with their husbands. Unfortunately, the women themselves accepted this assessment without question. Both of these reasons for division of labor into "women's work" and "men's work" is a testimonial to the power of myth over economic fact.

Women's Education Today
Eliminates the Need for "Women's Work"

Women are no longer the uneducated segment of society that they were 30 years ago, so they need not work at jobs for the unskilled. Statistics show that the average American woman today is far better trained than her mother. It is true that educational levels of both sexes is increasing, but the number of educated women is increasing faster than the number of educated men. In 1960 of all persons 25-29 years of age with a college degree, only 36 percent were females, but by 1970 this proportion had grown to 40 percent, and based on recent trends in college enrollments, especially enrollments for the last three years, it should be 50 percent by 1980.[2] Not only is the overall level of education of females increasing, but women are increasingly being educated in curricula that were formerly all-male. For example, Kansas State University has experienced a dramatic increase in the number of women students enrolling in management, accounting, marketing, finance, and personnel. (See Table 2.)

Women are also enrolling in professional training in many other fields that are non-traditional for women. (See Table 3.)

Table 2: Enrollment in the College of Business Administration, Kansas State University

Date—Fall Semester	Number of Men	Number of Women	Percent Women Are of Total
1965	650	101	13.0
1968	769	119	13.4
1971	950	188	16.5
1973	1128	297	20.8
1974	1076	374	25.8
1975	1094	471	30.1
1976	1142	553	32.6

Table 3: Women Enrolled in Professional Training, Selected Fields, 1966-1972

Year	Dentistry		Law		Medicine		Pharmacy		Veterinary Medicine	
	Number	Percent	Number	Percent	Number	Percent	Number	Percent	Number	Percent
1966	166	1	3,052	5	2,771	8	1,916	15	326	7
1972	511	3	12,728	12	6,066	13	4,689	25	888	14

Note: Percent refers to women as percent of total enrollment.
Source: Monthly Labor Review, U.S. Department of Labor, May 1974, p. 42.

As yet, the percentage of women majoring in, say, veterinary medicine is not very large, but if the trend of percentage increase continues another eight or ten years, women in these professions will be accepted equally with men, and "women's work" may further recede from view.

Women's Job Continuity Today Eliminates the Need for Women's Work

Employers' fear of losing time and money spent in training women employees for positions of responsibility and women's acceptance of this is also unrealistic today. The statistics do not uphold the myth of higher rates of quitting for women than for men. Labor Department figures revealed that voluntary "quit" rates for all workers were 2.2 per hundred male employees per month and 2.6 per hundred female employees per month in 1968. They affirm, however, that more than half of this small difference is attributable to the great concentration of women in occupations where quit rates for both men and women are above average.

A more meaningful analysis was described in the *Harvard Business Review*, which reported a study of over 5,000 M.B.A. graduates. The turnover rate was exactly the same for males and females.[3] It is true, some women resign to care for children or to move to new locations with their husbands. What many people fail to realize is that men also resign to take other positions, enter the armed forces, return to school, or even move with their wives to a different location.

Give a woman an exciting and challenging position, pay her well, and she will come to work regularly and will continue employment as long as the average man. What incentive is there for an intelligent, ambitious person to continue employment in a routine, dull job that characterized much of the so-called women's work?

As stated earlier, the women themselves as well as the employers must be made aware of the possibility of their continuous employment before they apply for management training positions. Part of this awareness may come from knowing the facts stated previously, but also an effort must be made to eliminate the last two fears the students expressed: fear of losing femininity and marriageability.

Women Can Be Executives or Administrators and Still Be Feminine

The concept of ideal man and ideal woman appears to be changing. In today's society there is a trend toward androgyny, or a blending of sex characteristics. We are rejecting old artificial forms. Vital statistics, education, and job patterns indicate that women will find themselves increasingly living in ways that parallel the lives of men. Even fashions in clothing, recreation, and social life are emphasizing the similarities between men and women and are playing down the differences.

The new conception of sex roles would allow both males and

females a wider range of permissible behavior. Conflicts have often arisen between a person's abilities and desires on the one hand and socially appropriate sex-role behavior on the other. Today females should not have to fear losing their "femininity" due to competency, and males can be kind and still be "masculine."

The fear of losing femininity is also based on the training each woman gets at home in being docile, helpful, loyal, and above all, not too smart. A woman Ph.D. was heard to say, "My mother said if I got a Ph.D., I'd never get married, and she was right." She probably did not get married because her mother told her she would not, rather than because of the Ph.D. Women graduating from college today need to reject advice like that given the Ph.D. because this is no longer the world in which their mothers grew up. In fact, the sexy woman today is more likely to be one who has achieved some success for herself, and not the helpless, ignorant person visualized by the last generation. Young men who are successful in any profession appear to be attractive and sexy. Women who achieve success appear to be attractive and sexy. There need be no distinctions. Success is attractive and appealing no matter who achieves it.

Finally, the fear of losing their femininity if they seek positions of authority is very real for some women because of the stereotypes people have developed over the years of a woman manager as a masculine, austere person. A woman who carries this stereotype in her subconscious is going to be fearful of stepping into a position where she thinks she will need to adopt masculine traits. *MBA Magazine*'s March 1972 issue was devoted to women in management. One of the articles, entitled "How Much of a Woman Should a Woman in Business Be?" quoted interviews with twelve practicing women executives, all of whom pointed out that there was no need to minimize feminine characteristics. In fact, many of them emphasized advantages of being feminine in executive positions. For example, Penny Kaniclides, President of Telstate Systems, New York, said:

> Women are ideally suited for major business responsibility. Lacking up to now were opportunity and self esteem. But those most womanly qualities—dedication, hard work, perseverance, thoroughness, compassion, and loyalty—are overcoming obstacles.

Edith Grimm, Vice President Merchandising, Carson Pirie Scott, Chicago, said:

> Being a woman is not a costume that can be put on or removed at will. A woman in business is successful because she is herself and not because she is an imitation of someone else. Talent doesn't have a gender, nor does intelligence.

Eileen Shanhan, Financial Reporter, *New York Times*, Washington Bureau, said:

> Be a woman? Do you mean passive and helpless? Nobody, regardless of sex, should be that. Or do you mean courteous and sensitive? Everybody should be that.[4]

As more women move into the decision-making ranks, the new college graduates will have role models to emulate on the job. Women executives who demonstrate their enthusiasm, intelligence, and femininity in work situations will be the best education for future generations of women who have the ability to hold positions of responsibility.

Women Can Have Both a Career and a Marriage

The last major fear, that of not succeeding at marriage, is closely associated with the fear of losing femininity, yet many of the role models currently in the work force are not only successful executives but also are married with families as well. It is by studying them that young women can realize that a two-career family is possible.

Lynda Holmstrom interviewed two-career families in the Boston area. She points out barriers imposed by society on the two-career family and how they can be overcome. The barriers divide themselves into three main categories: (1) the rigid structure of the professions which assumes a career person can change locations, travel at will, and devote massive amounts of time to promote the career; (2) isolation of the modern family, which means grandparents, aunts, and uncles, or other relatives are not in the home to act as baby-sitters or household helpers; and (3) the equation of masculinity with superiority.[5]

These three impediments to the two-career family are formidable, but they are not insurmountable as the numerous examples in Holmstrom's book illustrate. There is no uniform method of solving these problems, and each family has to develop its own individual solutions because society provides no institutionalized solutions. A two-career family is a very new social pattern, and some problems develop because of this very newness; but society appears to be moving in directions that will make two-career families easier to manage in the future.

The rigid structure of professions is being scrutinized by many social scientists and practitioners today. A special report in the *Harvard Business Review* emphasized that the changing workweek is no longer just an idea, it is a reality, and one that appears to be here to stay.[6] The authors maintain that some form of the flexible working-hours system, so popular in Europe, may well become the standard for U.S. companies. There is also a movement among some corporations to reduce the number of geographic transfers of executives because deleterious effects on family life have been demonstrated. Both the trends will greatly improve the workability of a two-career family.[7]

Isolation of the modern family means that in the typical family all household tasks fall on the wife. Holmstrom's survey showed that husbands shared the home duties in the two-career families and that much use was made of hired help and work-saving equipment. Some work was simply avoided by living with a lower housekeeping standard.

Eighty percent of the two-career families interviewed had children.[8] The mothers felt it was good for both child and mother to turn some child-care tasks over to hired help or day care centers. This conforms to many studies that point out the dangers of the mother-child relationship in which the mother's main preoccupation is giving continual care to her children.

The two-career family husbands all had very positive attitudes toward their wives' careers, and this translated into acts of positive support. One husband said his wife's career was part of her and could not be separated. He never thought of her in any other way.[9]

The third barrier to the two-career family, equating masculinity with superiority, is without doubt the most subtle and difficult of all the barriers. Feelings of competitiveness were evident in some husbands whose wives' careers were more successful than their own. The wives, however, did not feel resentful if the husband had the more prestigious job, because masculinity-meaning-superiority has been equally accepted by both sexes. Nevertheless, breakdowns in the marriage came most frequently as a result of this barrier. The wives were unwilling in those cases to play the subordinate role and forgo their own career plans. In each case of a marriage breakdown, the wife subsequently married a man who was supportive of her career.

Conclusion

The business community today is more willing to hire women for first-step executive positions than at any time in the past. They complain, however, that too few women apply for such positions. This article shows some possible explanations for the lack of enthusiasm for management jobs on the part of women who are qualified for them by education or experience.

Women have a fear of social pressure resulting from working at "man's work"; they fear a loss of femininity if they pursue positions of authority; and they fear they will be unable to have both marriage and career. Any university course or business training program to help women move into management positions must speak to these fears. If a woman can be assured that she can work as an executive without society's condemnation, if she knows she won't lose her femininity, and if she feels she can have both marriage and a career, she will be more likely to move into management positions in the future. Both industry and universities can help women do this by recognizing their fears and taking steps to combat them. Industry will benefit in the long run by having an increased pool of educated workers from which to choose their executives.

Footnotes

1. "The Woman Who Wasn't There," *Dun's Review*, June 1972, p. 63.

2. Fabian Linden, Women a Demographic, Social and Economic Presentation. Published 1972 by the CBS Broadcast Group, p. 19.

3. "Job-Hopping and the M.B.A.," *Harvard Business Review*, November-December 1971, p. 4.

4. *M.B.A. Magazine*, March 1972.

5. Lynda Lytle Holmstrom, *The Two-Career Family* (Cambridge, Massachusetts: Schenkman Publishing Company, 1972).

6. "Flexible Working Hours, It's About Time," *Harvard Business Review*, January-February 1974, p. 18.

7. Robert Seidenbeg, *Corporate Wives—Corporate Casualties* (New York: Amacom, 1973).

8. Holmstrom, *The Two-Career Family*, p. 23.

9. Ibid., p. 138.

Alan B. Solid *is Director of Admissions at MacCormac Junior College, Chicago, Illinois.*

17
The Woman Executive: Invincible or Invisible

Alan B. Solid

HELEN REDDY'S SONG, "I Am Woman," proclaims that women are invincible. A more appropriate statement, for women in executive positions, might be "Women Are Invisible." A study in 1972 showed that the ratio of men to women in top board and office positions was 600 to 1.[1] Such statistics do not hold much promise, but constant social and legal changes will inevitably improve the numbers game.

The major legislation against discrimination is Title VII of the Civil Rights Act of 1964 as amended by the Equal Opportunity Act of 1972. This Act prohibits sex, race, color, or religious discrimination by private employers of fifteen or more persons, state and local governments, and all educational institutions.

The Equal Employment Opportunity Commission was established to administer Title VII and has already filed some 250 employment discrimination suits. The most significant case was *Patterson* vs. *the American Tobacco Company*. "In that decision a federal district court required the company to appoint a woman or a 'minority individual' to the next position to become vacant at the supervisory level of its facilities."[2]

Another discrimination suit involved the Bank of America.

The California bank agreed to pay $3,750,000 into trust funds over the next 5 years to induce women employees to undertake management training or other programs to prepare them for management positions; to increase the proportion of women officers to 40 percent by December 1978, from 31 percent; to set goals in training programs for lending and operations officers to ensure that at least 45 percent of trainees during each of the next 5 years be women; and to assign women to overseas posts.[3]

Such court decisions are becoming commonplace, and some companies are becoming concerned. Rather than wait to be forced into compliance, many companies are initiating their own programs.

Union Carbide has assembled a list of promotable women, is counseling women on how to bid for jobs, and is encouraging female graduates to enter engineering as a career. Likewise, Avon is recruiting at Smith College and Atlanta University and is implementing an upward mobility and job opportunity program for women. Avon has also appointed a woman to its board along with naming two women as vice presidents.[4]

Only time can tell the effect of legislation and in-company programs on the woman executive. The higher she rises in the corporation the more she is faced with the vagaries and subjective factors that enter into promotions. Hopefully, male executives will realize that they only harm the corporation by not promoting the most competent people.

Attitude: Women's Major Problem

Stringent enforcement of civil rights legislation will remove some of the unnecessary barriers in the path of women in business. Legislation alone, however, cannot change the "myths" that surround women—myths often created by insecure men "locked in the organizational hierarchies of fear."[5]

No matter what their successes or achievements, women are confronted with the "weaker sex" syndrome. As the following cartoon shows, even women on boards of directors are fair game for satirists.[6]

THE NOW SOCIETY

© Chronicle Publishing Co 1975

9-19

"I made the broad on our board of directors cry."

It is a sorry society that cannot laugh at itself, but perhaps a cartoon aimed in another direction might be significant. This second cartoon sponsored by the National Organization for Women's Legal Defense and Education Fund attempts to correct an "Archie Bunker" mentality that pervades our society.[7]

"Hire him. He's got great legs."

If women thought this way about men they would be awfully silly.

When men think this way about women they're silly, too.

Women should be judged for a job by whether or not they can do it.

In a world where women are doctors, lawyers, judges, brokers, economists, scientists, political candidates, professors and company presidents, any other viewpoint is ridiculous.

Think of it this way. When we need all the help we can get, why waste half the brains around?

Womanpower. It's much too good to waste.

This "mentality" creates the problem of passing the corporate buck when it deals with equal opportunity for women.

The responsibility for it usually travels from the president to the vice president of personnel, industrial relations, or employee relations on down to the EEO manager. The average EEO manager has an uphill battle. Not only is he contending with government orders and guidelines, but he is also dealing with years of business tradition and cultural conditioning manifest in senior executives, in line managers, in his own staff and often in himself.[8]

Vice Chairman Jayne B. Spain of the U.S. Civil Service Commission described this problem succinctly when she said:

> These mental attitudes, are the greatest obstacles, and this is what I mean by stereotyping jobs. The ancient attitude about woman's place is so deeply ingrained that many people are not aware that they have it—in fact, they deny it—and that is why it is so hard to change. . . . The problem is not simply a matter of converting employers, for employers are the end result of an upbringing that encourages a bias against women working. It begins with the brainwashing of children that takes place in the nursery: "Johnny, boys don't play with dolls," and "Susie, football is not for little girls."[9]

Another problem is that women in business do not get the notoriety or press coverage as received by women politicians or journalists. Of the top ten women in business (according to *Fortune*) only Katharine Graham, publisher of the *Washington Post*, appears in a study of the fifty most influential women in the United States.[10] The woman executive is certainly influential; however, she is not visible. Her efforts do not appear in the society columns; her name is not seen daily on a by-line; and she has not been elected to a public office. Apparently, the woman executive's efforts appear only on the bottom line of her company's income statement.

However, there have been some recent changes in attitudes toward women. One of the most promising changes relates to the area of politics. A recent Gallup poll showed that 73 percent of the American public would vote for a qualified woman for president—a 7 percent increase from 1971 when the poll was last taken.[11] This same change in attitude is what the woman in business deserves.

Education: New Emphasis and Programs

Not only has legislation opened doors for women but recent developments in education also will provide women greater opportunity to utilize their skills. At present in the areas of business and commerce, women hold less than 10 percent of the bachelor's degrees, 3.5 percent of the master's, and a mere 1.6

percent of the doctorate's.[12] Of the master's degrees held by women, only 2 percent are MBA degrees.[13]

Even when women hold degrees, it takes them substantially longer to reach the supervisory level. "Nearly two-thirds of the successful women had four or more years of prior job experience before supervising the work of others, and 54 percent of these women were over 36 years of age."[14]

Part of the reason it has taken women longer than men to reach supervisory positions is that many are unsophisticated in leadership methods. Their initial dress, morals, attitudes, and goals develop a generation gap between them and the older employee.[15]

Lack of goal-directed behavior prompted Phyllis Haeger, executive vice president of Smith, Bucklin and Associates, to state, "If I'd known 15 years ago what I know now, I think I might have been president of General Motors."[16]

What Ms. Haeger is referring to is her association with Margaret Hennig and Anne Jardim through one of their seminars. These seminars reflect on the behavior of women in the workplace. The seminar includes techniques which enable women to compete more effectively for advancement. According to Ms. Hennig and Jardim, boys learn to be aggressive through competitive sports while girls are conditioned to take a more passive role. Women must learn to cope with their preconditioned experiences to compete in the male-dominated business world.[17]

This leads us to the development of the woman-oriented MBA program. Simmons College in Boston, where Ms. Hennig and Jardim are associate professors in management, has developed a special program for women. "The whole program is aimed at developing competence, not theory," explains Hennig. "It will provide women with the knowledge and skills to overcome the organizational bias that's built into the system."[18]

Another program at Pace University in New York is aimed at bringing women liberal arts graduates into the business world. Twenty-five women with BA degrees will enter the program each year for the next three years. After two years of study they will complete the MBA program, which will include work internship and career counseling.[19]

The MBA is becoming more and more important as women seek executive positions. "An MBA is one of the most marketable degrees you can have," says Carolyn Chin, 26, Harvard MBA and merchandise administrator for Macy's in New York (one of the first women there ever to hold this position). "A woman doesn't have to be like a man, but she has to learn the rules and play the game. That's where business school comes in. Not only do you get the entree, the credentials and the credibility, you get technical skills and management know-how."[20]

Changes are also taking place on the undergraduate level. Bryn Mawr has developed a whole range of programs in an attempt to inform their female liberal art students about careers in the business world. The programs include executives-in-residence, career conferences, seminars with businessmen, formation of business advisory committees, and business internships for students during midterm and summer vacations.[21]

These programs are all crucial to preparing women for successful management positions. As Philip Hogin, Western Electric executive vice-president and first executive-in-residence at Bryn Mawr, states, "We know that women are going to play a larger and larger part in management and we certainly don't want to rely on the typing pool as a source of future managers."[22]

Earnings: Never Quite Equal

It is a sad statement for our society that "the average woman college graduate who works full time all year ends up with about the same income as the average male high school dropout."[23] Other statistics are equally depressing. Even though forty percent of the total work force is female, only two percent of the managers earning over $25,000 per year are women.[24] Even if women managers and administrators are compared to men in the same field (nondurable goods manufacturing), the difference in their average salary is $7,181. This means that the male manager earns over twice that of his female counterpart.[25]

Several reasons explain these discrepancies. "Women often

work part year or part time and there are higher unemployment rates and lower educational attainments for women." However, these ". . . lower earnings of women are probably also the result of discriminatory hiring, promotion, and salary policies."[26]

Another reason is based on the career path taken by women. Employers often see the woman as a temporary worker and keep her in jobs where the skills are quickly learned and salaries are expendable. According to Dr. Nancy Smith Barrett, chairman of the Department of Economics at American University, "A 50-year-old secretary does not earn more than a 25-year-old secretary does."[27]

Even the government hiring policies have not adjusted themselves to the current trends. On October 31, 1970 only five percent of the full-time white-collar employees in federal government agencies were women earning over $20,000.[28]

The situation may be bleak, but there are certainly some strong glimmers of light. Mary Wells Lawrence, chairman of Wells, Rich and Green, stands out like the sun compared to a star. She is probably the highest paid woman in American business at $384,000.[29]

A study by *Fortune* shows that the top ten women in business average $76,700. These women are: Catherine Cleary, president of First Wisconsin Trust Company; Stella Russell, vice president of Norton Simon; Dorothy Chandler, executive of Times Mirror, Inc.; Mala Rubenstein, executive vice president of Helena Rubenstein; Tillie Lewis, director of Ogden Corporation; Katherine Graham, publisher of the Washington Post Co.; Bernice Lavin, secretary-treasurer of Alberto-Culver; Vera Neumann, president of the Vera Companies; Olivia Ann Beech, chairman of Beech Aircraft; and Ruth Handler, president of Mattel.[30]

The government does not pay as well as business. Marina von Neumann Whitman is the first and only woman member of the Council of Economic Advisors. She is one of the highest ranking women in government, and she earns $38,000.[31]

The best way for a woman to enter the high-earning ranks is to continue her education through to the MBA degree. The average salary for an MBA with no experience, straight out of college, is $14,500.[32]

In 1964 Barbara Franklin, now a member of the Consumer Product Safety Commission, joined Singer Company at a salary

$3,000 below the average of her other Harvard classmates.[33] So beware of earning discrimination, but don't price yourself out of the job market. As Jane Miller, president of I. Miller, says, "It's unfortunate that many men coming out of graduate schools set a specific high price on their heads. If they were willing to accept $8 or $9,000, they could get to $15,000 or more, more quickly, by having gone through the various training steps than by taking a job at $13,000 and sitting there for 2 or 3 years."[34]

Women at the Top

Although the female executive population is small, only .17 percent, there are enough top executive women to dispel all doubts of their effectiveness.[35]

Barbara Hackman Franklin was one of only 14 women in a class of 600 at the Harvard Business School. Since her graduation, she has been the assistant vice president at New York's First National City Bank and a White House aide whose responsibilities included recruiting women for top government jobs. Currently she is the youngest commissioner, male or female, of a federal agency in Washington. The agency is the Consumer Product Safety Commission.[36]

Ms. Franklin's wide experience and expertise in the area of women in business has led her to the conclusion that even though it is rough she would like to see more women pursuing careers in business. "I think things are getting better," she says, "but I still think there's a long way to go. We still haven't reached the place where women's career paths are developing the same way men's have, in which you enter at the bottom and work your way up to the top to become the head of it."[37]

Jane Evans is an exception to Ms. Franklin's rule. At the age of twenty-five, Ms. Evans became president of I. Miller, one of the largest women's shoe retailers in the world. Her formal education began at Vanderbilt, where she was preparing for a career with the State Department. Since her fluency in French would have indicated an assignment in Saigon, she decided to opt for a career in business.

After interviewing several other international corporations, Ms. Evans was offered a job as a special management trainee by

Genesco. Several months later she remained the only unplaced trainee. By begging the head of manpower, she was sent to New York where she was placed by I. Miller as an assistant shoe buyer.

> After I was the assistant shoe buyer, I became the hosiery and handbag buyer. I was responsible for buying these items for all of our stores. Then I went into wholesale and manufacturing and became fashion coordinator. As coordinator I was responsible for styling and selling all of the women's shoes that Genesco manufactures for Sears, Roebuck. It was a tremendous experience to go from buying high fashion merchandise for I. Miller to styling and interpreting the fashions for a volume market. I was actually working for Genesco Nashville division even though I had an office at I. Miller in New York. After two years of this, I was made the president of I. Miller.[38]

The success story of Jane Evans is remarkably similar to the success stories of most young chief executives. The only difference is that Jane Evans is a woman.

Another successful woman executive is Francine Gomez, the chief executive of Waterman, the well-known French pen-and-ink company. When the company was losing money in 1969 her mother, who had inherited control, turned to her for help. After only weeks as a "management trainee" she began to unload the top brass of Waterman. "She abruptly fired nine of Waterman's ten highest-ranking executives. She trimmed the total payroll from 1,200 to 715 and slashed the home-office staff from 200 to 55 persons."[39]

In 1972 profits rose to $1.5 million as compared to a loss of $560,000 before Ms. Gomez took control. Her attitude toward work is as succinct as any man's. "For me, business is a bit of a game and it's the aspect of competition that fascinates me."[40]

Mrs. Norma Pace also represents the successful woman executive. She is an economist who serves as director for both Sears, Roebuck & Company and Sperry Rand Corporation. She is the vice president of the American Paper Institute and was one of twenty-eight economists invited by President Ford to help set the stage for the economic summit. Mrs. Pace believes that picking the right employer is the key to success. "I tell young women they need to find innovative, dynamic people to work for, who can teach them how exciting and challenging business can be."[41]

Women are continually making strides into new areas. Mrs.

Louise K. Quarles Lawson recently became the first black woman to head a savings and loan association. She is the president and chief executive officer of the Illinois Federal Savings and Loan Association. In 1973, Mrs. Lawson was elected the first woman president of the American Savings Loan League, which is composed of sixty-six minority associations throughout the United States.[42]

Another first for women was achieved by Sister Jane Scully. She is the first Roman Catholic nun nominated for a major industrial corporation's board. She will serve on the board of the Gulf Oil Corporation. She is the president of Carlow College and in 1972 was named Pittsburgh's "Man of the Year" in education.[43]

The aforementioned women are but a few of the many successful women in American business. The extent of their success is but further proof that women are perhaps our greatest untapped natural resource.

Hints for Success

There are many steps worth taking in preparing yourself for a management position and for getting a job initially. Certainly education is of vital importance. The MBA is becoming an increasingly crucial degree for women as was mentioned previously. Other considerations, however, are equally important.

A woman's first experience with a company is an interview. Certain questions can help you determine if their hiring policy is discriminatory. In regards to education, "*Griggs vs. Duke Power* found that requiring employees to have a high school diploma or a specific score on an intelligence test has not proven to be necessary for job performance, was discriminatory to minority applicants, and was in the specific instance illegal. Similar situations could conceivably arise with regard to undergraduate or professional degree requirements."[44] In a similar manner, marital and family status, experience requirements, availability for overtime and night work, and extracurricular and community activities are all areas that, unless they relate to the job, may be subject to legal action.[45]

Certain traits have been identified which make women successful in management. First, they obviously must be competent and must have the necessary education. They must be realistic. With realism comes the knowledge that it will take them longer to get promoted and that they will have to work twice as hard as a man. The woman in business must be aggressive and self-confident. Women must be career-minded and yet not lose their femininity. They must develop a strategy and with it the support of an influential male.[46] Finally, they must utilize their uniqueness as women. "Women have a special something to offer in addition to a fine mind and ability—intuitiveness, sensitivity, understanding, fairness, enthusiasm and a fresh new approach."[47]

A final consideration for promotions is how to deal with the boss. Charles C. Vance has advanced three rules for dealing with superiors:

1. Don't be afraid to go in and talk to the boss. Part of his job is to listen. Talk about pay raises, promotions, work loads.

2. Be businesslike. Don't do what all bosses expect women to do—don't be emotional. Men are, but they get away with it. Know what you want to discuss in advance, rehearse it, and discuss it.

3. Prepare yourself, through night school, additional studies, whatever it takes for the next job in line. Train yourself to be thoroughly qualified. Tell the boss you are ready.[48]

No one can guarantee success. The aforementioned recommendations have proven successful in the past and your awareness of them certainly has to be to your advantage.

Conclusion

The obstacles that women must face in business become less every day. Changes in legislation, education, and attitudes are opening doors that were previously locked. Those women who are currently in executive positions are displaying a professional competence considered impossible in the not too distant "dark ages" of management thought.

It is for each individual woman to define her career goals, develop her skills, and implement a strategy to reach an executive position.

Women, your executive suite is waiting!

Footnotes

1. W. Robertson, "The Ten Highest-Ranking Women in Big Business," *Fortune*, April 1973, p. 81.

2. P. Meyer, "Women Executives Are Different," *Dun's Review*, January 1975, p. 47.

3. "Women Widen Job Rights," *Monthly Labor Review*, August 1974, pp. 87-88.

4. C. Smolowe, "Corporations and Women: A Decade of Near-Ms.'s," *MBA*, February 1974, p. 34.

5. J.C. Athanassiades, "Myths of Women in Management: What Every Businessman Ought to Know About Women But May Be Afraid to Ask," *Atlanta Economic Review*, May-June 1975, p. 8.

6. W. Hamilton, "The Now Society," *The Chicago Tribune*, September 19, 1975, Section II, p. 1.

7. J. Kreps, "Beyond the Statistics, Beyond the Rationales," *MBA*, March 1973, p. 12.

8. F. Fretz and J. Hayman, "Progress for Women—Men Are Still More Equal," *Harvard Business Review*, September-October 1973, p. 137.

9. J. Spain, "Job Stereotyping," *Vital Speeches*, July 1, 1973, p. 550.

10. "50 Women Named Most Influential in U.S.," *The Chicago Tribune*, August 17, 1975, Section I, p. 5.

11. G. Gallup, "73% Now Favor Woman as President," *The Chicago Suntimes*, September 18, 1975, p. 43.

12. R.E. Anderson and R.J. Tersine, "Our Working Women," *Business Horizons*, February 1973, p. 58.

13. Smolowe, "Corporations and Women: A Decade of Near-Ms.'s," pp. 33-34.

14. L.A. Koff, "Age, Experience, and Success among Women Managers," *Management Review*, November 1973, p. 65.

15. Ibid., p. 66.

16. "Learning How to Play the Corporation Games," *The Chicago Tribune*, August 4, 1975, Section III, p. 9.

17. Ibid.

18. "Why Women Need Their Own MBA Programs," *Business Week*, February 23, 1974, p. 102.

19. Ibid.

20. N.A. Comer, "Executive Jobs: How to Land Them," *Mademoiselle*, September 1974, pp. 160-163.

21. "How Business Is Introduced to Bryn Mawr," *Business Week*, April 20, 1974, p. 112.

22. Ibid.

23. B.R. Bergmann and I. Adelman, "The 1973 Report of the President's Council of Economic Advisors: The Economic Role of Women," *The American Economic Review*, September 1973, p. 509.

24. "Madam Executive," *Time*, February 18, 1974, p. 76.

25. D. Sommers, "Occupational Ranking for Men and Women by Earnings," *The Monthly Labor Review*, August 1974, pp. 34-35.

26. Ibid., p. 50.

27. "Women at Work: Why We Do What We Do," *Redbook*, March 1975, p. 88.

28. "Where Women Work," *The Monthly Labor Review*, May 1974, p. 9.

29. Robertson, "The Ten Highest-Ranking Women in Big Business," pp. 80-89.

30. Ibid.

31. "A Long Road for Women," *Time*, February 12, 1973, p. 69.

32. Comer, "Executive Jobs: How to Land Them," p. 160.

33. C. Shifrin, "Trailblazing in a Man's World," *MBA*, February 1975, p. 12.

34. "Men, Enjoy It! Says 28 Year Old Woman President," *The AMBA Executive*, May 1973, p. 8.

35. Robertson, "The Ten Highest-Ranking Women in Big Business," p. 81.

36. Shifrin, "Trailblazing in a Man's World," p. 12.

37. Ibid.

38. "Men, Enjoy It! Says 28 Year Old Woman President," pp. 1-2.

39. "Mme. Waterman," *Newsweek*, April 19, 1973, pp. 100-102.

40. Ibid., p. 104.

41. "It's Slow, But Women Are Moving Into the Executive Suite," *U.S. News & World Report*, September 30, 1974, p. 44.

42. "Lawson Is First Black Woman to Head an S-L," *The Chicago Tribune*, August 28, 1975, Section IV, p. 7.

43. "Nun on Board of Oil Company," *The Chicago Tribune*, April 23, 1975, Section VI, p. 9.

44. J.B. Johnson and P. Asinof, "The Interview and the Law," *MBA*, September 1975, p. 34.

45. Ibid., p. 35.

46. M.M. Woods, "What Does It Take for a Woman to Make It in Management," *Personnel Journal*, January 1975, pp. 38-41.

47. Ibid., p. 66.

48. C. Kleiman, "Women and Business Success," *The Chicago Tribune*, September 1, 1975, Section III, p. 8.

Anne B. Skae *is the National Branch
Manager—Health Care, Education and Govern-
ment for Honeywell Information Systems,
Inc., Waltham, Massachusetts.* Dr. Donald O.
Jewell *is Professor of Management and*
Carolyn R. Pollard *is Editor,* Atlanta Eco-
nomic Review, *School of Business Adminis-
tration, Georgia State University, Atlanta.*

*This article was published under the title,
"Women on the Executive Ladder: Performance Is the First Criterion,"* Atlanta Economic Review, *November-December 1976,
pp. 50-54.*

18
Performance Is the First Criterion

An Interview With Anne B. Skae

Donald O. Jewell and Carolyn R. Pollard

Anne—let's begin with an obvious question—how did you come to pursue a career in management?

Well, I wish I could say that from the beginning I had this all worked out, but that simply wasn't the case. In fact, my whole career up until recently has been a combination of accidents and opportunities. One of the first accidents was going to Washington after graduation from college to look for a job. I had been a history major, which afforded me a variety of experience, left me with the feeling that I was an expert in damn near everything, and an ability to write and talk well. Obviously, I was dangerous, but I didn't appreciate that at the time. I guess the people I interviewed recognized what I did not, and indicated an interest in me only if I were willing to be a secretary. Unfortunately, I couldn't type. Perhaps I should say fortunately I couldn't type, because this first accident led me to my first opportunity. I went back to Detroit and began working in my father's business. He had a manufacturing firm, and with a little arm twisting he gave me a job which would enable me to correct a glaring deficiency: I would learn how to type. That was in 1962.

Five years later, I found myself in Atlanta—and I still couldn't type. That was fortunate because it led me to my first "opportunity." I perceived very quickly that I could not maintain my standard of living on a receptionist's pay, and administrative positions were few and far between for women. Looking in the Help Wanted—Female column, I discovered computer programmers were paid about $500 a month. I began contacting different companies: computer users and vendors who were looking for trainees. Fortunately, I had a friend in Detroit who at that time was a Regional Director for Honeywell and was kind enough to write a letter to Atlanta to the Regional Director there requesting that he consider me for a position. At that time the Atlanta region and branch office was small and just beginning to expand. I started in January of 1967 as a programmer trainee for Honeywell in Atlanta.

Is that when you began your career with Honeywell?

Well, yes and no. I was a trainee at the time and was learning to program by the "seat of my pants." Toward the end of 1968, I had an opportunity to work as a pre-sales systems representative on the Georgia Hospital Computer Group. At that time I became interested in hospital computer applications.

In January of 1969, Honeywell formed three operational areas with staffs that were designed to support marketing efforts over a broader base. I had been interested in getting into marketing, but at that time selling wasn't "women's work." While I didn't have a lot of hospital experience, I had more than anyone else who was readily available. I got the job of Systems Specialist for Hospitals in industry marketing, and from that point started to build the career that I now have.

Our territory covered Baltimore, Maryland to El Paso, Texas and everything in between including Puerto Rico. We only had five hospital accounts, and monitoring those was not exactly a challenging job, so I learned enough about the hospital business to work effectively with the sales reps and really help them sell the systems.

With this sales experience, considerable success in expanding the base, and what amounted to a show of ambition, I was appointed Market Manager in charge of health care. At that point, while I was not involved in setting policy myself, I could see the impact that management had on an organization. In addition, I recognized that the higher up I went, the more readily I could see the impact of my performance on a broad scale. It was about this time I decided that management was where I wanted to be.

What did you like about it?

I enjoyed seeing people do things they didn't think they could do. And I felt that I had a talent in helping them accomplish those things. I think that's probably the real satisfaction in managing—watching people grow and develop and perform. There are other challenges, of course, which make management fun, and these are associated with the setting and accomplishing of heretofore "impossible" goals. Again, there was the element of accident and opportunity, because marketing provided me with an opportunity that perhaps I would not have had almost any other way. Interestingly enough, when I went to Honeywell looking for a job, I was certainly not looking for a career. I just wanted a job that would pay the rent and let me live in the South.

So at that point, you really did not have firm career plans.

That's true.

But then after you had some exposure to management, you started to enjoy it.

Yes. I've never had problems in making decisions or providing leadership. I'm the oldest in a large family and I've had a lot of practice in working through others. I really feel that now I've found my vocational niche, and contrary to where I was when I began with Honeywell, I now have a plan for my future.

What is your goal or plan for the future?

To be vice president of a major corporation by the time I turn 40, which at this point is less than five years. I might add that this would have to be a meaningful vice presidency, and not a position created for me because a company wanted a female vice president. Beyond that I think I would like to run my own business.

Do you have any aspirations to become president of Honeywell?

Of course, but I'm not sure I'll live long enough!

Okay . . . moving right along then . . .

Frankly, I am ambitious, but I also want to have as much fun between 40 and 50 as I am having between 30 and 40.

It sounds like it's not just the goals that interest you, but the process of attaining them as well.

You're absolutely right; I'm looking forward to moving up, but I fully intend to enjoy myself in the process of getting there.

Now that we have an idea of where you would like to be, let's talk briefly about where you are right now in the organization. What is your current title and what are your areas of responsibility?

My title is National Branch Manager—Health Care, Education and Government.

What generally are the duties associated with that title?

Basically, my job is to develop marketing programs for those three industries named in my title. In addition, I have the responsibility to see that those programs are implemented in the field. While our marketing programs contribute heavily to keeping and upgrading our current customers, new products and good programs sell new business as well. And new business is the key to expanding market share. The state government and health care markets are growing faster than the market as a whole. So there is additional pressure for really effective program design and execution.

It sounds like you're not only involved in planning, but also involved quite extensively in the day-to-day implementation of your programs.

That's right. I devise marketing plans for today and for the future, and then I work to develop and implement actual programs to accomplish these plans.

Okay, Anne, now that we've got some idea of where you've been, where you're going, and what you're currently doing, I would like to hear your thoughts concerning the movement of women into management. If you were asked by a young woman, how do I go about getting into management most readily, how would you answer?

Well, there's no question that there's pressure on employers to hire women, and employers are looking for those women who are interested in going into management and who have the skills necessary to be successful. I seem to find myself talking a great deal with young women, and I emphasize that they've got to be prepared both vocationally and emotionally.

Could you elaborate a bit on that?

Vocationally, most women who want to move out of clerical jobs into management simply don't have the skills or experience. Even those coming out of our traditional academic programs have little knowledge or experience that is relevant to the management process.

So what you're saying is that for the most part the women who have come up through our traditional educational channels have little to sell as potential managers.

That's definitely true. I encourage women who have completed their education, depending on their areas of interest, to get into areas such as planning, engineering, systems, sales, and marketing and for God's sake stay out of the secretarial pool. Once you've been pegged as a secretary, it's extremely difficult to change the image.

Would you recommend business school training for young women who are interested in management?

Absolutely. I believe that if women are going to be successful in management they are going to have to commit themselves to the kind of training that will prepare them to do the types of things that management calls for.

So while organizations are most definitely looking for women, they are not willing to hire just anyone and are looking for ones who will be successful.

Yes, but while I don't mean to sound contradictory, I'm not sure that they know what it is they are looking for. What I mean is I don't think they know how to recognize female management potential. I think many of the recruiters have difficulty recognizing management potential, period, but they're really at a loss when it comes to recruiting and hiring women.

Why do recruiters have problems recognizing female management potential?

For the most part because of conflicts in perceptions and attitudes. Many of the recruiters are men, and they tend to look at women in the traditional roles: as wives, daughters, and sisters—not really as business peers. They will not ask a woman the kinds of gut questions that they will ask men about their career objectives, about the relationships between work and their social life, and about how they plan to manage their career. On the other hand, there's a tendency to be turned off by the aggressive woman. The woman who comes on strong, who can clearly articulate her objectives, and who, in fact, can sell herself effectively may be written off by the recruiter as "pushy," when in fact all she is doing is portraying the same characteristics that a high-potential male would have.

Well how are companies making the decision, then, to hire a woman for a management position?

In many cases they're copping out and looking for women who are already successful in management.

You mean rather than growing their own, they're looking around for women who have made it in management in other organizations?

That's true. It seems that right now they're looking for women who already have both the title and the responsibility.

So from the long-term standpoint, the important thing is that women get the opportunity to get into management. If they can just do reasonably well, then the opportunities either within their own company or from outside will become available.

There's no question about it.

Well, then, if I am a woman who's already in an organization, how do I go about getting the opportunity?

First off, you've got to do a good job in your current position. Performance is the first criterion. Next, be knowledgeable about business and industry so that you can interact with peers and superiors.

How do you gain that expertise?

By reading. My choices are the *Harvard Business Review, California Management Review*, and *Atlanta Economic Review*—East Coast, West Coast and the New South! I also like *Forbes* and *Business Week*. Trade journals will offer specific insights into your own industry. I sometimes skim *The Wall Street Journal* but don't really have time to read any daily newspapers. That's why I stick to journals and magazines. I can read them on airplanes.

I want to talk about travel, but let's get back to getting the opportunity.

After performance and knowledge comes visibility. You've got to make yourself visible in a positive way. One way is by accepting opportunities to do things other than just your job. This is true within the organization as well as on the outside. At higher levels in the organization you want outside visibility; at lower levels you want inside visibility. Get involved in company bond drives, the United Fund, and don't be afraid to volunteer for special task-force situations, even if they are unrelated to your department. Community service organizations and industry and trade associations offer excellent opportunities for outside visibility. They depend exclusively on volunteers for their existence.

After a year or so as a worker, you'll normally be asked to take on a leadership position. And once you've made the contribution, tell people about it. Press releases should always find their way to the company newspaper—and so should a good picture!

I'd say there's no question that the visibility is needed, but how do I go about making certain that my visibility and its impact will be positively recognized?

If you can handle your job well in addition to significant volunteer activity and you've got what it takes to move up, they'll recognize it.

Anne, other women we have talked to indicated they felt that to get ahead they needed a sponsor within the organization.

Absolutely necessary. In my case, absolutely vital. The sponsor keeps you on track and can also keep you in an organization long enough to succeed on your own. Initially it's vital to gain credibility and support, and this is the role of the sponsor in any organization.

How do you go about finding this individual?

I was fortunate. I did not have to seek the individual out. The individual who developed as my sponsor happened to be the person who hired me. If you're working for someone that you respect, who appears to be respected by others, and who is moving in the organization, then I think your first one will be your own boss. If you're not working for someone who qualifies in these dimensions, then I think you've got to look around. I think you have to look for someone who is not many levels above you because you'll never get to them. It has to be someone you can relate to personally and someone who is known as a performer and who is going to move up in the organization. Then I believe you have to find an opportunity to contribute to their success—to build an alliance with the sponsor.

Staying on the topic of getting the opportunity, do you see any advantage in advanced degrees?

I don't think it would do a damn thing for Anne Skae, but it would certainly help someone who is recently graduated. I think it would be a good idea to get a job in the marketing, engineering, or sales area, and if you find that business is your area of interest, then go on and get an MBA. I'm not sure it makes much difference where you get your MBA, but when you're being considered for a position and are in competition with others, there's no question that advanced degrees are used in making choices.

We've talked a great deal about getting into management; what do you see as the primary benefits of being in management and what are the tradeoffs?

Naturally, I'm only speaking from my own perspective. I get a lot of satisfaction out of accomplishing things through other people. I also happen to particularly enjoy seeing people develop and being a part of that development. I think perhaps I have a little of Henry Higgins in me. During my career I have tried to help people remove the obstacles in the way of successful performance, giving them meaningful direction, challenging levels of expectation, and the support to help them make it happen. Another benefit in management is the ability to influence people and policy. To be successful as a manager, I feel you've got to be someone who likes to act and can be effective in combining knowledge and influence into decisive and positive accomplishment. If you are, you'll get considerable satisfaction from managing. Certainly, money is one of the rewards.

As for the tradeoffs, time is probably the one thing you'll run out of. You have to be very well disciplined to be a successful manager. You can't have banking hours; there are things that have to be done, and you're expected to accomplish them regardless of the time involved. I find myself doing a considerable amount of my paperwork before and after regular hours. It's easier to concentrate without the phone ringing. The time tradeoff probably impacts your sleep and your personal and social life most drastically. Time, or a lack of it, is the real problem. If you're going to gain satisfactions and still have any kind of personal life, you've really got to get your act together and get organized. At work, you have to learn to be tough enough to say "no" to those things that don't have high priority and will not allow you to do effectively the things that are essential. I also feel that there's no question that this time tradeoff is going to impact the social life of a single woman more than perhaps any other individual. Certainly more so that that of a male.

In that same vein, can you give any examples of specific problems or advantages females have that males don't?

Well, being a female in sales work can be quite an advantage, at least initially. The majority of buyers are male and are used to dealing with a man in a sales call. The thing a salesperson has to do is get someone's attention. The minute a woman walks in the door, she has it. You don't have to tell funny jokes, or give away the system. You don't have to wear a vest and wing tips. All you have to do is walk in the door. If you get the guy's attention the minute you walk in the door, it can save you two or three calls. It benefits the company. The problem is, sometimes you come across a buyer who wonders how badly you want the sale. It takes a considerable amount of experience to deal professionally, courteously, and pleasantly, but firmly, with the question of sex in business, because it does come up. If a female salesperson can't handle that question, she can't sell. One woman told me, "Well, I just eliminate the whole problem by maintaining a very cool attitude." Well, she was cool; she almost froze me right out of my office. I thought to myself, she's not inviting just a mere advance, but an out and out attack. It's a touchy area and you can turn a guy off. The problem is, if he wants to buy a computer, he might as well buy a Honeywell—but the sales rep doesn't go with the computer. Unfortunately, many men think of women simply as bed partners. They never think of them as having any brains—just woman in the kitchen, babies—the whole nine yards. But I believe this is changing. I'm not saying it'll go away, but maybe it won't be an immediate issue.

Anne, this isn't a completely fair question, but do you think that you are making it easier or harder for other women to follow you in careers at Honeywell?

I would hope that I will make it easier. One thing I can say with some certainty is that women who follow in marketing management, for better or for worse, will probably be measured against me. Given my position and visibility, I don't believe it can be any other way. I do think it's interesting to note that while there aren't scads of women in management at Honeywell, those who are are very good performers. They know their business, and they are good at it. One thing I have noticed concerning women in our organization bothers me. They don't seem to think in terms of planning their careers. Rather they think in terms of a specific job and view it as a job as opposed to a step in a defined career path. Women must begin planning their careers; they must gain enough perspective to avoid those situations which may consciously or unconsciously be designed as a program for failure. I sometimes have the feeling that many women are not willing to make career commitments. I hope that the kinds of things I'm doing and the success that other women may see me enjoying will help them feel more comfortable in making commitments to a career in management.

That's an interesting point. Could you pursue this issue of career commitment a bit more?

I think most of my feelings on this subject come from

conversations I've had with women regarding the way they perceive both the tradeoffs and the possibilities of success. Many have said that they feel they have to be super competent and put in more hours than males if they expect to be promoted. They are reluctant to give up what they see as important aspects of their lives in order to get ahead. Unfortunately, they use me as an example of someone who works a great deal. I'm always a little embarrassed that the main reason I have to work after five is that I can't honestly say I have my act completely together. I need those extra hours when the phone isn't ringing simply to catch up on the kinds of things I should be able to accomplish during the day. And, occasionally, everything is in total chaos. But everyone can expect to have a few fluffy days.

So you don't believe that women have to be super competent to get promoted?

No, not super competent, but there's no question that they will have to make commitments of time and effort if they are going to compete successfully with males. Most men see the extra hours as simply part of the job, many women see them as extra demands. There's no question that two to three extra hours a day is the kind of commitment that is necessary if women are to be successful in any organization. And it's not just extra hours in a day. There are certain times when I know I might as well just scratch off a social weekend. When we are into budgeting and goal setting or when we're reorganizing, the question is not one of time, the question is one of getting things done by a deadline.

What I hear you saying is that a career in management, for anyone, is going to be a time- and effort-consuming undertaking.

No question about it. Sometimes I'm amazed at the reactions of recent college graduates, particularly the women, when I begin discussing travel and working nights and weekends. I'm amazed because it seems to put them off, they seem to be looking for a 9:00 to 5:00 executive career. If one of these exists, I sure as hell haven't seen it!

It is necessary to plan ahead if you want to maintain some balance in your life. When I was traveling, I would leave town Monday and return Friday. I had to arrange my outside life in advance or by long-distance calls. I also had an answering service—that's just one of the costs involved. This brings up another point. I think it takes an extraordinary woman to be not only an executive in a company but also a successful wife and mother. Somewhere along the line, someone is going to get short-changed. It's for certain—if a woman intends to have a career in management and a husband, she damn well better pick the right guy. If half the husbands I know came home at night and found a message from the answering service saying their wife had just left for a week-long business meeting in San Juan, they would leap right through the roof. Hell, most of them wouldn't even know where to find their food. I'm not saying that a woman can't have both a career and a family, I'm just saying that the circumstances would have to be right, and the planning would have to be fantastic. I've found in my own life that unless I plan carefully, the sacrifices become greater. Planning is the key. And then, just when you've got your routine down, they move you or promote you and you have to start all over again.

You mentioned social life. Do you find it possible to have a "normal" social life?

I don't think I would go so far as to call it normal. Traditionally, women waited to be asked. Unfortunately, most men would wait until the middle of the week to ask me for a date on the weekend. Usually, I was out of town and I would miss the opportunity. Or, if your schedule is extremely complicated, many men are not interested in taking the time to keep calling. So I've gotten out of the habit of waiting to be asked. If I want to go to a party, or if I want a date, I'll call somebody up. I'm not sure I would have had the social confidence to do this just coming out of college, but I do now. I'll call someone and say, "Listen, I know you'd probably wait to call me Wednesday, but I'm not going to be here. Would you like to go to this party?" Generally, they laugh and accept. Interestingly enough, I'm beginning to get the feeling that there are an awful lot of men who are reluctant to make that first call themselves. So in some ways, I may make life easier for them. However, some men still have problems with my life style. For example, a guy I dated for a number of years finally stopped dating me because he got sick and tired of having to plan a week ahead of time what he was going to do on Saturday night. He preferred to be able to call in the middle of the week; not the week prior.

In many ways, my business commitments fulfill a lot of my social ambitions. I travel a lot and get opportunities to live it up at the best bars and restaurants with bright aggressive men and women. I really enjoy that. I like to travel and to meet new people. And after millions of air miles, I still get a kick out of flying.

I have been an active volunteer in my community for more than 15 years. In the last few years, as you know, I've had the opportunity to work with women just venturing into supervisory positions through speaking at continuing education programs for Women in Management at colleges and universities in the South. All of this makes for a pretty full life. As you might imagine, I don't find myself sitting home watching soap operas or TV serials or much of that. In fact, I don't have much time at home unless I specifically set it aside—which I try to do. But I don't have much time to think about whether I really like how those curtains fit.

So your career has in fact forced a change in the way you approach your social life?

Yes it has, but I find it works reasonably well for me.

Anne, let's get to a question that many women would be interested in hearing an answer to now. Do you think that being a woman right now is an advantage to you in your career?

Right now it's helpful to be a woman. True, it may not be easy. One way being a woman hurts you is that you have no really effective role models. But this is changing. And I'm part of that change. The positive side is that many organizations are looking for competent women for management positions, and there's no question that I can move faster at this point in time because I am a woman. Of course, I moved more slowly for the first nine years of my career, so I figure I'm just catching up.

Being a woman today is only an advantage if women will press it—by offering equal capabilities and equal commitment—by expecting equal treatment and equal standards of measurement—by giving equal performance—and by demanding equal opportunity and equal pay.

The opportunities are there in almost all industries and all companies. I know from my own experience—I've come a long way in nine years. And I'm not stopping now. The business world has changed a lot. Today organizations are willing to offer a woman an opportunity to compete and succeed—even if she does have an occasional fluffy day.

Marion M. Wood *is Assistant Professor of Management Communications, School of Business Administration, University of Southern California.*

Reprinted by permission of the publisher from S.A.M. Advanced Management Journal, *Winter 1976* © *1976 by S.A.M., a division of American Management Associations.*

19

Women in Management: How Is it Working Out?

Marion M. Wood

WOMEN MANAGERS have the same problems as men managers: pressures of responsibility, problems with subordinates, accountability to top management. But the woman manager also has some unique problems because she holds a position that has long been considered a "man's job." Where women are moving into the ranks of management, however, all the signs indicate that the problems are less than the women managers and their male counterparts expected. Even though many men—and women—continue their passive resistance to resocialization of the traditional male hierarchy, the consensus of nearly 100 male and female managers surveyed was that women managers are proving their competence and winning increasing acceptance. Some executives in key positions in the companies participating in the author's study are going out of their way to encourage qualified women to train themselves and to compete for higher level jobs. These supporters firmly believe that once the labor-force projection of increasing numbers of highly trained women becomes a reality, corporate management will be competing for their services. And this will be because of their potential for contributing to the organization, not simply because of the organization's need to meet affirmative action goals.

In late 1972, labor-force projections indicated the U.S. economy could look forward "to a substantial supply of well educated women" toward the end of the decade. Now, three years later, it would appear that little progress has been made by women in the higher echelons of the labor force. Following the industry's three-year concentration on affirmative action programs in response to "Revised Order Four" (Executive Order 11246, Revised Order Four [1972] made it imperative for federal contractors to establish affirmative action programs that ensure equal employment opportunities for women in all ranks), statistics show that women still represent less than one percent of the officials, managers, and professionals in the nation's major corporations.

These statistics, however, obscure the gains being made by women in individual organizations. To clarify these gains, a study of 14 Los Angeles companies where women have joined the managerial ranks was conducted by the author to determine how these women's new roles were affecting the quality of life at work. Much of the data was collected through personal interviews and observation, but a mailed questionnaire supplemented the informal method.

Even with this opportunity to speak anonymously, males and females expressed essentially the same opinions in writing as they did in the face-to-face discussions. In general, the men and women managers surveyed varied very little with respect to their answers to the questions asked. When asked to identify personal and organizational adjustments that had been made in fitting women into the male hierarchy, neither the male nor the female managers indicated that significant adjustments in either area had been necessary. Over half said they had not observed any noticeable effects on the overall operation. More women than men reported organizational changes, but none indicated that they had been traumatic.

All the participants in the survey seemed to be in general agreement on basic impressions of women's initial impact on the organization. On the plus side, the novelty of women in management apparently has been easier to adapt to than some of the managers surveyed had anticipated. Tension is subsiding, initial feelings of threat are easing, and status-role conflicts are slowly being resolved. The major problems, the persons queried said, are *not* in adjusting man-woman roles and relationships but rather in (1) finding or motivating qualified women within the organization to seek advancement and (2) gaining more general resocialization throughout the company. (Many in corporate management must still be convinced that promoting women is economically feasible.)

Finding and Motivating Qualified Women

Discussing the present scarcity of highly qualified women, both the men and women managers who have the responsibility of training, developing, and finding women for management positions admitted concern with the morality of pushing women—in fact, any persons—into something they don't want. When affirmative action was first required for giving equal opportunities to racial minorities, programs were developed to identify potential talent and motivate persons to set goals and seek them aggressively. Now training directors are trying to modify these programs for the recruitment and the training of women.

Of course, there is more than just an ethical question involved in implementing these programs. Until jobs can be guaranteed for every man and woman whom employers train for promotion, companies must accept the fact that they may be preparing their employees for other employers. And managers who are dedicated to helping women grow despite this risk face the additional fear of encouraging some women who may turn out to be not as qualified as they were thought to be at first. "All we need is one of these women managers to fail," said one man surveyed, "and it will confirm in some men's minds that women simply cannot handle the job at all. Sure, many men whom we push turn out to be disappointments," he admitted, "but these we're used to dealing with."

The woman who fails to meet the company's expectation of her sets the hopes for women way back—in that organization at least, if not on a far wider basis. Profit objectives have a higher priority especially today than do affirmative action goals; and the higher the employee in the company, the greater investment he or she is. A company must be convinced that promoting women into management positions is economically justifiable, and one bad example can easily tip the scales against further efforts by the company in that direction.

Knowing this adds to the pressure on a woman manager. So does the fact that even with everything else going for her, without the approval of her male counterparts, the gatekeepers, she will not be accepted in management. Consequently, in addition to proving her ability as a manager, a woman manager must sell a new image; she must help her male counterparts see the *self*-benefits in perceiving woman "as she is now rather than as how she always has been."

It takes a very strong and sensitive woman to put this across effectively, but even this kind of woman may be unable to meet the challenge if she is the only woman manager in the organization. One woman in a group of men is easily overpowered and will fall back into her traditional subordinate role if she is not prepared, alert, and determined. In a position of "damned if I do and damned if I don't," she runs the risk of alienation if she comes on too strong and of suppression if she comes on too weak.

This dilemma is frightening some qualified women from seeking management positions. Aware of the difficulties involved, they are reluctant to move into conflict, a fact that may explain at least in part the seeming paradox of women who have been fighting for opportunity being reluctant to use the doors that are now open to them. Many are doing very well in traditional roles in their organizations and question the logic of changing to something that apparently offers more frustration than security.

It is not altogether that women do not want to advance. It is just that until recently few thought about making careers in business; neither industry nor business schools encouraged them. But now the schools are busy trying to make up the time lag caused by industry's long antipathy.

Resocialization in the Company

In this social revolution, is it true that women have all to gain and men all to lose? According to some reports, this is a common perception. The study conducted by the author, however, did not reveal such thinking among most of the male managers surveyed. To some, women's ability to perform management functions is simply "a reinforcement of what I knew they could do, once given the chance." To others, it is "a pleasant surprise," "the end of another barrier," or "something that is long overdue."

Most of the men who made these comments have never held strong prejudices, though they did acknowledge that fitting women into their existing hierarchical scheme had taken some soul-searching. Adjusting to peer relationships with women who had been formerly subordinates or, more traumatic, accepting a female boss, had called for radical changes in self-concept and perception of society. The men had trained themselves to compete, particularly in terms of power, but nothing had prepared them for competing with women. As Michael Korda, author of *Male Chauvinism! How it Works*, wrote, "Behind their dogmatism and small guiles lies the fear that woman may in fact be a formidable competitor once she has made her choice."

The male managers surveyed did not cite significant examples of operational changes in their organization as a result of women's expanding role in management. They spoke candidly of efforts "to minimize or eliminate sex-role bias and misconceptions," and they specified obvious needs for change: special training for newly promoted female supervisors and managers, reevaluation of policies regarding salaries and hours, and new policies for business travel. There are problems with wives, one male manager admitted, "when men travel with attractive women in management." Other than this, the general feeling expressed was that women are making a significant contribution in their organizations.

How Competent Are Female Managers?

When asked to evaluate female managers' competence at decision making, their handling of emotions, and their response to criticism (three areas in which women are frequently stereotyped as being inferior to males), both male and female managers rated women high. Women evaluated themselves higher than men rated them as decision makers and in their ability to control their emotions. However, only two men graded women as less than moderately effective in decision making, and none considered them "not well in control" of emotions. The consensus among the men was that men in management tend to display their emotions more frequently than do women. Women, they explained, are trying so hard to break old stereotypes and create a new image that they keep their emotions well under control. In comparison, men will "blast off" at any provocation.

Only in the area of response to criticism did the men and women surveyed vary significantly in their evaluation of women managers. One fourth of the male managers sampled graded women as "somewhat subjective," and two men reported bad experiences that led them to evaluate women managers as "very subjective."

In general, however, the respondents felt that the sex of the manager does not affect ability or stability. In fact, most of the male and female managers queried were reluctant to assign unique characteristics to women managers. When crediting an asset to them, the man or woman was careful to qualify that the characteristic was not necessarily peculiar to women. Assuming, wrote one female manager, that women have met the same qualifications as required of men, unique characteristics of either are related to *individual personality*. Calling generalizations about women both "stereotyping and sexist thinking," the group sampled refused to make distinctions.

Nevertheless, in discussing the female managers' contributions to the organization, the male managers did point out that women have brought fresh new insights and new points of view to management and to the total organization. "Women are not steeped in traditional management," one male manager said. "They bring fresh ways of problem solving to meetings, and they bring a new value system to corporate policy making."

Better Balance in the Organization

Many of the male managers sampled indicated that women have brought a long-needed balance to the organization. In particular, stressed several, women are providing a better balance in marketing management. Their understanding of the female psyche has been valuable in marketing all products, not just those that are female-oriented. The general feeling expressed was that women are making a significant contribution in their handling of customers, particularly women customers, both in the office and out in the field.

Women tend to be people-minded, opined both the men and women surveyed. They are generally more aware of the human factor in business relationships and more sensitive and concerned about the personal feelings of their peers. This sensitivity was described as good for management. Women as a group, the male managers said, bring a degree of sensitivity (not to be interpreted as weakness or softness) to the management style that allows a broader perspective in determining course of action and decision making. One man's comment spoke right to the point: "Generally there is too much 'machismo' and misconceived need to be hard in business organizations; the stereotypical male sex role model needs some softening."

Women also have a good effect on the environment, according to the male managers surveyed. "They remain calm," said one, "when we're at the explosion point, and this helps to keep our discussions more objective, less emotional. Women managers tend to be more rational and more able to cope with the pressures of short turnaround, crisis situations." All of this adds up to a more pleasant place to work, the majority of the male respondents said. "For one thing," one claimed, "women have put a damper on the cutthroat competition found in my organization." "It's calmer around here," another noted.

Most of the men confided that they have had to clean up their language and jokes. At least temporarily! Apparently the male managers made this decision arbitrarily, not because the women complained. In fact, the women managers surveyed felt the issue is only a minor one, like opening doors and offering chairs. They want to concentrate on more important problems than these symbols inherited from another era. Still, the male managers felt that having women in management had made them "more thoughtful about employees," as one manager expressed it, and more respectful of females at all levels.

Role-Status Problems

Adjustment problems reported most frequently by the female managers were the role-status conflicts they experience when learning how to relate as a superior to secretaries and as a peer to male managers who have known them as secretaries. Both secretaries and male peers tend to regard the new woman manager in her former status. "I have to walk a delicate line to gain acceptance and respect," one woman confessed.

There were some women who said that they had had no personal problems adjusting to a peer relationship with men. They explained that they had always worked with men, they liked working with men, and they had been lucky to work with "good men." Only recently, because of all the discussion about the status of women, had some of these "old-timers" even become conscious of male chauvinism. Nor had any of the women with recent promotions into low-level management positions ever experienced male chauvinism. At the same time, these newcomers confessed that they had to frequently remind themselves to "stop assuming male colleagues are superior," to "be more assertive with ideas and opinions," and to "ask fewer questions." With each passing week and with helpful feedback from many of the men, they report they are feeling less tense about their role in the corporate hierarchy.

Overall, the women surveyed have found men not as difficult to work with as they had expected. For the most part, the women believe that their male counterparts are accepting them and expecting them to be advanced. One sure sign, one female manager said, is that "I haven't been asked to pour coffee or take notes at a meeting in two years."

Working Together—Its Problems and Promises

With rare exception, the male managers were optimistic that women can handle effectively the managerial positions they are assuming. They feel that the small problems women are experiencing right now are due primarily to lack of experience, a situation they will overcome in time. Emotional problems, several specified, cannot be helped. They will disappear, one male manager said, "with increased exposure." A number of the men reported having to help women get over their initial insecurity, gain confidence, and assume an active and not a passive role. But they spoke of these problems as temporary ones, not as issues of grave concern.

The two most critical faults of women managers, according to the men, are their demanding nature at times and their unwillingness to "reach out and help other females." "Women tend to be less flexible and to demand more from their subordinates—especially if their charges are also female," one male manager commented.

The female managers were less critical than the men with their comments. There was an occasional slur, such as "having to overlook men's running off at the mouth when they don't know an answer," and mentions of men's "emotionalism" and "over-reacting" at meetings, but, other than these observations, the women were not bitter or negative in their written or spoken comments. Just as the men evidenced understanding of women's need for more experience and time to adjust to their new role, women seemed to understand the conflicts that men are experiencing in working out new relationships with their female counterparts. The women managers said that they are ready to help face and overcome all the hangups and prejudices that exist, but they said that they do not feel it is altogether their responsibility. It should be a corporate venture, they pointed out.

It will be many more years, possibly decades, before women will be found more commonly in management. This is not because they are not doing a good job. They are. Nor is it totally because men are holding out. Many are, but women executives have the support of many others. This study has indicated that when asked for candid opinions, men have more commendations than complaints to make about women in management. When male management support will become sufficiently articulate and widespread to provide the freedom of choice that women are seeking is still subject to conjecture. But what appears to be clear is that whenever qualified women do make their way to higher positions in management, the worst of the struggle is over. Once there, men and women agree that the tensions, feelings of threat, and apprehensions rapidly disappear. Men seem to be surviving the changes. And they readily admit that, so far, there are more changes for the better than for the worse. That should be good news for women.

III
Gearing Up--
A Positive Response

THAT WOMEN WILL become managers is inevitable and desirable. Resistance to this change is inevitable and potentially destructive. How can organizations and society benefit from a new source of management talent, yet avoid the problems that accompany a change of this magnitude?

It won't be easy.

Society must work to prepare women to assume an unfamiliar role. Organizations must determine what type of woman can succeed in its managerial roles, and the resistance to change must be overcome constructively.

20
Guidelines for
Immediate Action

Rosalind Loring and Theodora Wells

To this end, I am now directing that you take the following actions:

—Develop and put into action a plan for attracting more qualified women to top appointive positions . . . this plan should be submitted to me by May 15.

—Develop and put into action by May 15 a plan for significantly increasing the number of women . . . in mid-level positions. . . This plan should directly involve your top personnel official.

—Ensure that substantial numbers of vacancies on your Advisory Boards and Committees are filled with well-qualified women.

—Designate an overall coordinator who will be held responsible for the success of this project. Please provide this name to me by May 15.

Richard Nixon
April 26, 1971

Top Policy Statement Is Formulated and
Announced Throughout the Organization

This is a policy statement from the top, essential to launching a program as pervasive as affirmative action for women, whether within the federal government or in some other organization. It is also an example of initial goals with a timetable—the parameters within which expected action is to take place.

Developing a climate for change of policies and practices in order to accept women as managers usually means revising some organization-wide procedures and many attitudes and relationships. So radical will these changes seem to some that little progress will be made without consistent committed leadership from top management.

Even with strong support from executives and trainers, this kind of organizational change requires a person near the top—a new manager, consultant or staff officer—to give it concentrated attention. A fresh way of looking at the familiar scene is essential. Analysis, identification, possible solution, collaboration . . . all will be parts of the puzzle for both the line and staff as more people become involved in the processes of change.

The puzzle, of course, is the design of an affirmative action program relating to women. The structure of the program will be variously designed depending upon the applicable compliance agency and the magnitude of the effort being applied. Guidance for planning and implementation, growing out of experience with other projects of organizational change, generally applies to affirmative action programs.

We are assuming that the mechanics and problems of spelling out the specifics of the plan in each organization are available most precisely in the local area and in working with compliance officers having jurisdiction. Developing timetables also entails estimating some elements on which there may be insufficient information at the start, or which are difficult to estimate on any other basis than a well-educated guess. We want to raise a number of considerations and ideas here that we feel need to be part of the thinking and approach in developing affirmative action programs for women, taking such factors and difficulties into account. We are using Revised Order 4 as a basic model. [Editor's note: Revised Order 4 refers to Executive Order 11246, which requires federal contractors to set up affirmative action programs for women and minorities.]

Affirmative Action Officers Need a Wide Range of Responsibility; Should Report to Top Management

The sheer size of the task of turning around an organization, its people and procedures means selecting an affirmative action officer who reports directly to the top management level. The position needs to include responsibility to . . .

● Review and approve: provisions and goals of the program; job opening announcements and ads; job descriptions and requisite qualifications; application forms; tests and other screening devices; other related areas where sex bias may occur in the selection and placement process.

● Review, report and recommend actions for on-going follow-through based on: personnel records; affirmative action files for promotion; reasons for termination, discipline, and rejected promotions of women.

● Review and recommend changes in: personnel policies to assure equitable treatment for women and men; insurance, health and retirement programs to equalize benefits for both sexes and their dependents; other fringe benefit and incentive programs; informal practices and stated policy about leaves, absences, and other time off; other support services such as child care, counseling, etc.

● Review and recommend changes in: training and development programs re: selection, content, results, and rates of job progress subsequent to training.[1]

Selecting the Affirmative Action Officer; Support Groups for Affirmative Action

The logical choice for the women's affirmative action officer is a woman. Why not put a man in charge of affirmative action for women? First, because of the credibility factor. Such a position usually pays well and carries some power in the organization. To select a man could be seen by women employees as meaning that top management intends to continue giving important positions to men. Second, it could appear that a male affirmative action officer is hired to whitewash sex discrimination, not eliminate it. Selecting a woman is *prima facie* good faith. Third, few men are fully aware of the subtleties of discrimination and how it has affected women's lives. Those men sensitive enough to sex discrimination to function effectively as affirmative action officers would well understand that most men in that position would have considerable difficulty in establishing credibility with some women, especially the more aware ones.

How should the affirmative action officer be selected? Requirements might include in-depth knowledge of women's needs, roles, attitudes; what's happening in women's rights activities; current psychological and achievement motivation research on women; organization and management skills; management by objectives; and government regulatory requirements. Experience as a manager, a change-agent or community development expert should be among the other qualifications.

To separate the unaware from the knowledgeable applicant, questions could well include . . .
● How do you recognize "non-conscious sexism" in action?
● How would you select a woman to become a manager with some prediction of her success?
● What work, if any, needs to be done with men managers to make a woman's affirmative action program effective?
● What problems are "women's" problems, "men's" problems, or just human problems?

Applicants will reveal many unconscious as well as conscious attitudes during the interview. Notice what she (he) thinks women are like. Does she (he) stereotype either men or women in her (his) discussion? Can you sense an attitude of vengeance, "getting back" at society in her (his) conversation? What jokes are made, and does hostility underlie them? Vengeance could be a problem but anger may be useful. Try to sense the quality of it. Or is she (he) somewhat anxious to please, looking for how she (he) is expected to respond? "Nice person," deferring qualities may be far less than helpful in this sensitive position. Openness, directness, honesty and self-confidence are vital. So is support for expressing these qualities.

One important caution. Many firms already have affirmative action officers who are minority men, due to the emphasis on minority affirmative action in the past decade. Minority women also hold many similarly visible positions. But problems arising from discriminatory practices against minorities are different from those women experience. Minority women experience both.

Second caution. It must be clear in policy and action that advancement of minority men will not be at the expense of women's advancement nor that women advance at the expense of minority men. This is one sensitive area that can be a key to management's good faith. To pit one group against the other is to undermine the objectives of both. One way to avoid such problems is to select an aware woman who can work with the minority man who is now in affirmative action work. Equal status between them eliminates possible conflicts of interest and makes visible management's equal commitment to both groups. This delicate social balance in black/white, male/female advancement must be weighed in the final selection and placement of affirmative action officers as well as in implementing the program.

Additional people on the affirmative action teams could well include:

● An advisory committee, made up of women and minorities to solicit community and employees' views, to review and comment on policies, grievances, and the administration of the affirmative action program, to propose programs and procedures, and to consider special problems of minority women.

● Personnel staff who have sensitivity and commitment to affirmative action purposes, as evidenced by their work in feminist organizations, and minority communities.

● Supervisors and employees trained to have sensitivity to different attitudes, self-concepts, traditional social roles, and cultural differences among men and women of different ethnic groups.[2]

Responsibility for the success of the program must rest with top management on down through line supervision. Managers and supervisors should be held responsible through their performance reviews for meeting goals and timetables. If they have not met them, the reasons should be made clear. Eventually this information will be requested by compliance officers. Even without that pressure, the realistic problems and needed changes in plans are important for future planning.

Determining the Present Status of Women in the Organization

A survey to determine the practices, policies and attitudes which affect women should also canvas the experiences women have had in the organization and the ambitions they hold.

First, the survey should determine where women are in the organization by work-unit and by levels. When the search turns to women in management it will be necessary to *define a manager* for the purpose of the count. Without a precise definition, some departments may try to appear more progressive to higher management by including doubtful positions as management roles. In fact some organizations, straining hard, have even included executive secretaries as managers. Some include first-line supervision in management, others start at first-line management, which differs according to the size of the organization.

What defines management will have to be determined by each organization individually. The Department of Health, Education and Welfare bases management on pay-grade level. A major banking operation does not include first-line supervisors in its classifications of officials and managers. Their managers include those who supervise other officers, or are responsible for lending, managing and operations functions.

The basis for defining management—whether by pay-level, function, or numbers of people supervised—must be consistently applied by all managers and supervisors. The survey should include questions covering requirements of the guidelines of Revised Order 4 which call for analysis of:
● The composition of the work force and applicant flow by minority group status and sex;
● The total selection process—position descriptions and titles, worker specifications, application forms, interviews, tests, referrals, transfer and promotion practices;
● Seniority;
● Facilities and company-sponsored recreation;
● Special programs including educational assistance;
● All company training programs;
● Work force attitude; and
● Under-utilization of women in specific classifications.

Lateral or vertical movements should occur at similar time rates for women and men. Position descriptions should accurately describe all actual functions and duties. Tests for selecting women should be validated, or be clearly capable of being validated should they be questioned for sex bias. Women should be participating in company activities and programs and be proportionately represented in training and development programs. A well-designed survey will reveal how men and women are experiencing the prevailing policies, practices and attitudes which affect their progress.

Written policies of the organization should be analyzed for sex bias by the affirmative action officer. Unwritten policies are more subtle and may be discovered via the survey which can include questions that focus on some of the old discriminatory practices of differential interview questions, pay, expectations, promotional opportunity, eligibility for further training among others.

More information can be gotten from observing the results of prior bias, such as the invisible ceiling, assumed responsibilities in housekeeping functions, and what positions are most sex-typed. These evidences can be traced back to how they started. This "audit trail" points back to a source of discrimination where differential ways of treating women from men is evident at the interface with the external market. For example, observe the double message in the employment ad that talks about looking for a man to head up a department, and which also states at the bottom of the ad, "an equal opportunity employer."

Another useful means for locating discriminatory practices is to ask the same questions of men and women, tabulating different patterns of answers. Also, when sex reversal questions are asked (those where the customary sex is replaced with the other sex) any absurdity is a solid clue that sex discrimination is present. Using sex reversal is most revealing of old habits of thinking and brings the habit into conscious awareness.

Interviews and group sessions, as well as casual conversations can also be a rich source of information about how women feel. Care must be used, however, in interpreting these comments, as well as survey results. They reflect attitudes as of the time expressed, which may change, sometimes very rapidly. In general, most women tend to say what is expected of them, especially to men to whom they have been socialized to defer.

It's part of being nice. However, as women become more aware that the price of being nice may be high, they may become more open with their formerly unexpressed viewpoints and experiences. This is the first move toward stepping out of some self-limiting behavior and can identify a potential candidate for career development. New awareness in women may be difficult to understand in comparison to former behavior, but it is a strength that is being released. Once released, it tends to grow.

Finding and Recruiting Women to Fill New Positions

Once the status of women within the organization has been determined, a plan for increasing the number of women and minorities at all levels is set up. Specific targets within definite times are part of this plan. Sometimes there is a point of "operational discrimination"—where the necessary changes seem impossible. If this happens, try making a parallel with other "impossible" situations. Usually they just take a little longer! When you decide "We'll find a way," new possibilities begin to open up. This is "good faith." Finding women who are capable of becoming managers may be somewhat easier than it seems. Thus some thoughts on how "good faith" works . . .

Colleges and Universities

Recruitment from colleges and universities is a major source for potential managers who are men. Women graduates typically have been avoided by the campus recruiter. Even women with Harvard MBA's have had this experience.[3] The fact that 30 percent of recruiting companies went to women's colleges while 60 percent went to men's colleges[4] is a sure indicator of intent not to recruit women. Women's colleges as well as coeducational institutions are the primary source for recruiting women for entry-level management positions. They are also the place to find well prepared professional and technical women.

Now that the demand for educated women for higher-level positions is increasing, more effective recruiting practices are necessary. What changes can improve the effectiveness of recruiting? In the past, women have been formally recruited but informally excluded. They have been sought as "tokens," recruited on a basis different from men.

Briefly, here's what has been happening. Recruiters may perform formal interviews to give the appearance of active interest, knowing that an "out" will be available. They avoid the possibility of the woman student suspecting sex discrimination. This works well if the men and women students do not exchange information after their respective interviews. Many do. Even if recruiters are careful to ask the same questions and give the same explanations to both women and men students, it is becoming easier to spot lack of seriousness. Women graduates are learning what to look for. The most difficult position for a recruiter is to be seeking a qualified person for a position where the department head refuses to hire women. The recruiter is put in a personal double-bind and a long-term result may be that women graduates learn of this company's poor reputation and avoid interviews.

Recruiting a token woman is usually discovered by the woman graduate who is likely to ask about the invisible ceiling in that company. This is an excellent indicator of how serious the company is in integrating women into the managerial ranks. Some women don't want to be the token, fearing it may be another terminal position. Their concern is with being used to conceal exclusionary practices.

Equal pay for equal work is not yet a reality in campus recruiting policies. The U.S. Department of Labor reports that women are consistently offered lower starting salaries for the same job than are men. In 1970 men received offers averaging $86 a month more than women. In 1971 the difference averaged $68 a month.[5]

Some recruiters are still asking biased interview questions such as the old saws, "How will you be able to combine marriage and a career?" (as though men did not combine them all the time) and, "What will your husband say if you don't get his dinner ready by 6 p.m.?" To ask such questions of women concentrates more on her personal situation than on her capabilities. It implies that her skills are of minor importance to the job and devalues her educational achievements.

Finally, some companies do actively recruit women on the same bases and qualifications as men. We predict this practice will increase sharply, stimulated by Revised Order 4. Personnel managers and recruiters can do a major turnaround in their recruiting work when they are backed by solid policy and follow-through. It is vital to establish credibility of serious intent and action over a long period of time. One way to start is by offering equal beginning salaries. The word spreads among students, and certain firms will be avoided if actual experience of graduates differs from that represented. Young women are more aware of the sex bias they face. They are not gullible when they feel a solid personal commitment to actively use their education for achievement and advancement in their chosen profession.

Executive Search and Placement Agencies

Next, executive search and placement agencies and consulting firms are a rich source for management men, but not for management women. There are few, if any, who will handle women even though this is in violation of Title XII. Head-hunters are caught in the middle: the law requires them to handle persons for whom there has been no market. It's an open invitation to pass the buck.

In Atlanta, for example, the local NOW chapter undertook to disexigrate want ads. In the process they were successful in persuading personnel and executive agencies to insist on sending women applicants for all openings formerly designated as "male" positions. As these agencies made their client companies aware of the legal requirements to do this, more women were considered for higher positions.

Search practices can be reversed. Organizations can easily require their recruitment agencies to search and send women on all job openings they place. When it's necessary for earning their fees, agencies will become primary sources for higher-qualified women of all kinds. They have proselyted before and possess considerable creative talent in generating new sources when they apply their minds to it. Without question, the agency deciding to develop this market will find itself an innovator with a rich potential for new income. . . .

Some other sources for management women are such organizations as the American Association of University Women, the Business and Professional Women's Talent Bank,

National Organization for Women, Federally Employed Women, Women's Equity Action League and the Women's Bureau. In Washington, D.C., Washington Opportunities for Women, a private, non-profit organization provides job matchmaking for people in that area. Other large cities have new agencies forming for this purpose, as well as local chapters of women's organizations.

Recruiting from Within

Probably the best source is women currently employed in the organization, especially those who are bumping their heads against the invisible ceiling. Although there may be no *formal* restrictions to keep women from advancing, practice demonstrates clearly that they will go no higher. The rationale for the ceiling goes, "It's never been done before," and "This is not a good time to try it," or "Our customers wouldn't accept it; they expect to do business with a man."[6]

Women at the invisible ceiling may be in executive assistantships, staff or administrative capacities or in various supervisory positions. Many have trained one or more male bosses for the next-level position for which they may be well qualified themselves, but have not been considered for promotion. Not uncommonly, a less qualified man will be given the promotion and a woman asked to "show him the ropes." Even if a woman holds a position in an acting capacity and is rated excellent in her performance, she seldom gets the promotion permanently. Such women represent a valuable pool of under-used, well-trained, and proven, high-potential management talent.[7]

Problems in Assessing and Selecting Women for Management Positions

Many men may find it difficult to evaluate the technical and professional competence of women. They may feel they can spot these capabilities and potentials in another man, but doubt their judgment about them in a woman. If the woman is attractive, sexy or appealing, how can he be sure he's evaluating her professional and intellectual capabilities rather than being swayed by her physical appearance? Further, when he is used to women performing only as secretaries or perhaps executive assistants, how can he visualize any woman as a manager? On what basis can he choose a woman over a man with sufficient certainty that he is willing to withstand expected pressures from other men? It may even seem like too much trouble, especially if he suspects this is only the beginning of similar problems.

To mitigate this difficulty, male managers may want to consider thinking through the kind of managerial job to be done and what it takes to do it *before* thinking about the sex of the person to fill it. To be fruitful this process will have to explicitly include envisioning a woman filling the job. Most managers are so used to looking for "the best man for the job" that they rarely hear their own assumption that only a man can qualify. This sex-linked assumption must be questioned each time it appears. For some time to come, it may be necessary to seek "the best woman for the job." Whether it is a woman or a man who is finally selected, this way of thinking the matter through will be more thorough, more certain to make the best selection, as well as helping to minimize sex bias.

Almost no woman would want to be selected for promotion solely because she is a woman. Similarly, it is hard to believe any man would want to be selected solely because he is a man. On the other side of the coin, it's frustrating for any woman to realize she is *not* being promoted solely because she is a woman. Yet many a woman has been forced to that realization and to the realization that men do not have parallel experiences.

Not all women employees with the requisite capabilities are good candidates for managerial positions. Many women are conditioned to think of themselves as wives and mothers first and only secondarily as employees. Those women may not be ready to become managers. There are ways, however, of spotting a woman with a primary, long-range interest in her career. She is an achieving woman who has:

● A high level of motivation and achievement need.
● An identification with a field or profession.
● A high degree of individuality.
● A strong self-esteem.[8]

Recent studies have shown that career-oriented women, more

than traditional women, have an experience history and background that contains:
- A working mother who served as a role model.
- Strong influence by teachers, professors and people in the chosen profession.
- As high school girls, infrequent dating and enjoyment from studying and reading, but dating as much as others in college.
- Professionally educated parents with a high socio-economic status from a metropolitan area.
- Experience of being out-of-phase; late physical maturity, not belonging to high school cliques, moving frequently.[9]

An achieving woman has more commonly developed from such a background, but this background does not guarantee the development of achievement motivation nor is it the only background in which such motivation can develop. Thus, the sociological factors found in these studies should not be used as selection criteria. Rather, a direct assessment is needed of her character, high tolerance for ambiguity, and plenty of energy and endurance, which she'll need!

Unfortunately, individuality, energy and an outside identification can be seen by an interviewer as indicating a nonconformist and potential trouble-maker. Such a woman does not fit "feminine" expectations. Yet the qualities for managerial functions are not standard female role expectations. Fear of a "trouble-maker" may be fear of an independent thinker. The interviewer's bias, if any, must be compensated for by using another interviewer who does not share a similar bias.

Assessment Centers Need to Include Women Among the Managerial Candidates

Some large companies such as Standard Oil and the Bell System have been using assessment centers for several years to identify men as candidates for management positions. Some of the methods being developed are proving successful in predicting future success among men over a long period of time. Longitudinal studies are being done.[10] The programs had no women involved at their inception. Therefore, there is no assessment center information available today for predicting the success of women in managerial roles. Where there are early identification plans and assessment center programs, it is urgent that women be included now to start building data for identifying future women managers.

One of the key innovators in this field, Douglas Bray, quickly recognizes the difficulty managers have in identifying unrealized potential in men, and how much more difficult it is for women. He comments that "even her own boss may be skeptical about advancing her, since the undemanding nature of many entry jobs for women does not allow for a real demonstration of ability."[1] This is organizational bias, structured into the entry-level position system.

Clearly, an objective assessment of ability is needed, not only to persuade men supervising new women managers, but to determine that she actually has the required capabilities. Considerable new work may be needed in this assessment process to take into account the effects of cultural sex bias. The final selection criteria must, of course, be the same for both men and women. But the means to getting there may be quite different. Substantial changes in self-concept can and do take place in many achieving women. Such changes are less centrally important for men. Cultural expectations for each sex create these differences.

Sponsorship as a Means of Preparing Women for Managerial Responsibilities

In deciding how to move women ahead in management, employers might examine how men get ahead and compare this with how women are advanced. Social psychologist Dr. Martha White has found one such difference for women in science. Women are left out of the informal sponsorship system through which a young man advances by virtue of being the protege of an older, established person.

"Unfortunately, a man may be hesitant about encouraging a woman as a protege," Dr. White says. "He may be delighted to have her as an assistant, but he may not see her as a colleague. He may believe that she is less likely to be a good gamble, that she is financially less dependent upon a job. Because of subtle pressure from his wife, he may temper his publicly expressed enthusiasm or interest. Furthermore, he may fail to introduce her to colleagues or sponsor her for jobs."[1][2]

Management-directed women find few women mentors available and it is rare for a man to choose a woman as a protege. This sets up an insidious cycle: women do not advance rapidly in part because they lack the insights and contacts women managers could give them, resulting in very few women managers to serve as mentors for younger aspiring women.

Women executives and managers should be encouraged to take on such a role, *but* it must not be women alone who are made responsible for women.[13] That would ensure the future numbers of women in management would remain almost as low as today. Men managers, too, must identify women subordinates who have potential as managers and sponsor them as they would men. In fact, men managers should be expected by their superiors to coach aspiring women toward managerial preparation, and later sponsor them.

Re-examining Relevancy of Past Experience Can Prove Fruitful

For the mature woman with some relevant experience, the career ladder should be open for entry or re-entry at the most appropriate rung instead of automatically starting at the bottom. Positions which provide equivalent development experience but are not now considered part of the management development sequence should be reconsidered for their relevant value. For example, a mature woman's community experience may have been extensive in budget and finance, personnel, coordination and planning. Some few organizations now recognize such experience on their personnel forms and in hiring, placement and training decisions. Indeed, social agency experience at the board or committee chairman level is highly comparable to some middle and upper management positions of small and medium-size profit organizations. Or, complex political campaign administration can require similar capabilities as are needed for certain middle management and staff positions. Finally, most difficult to subjectively identify are latent "natural" capabilities that come into use in the challenge of increased responsibilities. Objective assessment methods are needed to assist managers in these choices.

Because most women's life-styles are different from most men's does not automatically make them less valuable—only different. Relevant experience can be garnered from many sources. Any other assumption could produce biased effects.

Awareness Training Is a New Idea in Changing the Climate

Awareness training is a new concept developing with women's affirmative action programs. There are at least three kinds worth considering:

1. Management awareness of cultural bias and sex-role expectations that prevail in the organization and in attitudes of managers at all levels.

2. Women's awareness of their perception of themselves in their career development objectives and considering many new alternatives. For those women who are already aware, the next phase is coping with change in reaching their new objectives, including their part in changing the stereotypic expectations they may face and their responses to them.

3. Men's awareness of what it means to them to be involved in many new working relationships with women as colleagues and sometimes superiors. Changes in women's roles as they move up in managerial expertise will certainly impact men's roles and responses as managers.

Among management training and development people, there is considerable interest as well as concern about such programs and how they should be conducted. Without question, the subject of sex factors in employment, especially management, is potentially volatile in today's climate of active feminism. Polarization between the sexes is just one of many long-buried attitudes that may surface with some intensity as these changes are explored. Objective recognition of the sub-rosa attitudes can greatly facilitate their being handled or resolved. While certain behaviors are now illegal, attitudes are personal even though some may be less than generally acceptable. In awareness training, changing standards of acceptability are also explored.

Films, Discussion, Role-Reversal
Are Tools for Awareness Training

Many new tools for conducting awareness training are currently being developed. Films, discussions, experiences in role-reversal situations are among the early developments. One film, *51 percent*, is valuable in opening up discussion and awareness in managements where the subject is new. It presents three women from different experiential and educational backgrounds, through whom the changing roles of women are played. Viewers see how their attitudes and actions can change the work situation to help reduce barriers to using women's potential for management. It treats the subject generally and is useful as an opener to awareness.

A new film, *Women: Up the Career Ladder*, which this [article's] authors cooperatively designed and produced, goes into work patterns and feelings more deeply. Eight women discuss and cope with their own real problems and possible solutions. Employee follow-up discussion of the various issues in the film usually brings to the surface responses which reveal more underlying expectations that men and women have for each other. It has been used variously: with groups of women only, with mixed groups, with management levels, or with only middle and lower supervision levels.

The Civil Service Commission has an excellent film, *What's the Matter with Alice?* that focuses on those attitudes around a minority woman that can limit her advancement and full use of her education. The process of non-conscious discouragement and non-communication is clearly portrayed and insightfully done.

A variety of pencil-paper tools and awareness readings are also being developed which bring to the surface some of the attitudes that carry a double standard or reflect cultural expectations.

Self-concept inventories are being developed to give persons taking them some insights on how they see themselves and their aspirations in a context of sex-roles. Some of these may develop into new selection tools for management development.

It is our feeling that management awareness training of the first type should be done with all managers and supervisors as one of the first implementation steps of an affirmative action program. The other two types can best be handled as a part of the regular management development program, first on a separate-sex basis, then together. Various task exercises can be used that involve a "trading of expectations" between groups. Many such training tools have already been developed for use in minority awareness programs, as well as in resolving interdepartmental conflicts. With appropriate modifications to fit the subject of sex-role bias, there are a number of useful communication exercises and team-task projects that can be adapted. Care needs to be taken that they accomplish the purpose intended. Review by the women's affirmative action officer is vital before using them in training situations.

This initial awareness training attempts to activate required behavior changes and begins to develop an awareness of attitudes that take longer to perceive.

Management Development Implications for Women—And Men

A woman can't become a good manager without appropriate training any more than a man can. She must develop her skills by moving into progressively more responsible positions where she can use her capabilities and be held accountable for the results. She also needs to attend the same management and supervisory training programs available to similarly qualified men. In addition, some women working in a male-valued environment may need training programs that deal with new working relationships with men. And certainly men may need to reconsider their old attitudes about a woman when she, formerly a subordinate, becomes a peer.

As noted previously, a good assessment program is essential to be able to objectively measure both women and men in their management capability, progress and advancement potential. Objectivity needs to prevail, whether it's a small-scale program, or a major management assessment center program.

In the first phase of management development, basic managerial skills need to be emphasized and provision made for advance preparation in weak areas. Key processes, that all managers must have a good grasp of, should be defined by the organization and would include such items as:
● Having the ability to develop goals and objectives

- Being able to build a plan to implement these goals interrelating them with others
- Capable of effective communications, especially with people but also written and formal presentations
- Able to resolve or balance conflicts between work, interests and people
- Good at problem solving in all its phases, with work processes and people problems
- Balanced decision making, carefully weighing the important elements and generally using good judgment
- Able to determine priorities with flexibility, to change as needed, and stick with them when necessary.

Undoubtedly there are others considered essential in some places and not in others. In addition to this general managerial ability list, there usually are further areas that the new woman manager may want or need in her personal development. Moving from subordinancy and relative powerlessness into a position of a different kind of subordinancy with possession of some power can present a woman manager with many new questions. The initial bridge, with open discussion of concerns and alternatives, can be critical at this stage of development for some women. Certainly not all will find this change difficult.

It is later, when moving from middle management into higher management that many successful women have experienced some identity crises and have broken through the competence-femininity conflict into a "fully-functioning person" self-concept.[14] Early awareness of these double-binds can help resolve them before they reach high conflict proportions.

The focus here is on some of the male-female dimensions of management development. It is assumed that the qualifications educationally and technically are present, or being developed in preparation for management development. If the organization is under pressure to have more women in management training, they may feel a need to select a woman who is not ready for such training. If this is the case, it is essential that she be given sufficient preparatory training to give her a basis for additional management training work. When both are done simultaneously, the added pressure on the woman must be taken into consideration when evaluating her achievements.

To knowingly select a person who is underqualified without giving the essential support for probable success is a waste of time and effort on the part of the organization and the woman trainee. It will be better to take more preparatory time and adjust the timetable for accomplishing an increase in the number of women in management training. However, it will be necessary to convince most compliance officers that any delay is not, in fact, lack of good faith. Objective evidence of the need to delay management training pending further preparatory training may be required. Surely some indication that such training is in process is essential. The pressures for promotion will undoubtedly increase as affirmative action programs are implemented.

Promotion Is Where the Barriers Based on Sex Become Most Apparent

Often the very structure of an organization makes it almost impossible for a woman to be promoted. Male managers may be quite willing to promote women, yet find it impossible as long as they follow company rules and policies. Sex-segregated jobs make it difficult for women to achieve promotion because managerial positions in such an organization typically require "male" job prerequisites. The EEOC's investigators have found this to be the case in several companies.[15]

Seniority, in some companies, may be a barrier to women's advancement. When seniority is considered to be total time spent working for the company, women are considered equally. But when seniority is based on time spent in a department and potential managers come only from male-dominated departments, it works against women. Further, if women lose seniority because of maternity breaks in employment, they suffer a sex-linked, discriminatory disadvantage. Seniority rules of that kind are now in violation of the law. Career ladders with vertical and lateral transfers must be developed to provide ways for women to move out of the traditional pattern of dominating the lower job categories. Long-term improvement hinges on there being known ways to advance within the organization. This fact must be made credible by evidence of women having been promoted from within.

Where women are being introduced for the first time into a particular management level or into an all-male work unit, consideration must be given to the best way to introduce such change. Tokenism with its deleterious effects should be avoided if at all possible. One way to avoid it is to bring more than one woman into previously all-male positions or work units. Women coming into higher responsibilities may need some preparation for coping with being pioneers. Certainly the men in the all-male climate may need some preparation for coping with this change.

As one training officer of a major electrical company said, "Our men have gotten their early education in all-male classes, often studied at male institutions, have worked in and been promoted to positions where only men work, and now our management is all male. They just don't know what to do with the idea of working with women as co-professionals." Too often this is the stark reality of long-standing cultural bias. This group will need awareness training, probably of the introductory kind as well as in more operational depth. . . .

Footnotes

1. Excerpted from "Affirmative Action Programs for Women: Requirements and Recommendations," Womanpower Consultants, Berkeley, CA 94703. October 1, 1971, p. 3.

2. Ibid., pp. 3-4.

3. Caroline Bird, *Born Female: The High Cost of Keeping Women Down* (New York: Pocket Books, 1st printing, May, 1969), pp. 43-44.

4. Charles D. Orth and Frederick Jacobs, "Women in Management: Pattern for Change," *Harvard Business Review*, July-August, 1971, p. 144.

5. *Fact Sheet on the Earnings Gap*, U.S. Department of Labor, Employment Standards Administration, Women's Bureau, December, 1971 (rev.), p. 5.

6. Theodora Wells, "Woman's Self-Concept: Implications for Management Development," Chapter in Gordon L. Lippitt, Leslie E. This, and Robert G. Bidwell, Jr. (eds.), *Optimizing Human Resources* (Reading, Mass.: Addison-Wesley Publishing Co., 1971), p. 303.

7. Ibid., p. 304.

8. Summarized from Bird McCord, "Identifying and Developing Woman for Management Position," *Training and Development Journal*, November, 1971, p. 4.

9. "How Are Career-Oriented Women Different," *Capsule* (published by ERIC Counseling and Personnel Services Information Center, Ann Arbor, Michigan 48104), Spring, 1971, p. 10. The article is a summary of three recent research studies comparing "college women who chose conventional career goals with those who chose unconventional career goals (an occupation which is now dominated by men)." The studies are: Elizabeth M. Almquist and Shirley I. Angrist, "Career Choice Salience and Atypicality of Occupational Choice Among College Women, *Journal of Marriage and the Family*, 1970, 32(2), pp. 242-248; Florence S. Tangri, "Role Innovation in Occupational Choice Among College Women," Michigan University, 1969; and Mary L. Walshok, "The Social Correlated and Sexual Consequences of Variations in Gender Role Orientation: A National Study of College Students," Indiana University, 1969.

10. William C. Byham, "Assessment Centers for Spotting Future Managers," *Harvard Business Review*, July-August, 1970, pp. 150-160.

11. Douglas M. Bray, "The Assessment Center: Opportunities for Women," *Personnel*, Sept.-Oct., 1971, p. 31.

12. Martha S. White, "Psychological and Social Barriers to Women in Science," *Science*, October 23, 1970, p. 414.

13. Orth and Jacobs, "Women in Management," pp. 145-146.

14. Margaret Hennig, "What Happens on the Way Up," *The MBA*, March, 1971, p. 10. This article is a summary of her dissertation research for her DBA from Harvard, entitled "Career Development for Women Executives."

15. For an example of a thorough analysis of how this allegedly operates in the Bell System, see "A Unique Competence," Equal Employment Opportunity Commission, Washington, D.C.

Sandra Ekberg-Jordan *is Director, Graduate Management Program for Women, Pace University, New York, New York.*

This article is reprinted with permission from Atlanta Economic Review, *March-April 1976, pp. 47-50.*

21
Preparing for the Future: Commitment and Action

Sandra Ekberg-Jordan

MANY COMPANIES will have to initiate more vigorous affirmative action programs if larger numbers of women are to be brought into management soon and given the opportunity to experience the same sense of options about their careers that men have. If a business organization wishes to improve its compliance with EEO requirements and to be known as progressive, it should incorporate many of the following concepts into its affirmative action program. I would suggest the following steps:

1. Discussion of the company's written affirmative action policy with, and distribution of the policy among, as many employees as possible. Fears may exist among some men that they will be replaced by women; thus any step the organization takes to clarify its objectives and their implementation will help to create a more realistic and favorable atmosphere for acceptance of the affirmative action policy.

Employee meetings also serve to reinforce top management's belief in affirmative action and intention to correct any existing imbalances. Where programs exist only on paper and are not reassessed and reaffirmed at regular intervals—at least annually—little attention is likely to be paid to the programs.

2. Appointment of an affirmative action officer who reports to top management. In most organizations it makes sense for a woman to be appointed to this position, in part because such an appointment publicly affirms the company's belief in giving women good jobs. In addition, a woman is more likely to be sensitive to the problems experienced by other women in the organization and is thus more credible to them.

In those companies in which equality of opportunity is a genuine goal, the affirmative action officer should be assigned internal responsibilities—meeting with department managers, women employees, and advisory committees within the organization and top management to report on progress and problems and to recommend new action.

3. Recruitment and hiring of qualified women. This can be accomplished through on-campus recruiting programs and by using the services of executive search firms that specialize in finding women for all levels of management jobs.

If a company is honest about its efforts to hire women, it also will take a close look at its annual report and its recruiting materials. One thing that discourages potential women applicants is company literature that makes no reference to women. Many larger corporations have been revising their materials to include photographs of women in professional, technical, or managerial positions and references to managers as "she's" as well as "he's." As women develop greater awareness of the subtleties of employment discrimination, they will look more critically at a company's written materials.

4. Reassessment of career paths. No longer should any woman who expresses interest in a career be placed in a dead-end job, whether it be at a clerical or staff level. To assure all interested employees of career ladders, many firms may need to analyze existing positions and possibly reassign job responsibilities so that upward mobility will be possible from a larger number of positions. Salary scales for all positions should be equal for both men and women.

5. Career counseling for women employees. Women employed by the organization may never have had career counseling during their school years, and they may be unaware of the need to think ahead about career paths. Regular meetings

led by personnel staff or outside consultants to talk about affirmative action plans and the company's career ladders can help currently employed women to learn what career options exist and to define long-range career goals. Such meetings also will assist corporate personnel staff members in learning which women may be interested in further responsibilities and which may prefer to remain at their current level.

6. Informal meetings for new women in management. Established women managers employed by the company or by other companies in the area should be invited to meet with new managers. The experienced women will serve as role models for the newer managers and may be able to offer advice and to share experiences that will be helpful to the neophytes.

7. Encouragement of women to improve their knowledge. Information should be made available to women about credit courses that will prepare them for new levels of responsibility as well as conferences and professional meetings that will contribute to their personal development.

If women have not had an opportunity to complete undergraduate course work and if having degrees is important to their long-range career goals, they should be encouraged to look not only to traditional undergraduate programs, but also to those programs that offer adults credit for skills learned on the job or through workshops or other noncredit courses.

Those for whom graduate business course work is considered an advantage should be encouraged to investigate special MBA programs designed for working men and women. At Pace University two daytime master's level business programs have been established to encourage corporate employees to return to school. One is the Executive MBA Program, which is designed for those with at least eight years of business experience. Its classes meet alternate Fridays and Saturdays. The second is the Friday/Saturday Program within the Graduate Management Program for Women. The latter is open to those with undergraduate degrees and no specific business experience. Classes meet all or part of the day Friday and Saturday during the first year of study and are supplemented by special seminars, a communications workshop, and assertiveness training, features which are designed to help new managers become more effective on the job. During their second year of study, students continue their course work at night.

8. Development of an assessment technique to measure the progress made by women in different departments. If individual career programs have been developed for all women selected for management level positions, an affirmative action staff member will be able to sit down annually (or more frequently) with each department manager to learn how each individual woman under his or her supervision is doing, what additional training or experience she needs, how she can best obtain it, and when she will be ready for further responsibility.

To assure that women managers are being groomed for continued advancement, each department manager should be held responsible for the development of women within his department. If his own performance evaluation includes an assessment of how well women have been counseled and given the professional exposure they need, the department manager will be motivated to treat the women under him as seriously as he would the men.

9. Public posting of all open positions and access to personnel representatives with whom to discuss the openings. The installation of bulletin boards in prominent locations for posting weekly listings of new openings can help to make women aware of what advancement possibilities exist.

10. Establishment of a Women's Advisory Committee to recommend programs and policies to the affirmative action officer or to senior management. This committee might be composed of men and women representing different departments. Permitting women to select some of their own representatives will be helpful in getting legitimate feedback as to the women employees' true feelings.

11. Sponsorship of sensitivity workshops for men and women at managerial levels to explore their attitudes and develop an awareness of how they feel about women in management. Their purpose would be to dispel stereotyped attitudes and to change discriminatory behavior. Such workshops might be led by consultants specializing in affirmative action or by trained staff members.

12. Development of a sponsorship procedure for women managers. In many professions and businesses, an older man will assume sponsorship of a younger man, introduce him to colleagues, and generally acquaint him with the informal customs and rituals of the field. Similarly, corporations need to

encourage middle and senior male managers to act as sponsors of women.

13. Establishment of flexible hours and part-time positions where possible, which will allow women, as well as male employees, with young children to work different schedules from those of regular employees. The government has been attempting to develop increased numbers of part-time positions, particularly as a means of allowing educated women to balance family responsibilities with the use of their skills and experience.[1]

14. Reevaluation of policies regarding maternity leaves, making it possible for new mothers to return after a specified period without loss of credit toward vacations, retirement, or other benefits. In addition to maternity leave, companies need to consider paternity leaves, as many young couples are interested in sharing the parenting process.

15. Review of relocation policies. Concern over the need for relocation is expressed by employers and by potential and actual women managers. Although some single and some married women may view relocation as an exciting prospect, others may consider it unpleasant or impossible. Some single women object to transfers as they feel it is more difficult for them to build a social life in a new community than it is for a family, which, through the children's school and the community associations developed by the wife, can readily acquire new friends.

For married professional couples who do not wish to live apart, a relocation decision may rest on economic considerations, with the highest wage earner having the most say in any decision. A few married couples—with or without children—prefer to pursue their individual careers in whatever directions they may take them and to commute weekends so as to spend time together.[2] Although the latter concept has not been widely adopted, it may become more popular—at least among childless career couples—in the future.

Two-career families may well become more commonplace in the future; thus assessment by a company of its relocation policies is important. Is it really necessary for someone to relocate in order to gain the experience thought necessary for career development? Or will some other kind of experience, not requiring relocation, do as well? The need for reviewing relocation policies should not be based on a desire only to accommodate women. Undoubtedly, as both husbands and wives work and share more equally in their financial contributions to the family, men, too, will begin asserting their preference not to move.

16. Funding of day-care centers. Thus far, our society has not accepted the position that good child care is a government responsibility. Existing child care centers are available to only a few, and the care of children has remained largely a personal family responsibility. Supporters of women's rights are seeking alternate solutions, for private arrangements are costly and government tax allowances for private child care deductions are limited to certain income levels. In the future, companies interested in attracting women with young children may offer day-care services for their employees. In an area where several companies are clustered, a center might be jointly built and operated. Parents with young children could leave their offspring during working hours and visit with them at lunch.

Conclusion

Women are becoming more optimistic about what the future holds for them. This is especially true for younger women, many of whom are excited about job opportunities. According to a 1974 Roper poll, more than half of the women surveyed indicated that they plan to combine careers with marriage and children.[3] Thus, the female job applicants with whom corporate recruiters and personnel managers talk in 1976 and the decade ahead will expect many more opportunities for advancement than did women employees of 5 or 10 years ago.

Women also are becoming more knowledgeable about their legal rights, and are being urged through the media and by women's groups to ask for their legal due. Women are bringing suits against companies, the effects of which can be financially costly and damaging to the organizations' reputation. John Kenneth Galbraith has argued that legal pressure is needed to break the male monopoly on jobs and has recommended that major corporations be given a ten-year period in which "to bring the representation of women at various salary levels into general accord with their representation in the work force as a whole."[4] Galbraith's view is not universally shared. Others have argued that giving companies a set number of years in which to bring themselves into compliance provides the companies with convenient excuses for not bringing about real change in the interim.[5]

Whether corporations are given a ten-year grace period or less, all business organizations face the need to develop the policies and programs that will make it possible for women to experience true equality on the job within the near future. It's up to each business to contribute to societal change through a commitment by senior management to an affirmative action program that guarantees elimination of sexist policies and practices. The time to make that commitment is today.

Footnotes

1. U.S. Civil Service Commission, "The Federal Women's Program—A Point of View" (Washington, D.C., U.S. Government Printing Office, 1972).

2. Francine E. Gordon and Myra Strober, *Bringing Women into Management* (New York, McGraw-Hill, 1975), pp. 139-147.

3. "The Virginia Slims American Women's Opinion Poll," vol. III (The Roper Organization, 1974), p. 1.

4. John Kenneth Galbraith, *Economics and the Public Purpose* (Boston, Houghton Mifflin Company, 1973), p. 258.

5. "Female Employment Opportunities: Some Recent Research Findings" (Philadelphia, Hay Associates, June 1974), p. 9.

Dr. Rae Rohfeld *is Director of the Clearing-house for Research on Women and Employment, Institute of Urban Studies, Cleveland State University.*

22
Women in Management: Can Education Fill the Gap?

Rae Rohfeld

DESPITE EQUAL EMPLOYMENT opportunity laws, despite pressures of the women's movement, and despite rumors of preferential hiring of women, employment and salary figures show women are still second-class citizens in the executive suite. In 1973, fourteen percent of employed men were managers and administrators, but only five percent of employed women held such positions. The median income for those women who did attain such jobs was fifty-three percent of the median male administrators' income.[1] Women's groups and government agencies press employers to correct these inequalities. Employers reply that they cannot find qualified women; that they would love to hire women if only they had the right training.[2]

This article reviews research which confirms that women have indeed continued to train for traditional fields despite exhortations to go into business administration, engineering, or other nontraditional fields. It indicates that changes in female education may finally be occurring and suggests steps that employers can take to encourage or assist women in achieving appropriate education. It also discusses research that places limits on the lack-of-training explanation for the paucity of women in management and suggests that women may still have to be "better" than men to be considered qualified.

Present Career Plans of Women

According to the U.S. Women's Bureau, nine out of ten women will work at some time in their lives,[3] and the average woman will spend twenty-five years in the labor force.[4] The more education a woman has, the more likely she is to work. Chances are, therefore, that a woman's college training will be far more than "something to fall back on, just in case. . . ." Research shows that a portion of college women do recognize this likelihood; however, just what portion is open to some question. One study found that forty-three percent of the females sampled were career-oriented;[5] another forty-eight percent;[6] and still another, seventy percent.[7] The highest percentage of female students reporting career plans was eighty-two percent in a study conducted at Macalester College.[8]

To what extent are these women who are planning careers looking toward management fields? Available research is not encouraging to those seeking a rapid increase in the number of women candidates for management, although some very recent figures suggest change may at last be occurring.

When Helen Astin and Ann Bisconti studied career plans of 1965 and 1970 graduates, they found only two percent of the women *in both classes* chose nonclerical, business careers.[9] Teaching remained the single predominant choice of half the women. Furthermore, during their college years, women in both classes shifted out of fields deemed "masculine" and generally turned to teaching.

Some evidence of changing patterns did emerge for the class of 1970. Keeping in mind the very small number of women starting in the "male" fields, the Astin-Bisconti study found that those women were less likely to shift out of the "male" fields to teaching than those surveyed from the class of 1965, and more women shifted from other fields into business. Further, the proportion of women business majors planning to be business executives rose from thirteen percent to thirty percent.[10]

Since large proportions of both men and women are liberal arts majors, it is instructive to compare career interests that Astin and Bisconti found among these students. Women liberal arts majors did not appear to have strong interests in business careers. This was quite unlike the picture for men, many of whom expected a liberal arts education to be applicable in business settings. Thus, in both professional and liberal arts curricula, aspiration to business leadership remained part of the male role concept.

A study of degrees conferred during 1973-1974 in the Cleveland Metropolitan Area confirms the sex segregation of many educational programs, both locally and nationally. In the area's associate degree programs, "every individual occupational program was segregated or stereotyped by sex, with at least two-thirds of the graduates in each program being of the same sex."[11] Men received more than ninety percent of the associate degrees in business management. A similar pattern occurred at the bachelor's level where ninety percent of those business management degrees were also received by men. Cleveland's figures were very close to the national level, where only about two percent more women received bachelor's degrees in business.[12] The most current figures show the effect of special attention being given to attracting women. The Boston University School of Management reported twenty-eight percent of its 1974 entering class was female after the staff made a strong effort to recruit women. The Stanford Graduate School of Business reported nearly twenty percent of its 1974 entering class was female—up from one percent five years before.[13] The amount of change required for women to recognize business opportunities to the same extent that men do, however, is so great that special concern about how to motivate women to seek those opportunities will be required for some time.

How Women Choose Careers

In the days before the current women's movement, traditional patterns were attributed to the natural interests of the sexes or to women's almost universal desire to plan for a home-centered life. Now it is most common to attribute occupational choices to learned behavior—to socialization to particular sex roles. For the most part, researchers assume that since sex roles are learned they can also be changed.

Socialization to sex role begins almost at birth. In studying mothers' behavior, mothers of girl babies were observed touching and talking to their babies more often than mothers of infant boys. By thirteen months these girls and boys interacted differently with their mothers.[14] Continuing input from family, media, and associates teaches pre-schoolers to distinguish between male and female roles. By the age of three, children begin to express sex-role preferences; by four, their preferences are stronger.[15] Thereafter, children intensify these sex-role differences, and society rewards them for doing so.

Of course, experiences intervene in the lives of many to counteract the forces toward stereotyped behavior and to allow people to accept more options in their lives. The factor most consistently associated with both a positive view of female competence and career commitment among young women is the mother's presence in the work force. While work force activity of parents and attitudes of family members toward work have already had their effect on today's young women, other experiences which take place during college years also seem to have an effect on career commitment of women. These are the areas in which faculty and employers can encourage exploration of new ways for women to develop their potential.

Women who are oriented to careers, and particularly to nontraditional careers, report broad exposure to a variety of experiences. Almquist and Angrist found that women desiring nontraditional careers identified their career choices as similar to their male friends. They also had more jobs and a greater variety of jobs than women not seeking such careers.[16] This would suggest that contact with people in varying occupations through campus visits and opportunities for experience through field work and internships could open new career possibilities for women. Such opportunities could be increased if employers and educators worked together to plan them.

In addition to having a broad base of experience, women interested in traditionally male careers have reported that the influence of faculty and workers in the field was of major importance. According to Almquist and Angrist, these women perceived professors as having a more positive evaluation of their abilities than did the non-career-oriented women.[17] Tangri found that women who were "occupational role innovators" received support from faculty in their major fields.[18] Whether or not a student senses faculty support may be due to either internal conditions—her own self-esteem—or external conditions—the feelings and behavior of the faculty member. Some women may be more prepared to recognize faculty support and encouragement than others. Nevertheless, faculty members who are aware of the influence they can have on women's career plans might take the initiative more often to encourage women to explore their interests and the fields that are available to them.

Peer support is also important in encouraging women in whichever direction they take. Tangri found that occupational role innovators had the support of both male and female college friends.[19] Angrist and Almquist found that career-oriented women identified with male peers. On the other hand, a high proportion of their non-career-oriented women were sorority members, and these students felt their families or their peers had been their primary influences in determining their future roles.[20] The women in both studies may have selected friends and associates who had similar values to begin with, but they would be unusual college populations if there were not many among them who were uncertain of their interests and were susceptible to peer pressures.

The importance of peer acceptance and support is additional reason for exposing all students to experiences, studies, and counseling that enables them to recognize that many options are open to them which will not violate their sexual identity. The key word here is "options." Many women (and men) will continue to choose occupations or adopt life styles that reflect more traditional sex roles. But it is an objective of educational institutions to help students understand their society and culture. Focusing on changing roles aids students in their intellectual and their personal growth. The topics can be approached from both theoretical and experiential directions. Attention to these issues can enable students to take advantage of new opportunities if they choose and also to give support to the explorations and choices of others.

Thus far, the discussion has centered on issues involved in encouraging young women just entering the work force to plan and train for management. We do not want to overlook women already at work as a resource for management. In a recent survey, fifty-two Cleveland business firms reported that during 1974, 167 women moved into 150 jobs not previously held by women in those companies. A large majority of these women received the new positions by promotion.[21]

Utilization of employed women as a resource necessitates consideration of company training opportunities and practices. In 1973 labor economist Hilda Kahne stated, "It is regrettable that even today relatively few companies include women in their training programs, and they do not evaluate managerial capabilities of women when recruiting for entry-level jobs."[22] Dr. Kahne called for small working conferences in specific areas to think through concrete policies for enabling women to participate in management "within a reasonable period of time."[23]

Discrimination Against Women in Hiring

Having argued that attention to education and training may go far toward enabling women to reach their potential as managers, we must point out that it is not the total answer. It appears that women's underrepresentation in management is not due solely to a lack of appropriately trained women.

Women students have heard a great deal about opportunities available to them if they have the training, but credibility is still an issue. A study of job candidates in the fields of business, engineering, and science at Pennsylvania State University found that many recruiters asked different questions of male and female candidates. For example, they asked women, but not men, about family plans. They also appeared to assume men were planning long-range careers, but there were no such assumptions about women. The majority of the female candidates thought the recruiter discouraged them from employment because of sex.[24]

Many female job candidates never see a recruiter on campus. Dr. Kahne reported in 1973 that only thirty percent of the companies which recruited on college campuses went to women's colleges. Twice that number went to men's schools. She also believed that even those recruiters who did visit women's campuses did not seek women for the key entry-level positions representing the first step into management.[2][5]

Another aspect of sex-segregated recruitment is illustrated by a pilot study of 1973 psychology graduates of Cleveland State University. These were liberal arts graduates, open to applying their training in a number of directions. A survey elicited information concerning the jobs they had obtained. Those men and women who found employment in public or non-profit agencies occupied similar types of positions, and their mean salary was also about the same. But men and women who took jobs in private industry were frequently placed in "male" and "female" positions. Examples of women's jobs were secretary, administrative assistant, and dress shop manager. Examples of males' jobs were industrial sales, customer relations, and insurance claims adjuster. The sex segregation also showed up in the salaries paid by private firms where the mean annual salary for women was $4,400 less than that of men.[2][6]

The Clearinghouse for Research on Women and Employment at Cleveland State University hopes to expand this study in order to understand these phenomena better. It is possible that more research will uncover differences earlier in the socialization process which override the similarity of the college education. At present, however, the results of this small survey certainly suggest some differences in the recruiting of men and women among the private employers represented. Men have long risen in business on the foundation of a liberal arts education. Are women with the same background to be declared "not qualified"?

Implications for Employers

The research discussed previously suggests a number of ways in which business and industry can join higher education institutions in developing the management potential of women. First among these is providing opportunities for women to observe and experience nontraditional jobs through various types of field experience. Existing programs providing field experience need to be evaluated in terms of introducing students to nontraditional occupations. Many such programs simply serve to provide practical experience in occupations already decided on. But cooperative education programs, in which students alternate work and study quarters, may offer one model for broadening horizons. While not all students would find a complete co-op program suitable, many would benefit from other special efforts to provide vacation jobs with the specific purpose of exploring career options. Higher education institutions can coordinate and facilitate such programs, but employers have to take the initiative in providing jobs or non-paid educational experiences.

A second need is for the reevaluation of the means used to identify and train women who are already employed. This could involve clarification of the characteristics which the firm uses to identify management potential and consideration of ways to motivate women who have this potential. It would also require a review of training needs and possibly the development of new training to meet the special needs of female managers as well as the needs of males in adjusting to females as colleagues and superiors. The training itself could be done in cooperation with universities.

Third is the need to review initial recruitment activities. This might lead to the hiring of female recruiters and to programs to sensitize male recruiters to subtle forms of discrimination they must avoid. Recruiters can also play the role of educator and counselor, helping women with liberal arts training to explore the same job options their male classmates are considering. Thus recruitment will take on a more creative aspect.

Business and industry have a clear educational task in the process of developing and utilizing female management skills. Employers are the people most knowledgeable about what particular fields are like. If students are to have access to more role models, more work experience, and more support for their choices, both employers and faculty will have to recognize employers' roles as educators.

Women in management—can education fill the gap? Given the small numbers of women currently in training, the answer is "no." But business and industry do have the power to encourage young women to consider and to try out business careers, and they have the power to develop the skills of women who are already employed. We can make education fill the gap in female management if we attend to the shortcomings both in higher education institutions and in industry and if we make totally credible industry's desire to utilize the management skills of women.

Footnotes

1. U.S. Department of Labor, Women's Bureau, *Women Workers Today* (Washington, D.C., U.S. Government Printing Office, 1974), pp. 5-7.

2. U.S. Department of Labor, Women's Bureau, *Counseling for Careers in Business* (Washington, D.C., U.S. Government Printing Office), reprinted from *The Personnel Women*, July-August 1973, p. 1.

3. U.S. Department of Labor, Women's Bureau, *Twenty Facts on Women Workers* (Washington, D.C., U.S. Government Printing Office, 1972).

4. U.S. Department of Labor, Women's Bureau, *The Myth and the Reality* (Washington, D.C., U.S. Government Printing Office, 1972), p. 2.

5. Linda G. Erikson and Margaret L. Nordin, Sex role ideologies and career salaries of college women: A preliminary report (Washington, D.C., ERIC, 1974), from *Women Studies Abstracts*, vol. 4, no. 2, Summer 1975, p. 19.

6. Mervin B. Freedman, "The Role of the Educated Women: An Empirical Study of the Attitudes of a Group of College Women," *Journal of College Student Personnel*, vol. 6, no. 2, 1965, pp. 145-155.

7. Alberta E. Siegal and Elizabeth A. Curtis, "Familial Correlates of Orientation Toward Future Employment Among College Women," *Journal of Educational Psychology*, vol. 54, no. 1, 1963, p. 35.

8. Dorothy Dodge, *Attitudes of Undergraduate Women toward Careers*, Research report (St. Paul, Minnesota, Macalester College, June 1974), p. 5.

9. Helen Astin and Ann Bisconti, *Career Plans of College Graduates of 1965 and 1970*, Report No. 2 (Bethlehem, Pennsylvania, The CPC Foundation, 1973), p. 9.

10. Ibid., pp. 14-15.

11. Laverne C. Zell and Edric A. Weld, Jr., *Women's Participation in Higher Education: A Case Study of Degrees Conferred by Field of Study by Nine Colleges and Universities in the Cleveland Metropolitan Area, 1973-74* (Clearinghouse for Research on Women and Employment, Institute of Urban Studies, Cleveland State University, 1974), p. 6.

12. Ibid., p. 23.

13. *On Campus With Women*, No. 11 (Washington, D.C., Association of American Colleges, May 1975), pp. 8, 10.

14. Lenore J. Weitzman, "Sex-role Socialization," in *Women: A Feminist Perspective*, Jo Freeman (ed.) (Palo Alto, Mayfield Publishing Company, 1975), p. 112.

15. Willard W. Hartup and Elsie Zook, "Sex Role Preferences in Three and Four-Year Old Children," *Journal of Consulting Psychology*, vol. 24, no. 5, 1960, pp. 420-426.

16. Elizabeth N. Almquist and Shirley S. Angrist, "Role Model Influences on College Women's Career Aspirations," *Merrill-Palmer Quarterly of Behavior and Development*, vol. 17, no. 3, 1971, pp. 270-271.

17. Ibid.

18. Sandra Schwartz Tangri, "Determinants of Occupational Role Innovation Among College Women," *Journal of Social Issues*, vol. 28, no. 2, 1972, p. 190.

19. Ibid., pp. 191-192.

20. Almquist and Angrist, "Role Model Influences," pp. 269, 273.

21. Businessmen's Interracial Committee on Community Affairs, Action Group-up Project. 1974 Breakthrough Survey (Cleveland, Ohio, July 1, 1975), pp. 3-4.

22. Hilda Kahne, *Women in Management: Strategy for Increase* (Washington, D.C., Business and Professional Women's Foundation, 1974), p. 6.

23. Ibid.

24. Jean Baker Driscoll and H. Richard Hess, "The Recruiter: Women's Friend or Foe?" *Journal of College Placement*, Summer 1974, pp. 42-48.

25. Kahne, *Women in Management*, pp. 5-6.

26. Morton Slobin and Laverne C. Zell, *Jobs of Cleveland State University Graduates in Psychology*. Unpublished report, 1975.

Ms. Jayne I. Gackenbach *is a doctoral student in experimental psychology at Virginia Commonwealth University.* Ms. Marian Burke, *a doctoral student in the Graduate School of Management at the University of California at Los Angeles, was formerly an Instructor in the Marketing Department of the School of Business at Virginia Commonwealth University.* Dr. Stephen M. Auerbach *is Assistant Professor of Clinical Psychology at Virginia Commonwealth University.*

This article is reprinted with permission from Atlanta Economic Review, *March-April 1976, pp. 32-37.*

23

A 'Women in Business' Seminar: Exploring an Approach to Change in Sex-Role Awareness

Jayne I. Gackenbach, Marian Burke, and Stephen M. Auerbach

THE ROLE OF women in the corporate structure has become an increasingly active and controversial issue. Women are demanding equal opportunity to compete with men in the business world; and, given the present climate determined by recent EEOC decisions, it has become clear that there are no legal barriers to women in management. Yet, strong attitudinal barriers to female corporate advancement continue to exist. The present article deals with the usage in business and academia of seminars or courses designed to modify those attitudinal barriers which continue to impede the progress of women in management. Specifically, it will center around a discussion of the procedures involved in presenting such a course and in evaluating its impact on participants using attitudinal and personality measures.

The nature of the attitudinal barriers prevalent in the business world has been discussed by many writers, with analyses including conceptual formulations as well as empirical findings. From a conceptual point of view, Daddio discusses four behavioral systems in management which hold women back: the visibility, property value, sponsor-protege, and legal systems.[1] Women must be seen, not simply in terms of their sex but in relation to their abilities. In terms of dollar value, "women's jobs" are associated with less prestige and salary. Regarding sponsoring for higher level positions, the route to top-level executive positions is closed by male sponsors who cannot conceive of a woman taking over their jobs. Finally, legal pressure from other influential minority groups to place their constituents also contributes to the deceleration of women's advancement in the corporate structure. Shah talks about the many negative and misleading myths held by management about female workers.[2] These myths, ranging from "women are sick more" to "they don't really need the money," generally are based on the perceived inferiority of the feminine sex role in contemporary society.

Empirical evidence is offered by Rosen and Jerdee, who established that these attitudinal barriers are not held exclusively by males.[3] Males and females agree on what constitutes sex-role appropriate behavior for individuals in supervisory positions; both sexes value "male" traits above "female" traits.[4] On the basis of a survey of *Harvard Business Review* subscribers regarding sex stereotyping in business settings, Rosen and Jerdee further concluded that there are two general ways in which subtle sex discrimination is practiced: (a) through greater organizational concern for the careers of men than for those of women and (b) as a reflection of skepticism regarding women's abilities to balance work and family demands. In this regard, it is noted that this discrimination is practiced by males despite outward attempts to appear "liberal" and nondiscriminating toward females.[5]

Many recommendations have been made as to how to eliminate these debilitating attitudinal barriers, with suggestions ranging from the implementation of an affirmative action program to the development of management awareness seminars.[6] In terms of the latter, M. Barbara Boyle, President of the New York consulting firm Boyle/Kirkman Associates, reports success with in-house awareness seminars designed to develop manager awareness of the unconscious discrimination against women. Career awareness sessions also have been held for women to examine their motivations and ambitions.[7] The objective of such seminars is not to make all women managers.

Rather, the goal is the destruction of myths through attitude change, employing a variety of techniques including role-playing and role reversal. Interest in women's role in management is not limited to the corporate world. Seminars and special courses concerning women in management have been cropping up in business schools across the country. Margaret Hennig conducts a doctoral seminar at Harvard, "Women in Industry: Facts and Issues," and Francine Gordon and Myra Strober offer "The American Woman at Work" in the Graduate School of Business at Stanford. To date, little empirical evidence has surfaced to demonstrate the success of such seminars.

In the spring of 1975 the Marketing Department at Virginia Commonwealth University (VCU) in Richmond, Virginia, offered a seminar, "Women in Marketing and Business," to young men and women about to enter the business world. The overall aims of the seminar were: (a) to construct a training experience for the students that would also provide information about and serve as a model for the development of similar approaches within a university setting, (b) demonstrate the efficacy of utilizing sex-role related self-report measures as a means of monitoring the impact of such a course on the participants, and (c) to provide objective data using these measures which would provide descriptive information about the present seminar, thereby improving the quality of future seminars, and generate questions to be pursued in future research under more controlled conditions with larger samples of subjects.

In order to assess attitudinal and personality changes resulting from participation in the seminar, the measures were taken on a pre and post basis. The particular attitudes and personality states measured were chosen by the authors on the basis of hypotheses developed from the current sex-role literature in psychology, results of their previous research, and business-related questions raised by enrollment in such a course. Before moving to a detailed description of the seminar and the results of the evaluation, we will briefly discuss the hypotheses of the study and some general findings as they relate to the psychological literature on sex roles.

O'Leary, in a recent conceptual article, attempts to account for women's lowered status in the business community from a psychological perspective.[8] Among the attitudinal barriers she discusses are societal sex-role stereotypes, attitudes towards female competence, the prevalence of the "male managerial" model, and other influences which are external to the woman herself. She also notes the import of internal barriers such as fear of failure, low self-esteem, role conflict, and fear of success, which also serve to inhibit upward mobility in women. Particular emphasis is placed on the notion that women generally have poorer self-concepts than do men. Maccoby and Jacklin, however, argue that the sexes are similar in their overall level of self-satisfaction and that any sex differences are situation-specific.[9] Girls rate themselves higher in the area of social competence than do boys; boys see themselves as strong, powerful, dominant, competitive, and aggressive. Thus, when women enter the business environment they are stepping into a masculine domain, a situation which would be expected to result in low self-esteem due to increased role conflict for the woman. She is expected to be professional, independent, and rational in the business world and at the same time fulfill the typically feminine roles of nurturance and dependence. To the degree that she sees herself as having masculine characteristics and performing competently on the job, but also has interests in marriage and family, she more profoundly experiences this role conflict. If the conflict is strong enough, it will result in the suppression of achievement striving and a lack of desire to move up in the corporate structure.

Since degree of role conflict seems to be of central importance, in the present study two measures of attitudes towards women's changing sex roles were obtained. One measure evaluated these attitudes specifically in the business environment; the other focused specifically on the home/personal environment. It was found that both male and female students participating in the seminar were able to differentiate between sex-role appropriate behaviors in the home and those in the business environment. This tendency to perceive the home and business environment as differing regarding sex-role appropriate behavior may indicate that women may be able to alleviate role conflict by developing different sets of behaviors for each setting ("feminine" at home and in personal dealings, competitive and achieving in the business setting). Further support for this notion was obtained by Paloma and Garland, who found that in dual working couples there was no real change in family life or in the division of household tasks; when women go to work they add a role, they do not drop one.[10] Also relevant in this regard are the findings by Hawley and by French and Lesser that the emotional support of a significant male is critical in lowering a career woman's role conflict and therefore in increasing her self-esteem at work.[11]

As noted previously, this role conflict in women, if sufficiently severe, can result in a suppression in achievement striving. There is evidence to suggest that a woman's achievement strivings are mediated not only by worry over failure, but also by fears of the cost of success (success not being in accordance with her prescribed sex role). This "motive to avoid success" in women has recently been popularized by Horner,[12] though Tresemer has suggested it might more appropriately be termed "fear of sex-role inappropriateness."[13] Regardless of the terminology, if such fears do indeed exist they certainly could explain some part of women's past reluctance to assume managerial positions, and it would appear to be important to develop ways to alleviate these fears if females are to advance in the corporate structure. Thus, in the present study, a measure of fear of success was obtained from the students both prior to and subsequent to participation in the seminar, and scores on this measure in fact did decline somewhat among women students.

Method of Study

The students enrolled in the seminar were 7 male and 14 female junior and senior marketing majors in the College of Business at VCU. Their ages ranged from 19 to 28 years, and most were single. Although most were unemployed when they enrolled in the seminar, all had an employment history. Four black women were among the enrollees.

Seven measures were given the students on the first and on the last day of class. Four of these were attitude scales, and the other three measured general affective states. Two measures of sex-role attitude and one of sex-role identity were taken, as well as a measure of the achievement motive "fear of success." The affective states measured were anxiety, hostility, and depression.

The two sex-role attitude scales were employed since it was necessary to measure acceptance of the changing sex roles of women in society as these sex-role attitudes pertained to different environments (specifically the home/personal environment and the business environment). Consequently, the Spence and Helmreich Attitudes Towards Women Scale (AWS),[14] a 55-item self-report scale designed to measure "attitudes toward the rights and roles of women in contemporary society," constituted a measure of sex-role attitude in the home and personal environment. Peters, Terborg, and Taynor suggest that although the AWS contains items that deal with attitudes toward working women, the scale is too general to "be used exclusively for assessing stereotypes about women in management positions."[15] These authors therefore developed the Women as Managers Scale (WAMS), a 21-item questionnaire which measures sex-role attitudes in the business environment. This scale also was administered in the present study. It should be noted that analysis of the present data yielded no correlation between WAMS scores and scores based on a factorially derived subset of items on the AWS which purportedly get at vocational-educational attitudes. This further justifies usage of the WAMS in the present study.

A measure of sex-role identity was obtained from the Masculinity Femininity (Fe) scale of the California Psychological Inventory. The Fe scale consists of 38 items and measures "the masculinity or femininity of interests."[16]

Horner, as noted previously, identified a motive to avoid success in women. Due to the nature of the seminar it was thought pertinent to obtain some measure of fear of success. The motive to avoid success scale is a 29-item self-report scale designed to measure the degree to which an individual fears success.[17] Auerbach and Bowman have found that this scale correlates highly with the projective technique employed by Horner for measuring fear of success.[18]

Pre and post measures were also obtained on the emotional dimensions of anxiety, depression, and hostility. These were obtained from the Multiple Affect Adjective Check List, a 132-item adjective list that has been used extensively to measure state and trait anxiety, depression, and hostility.[19]

The course itself was an elective in the marketing curriculum. From the standpoint of the student, it was designed to serve as a sort of buffer between the rather protected academic environment and the reality of the business world. The purpose was to expose the students to the various types of discrimination and prejudice they may encounter, in themselves as well as in others, and to alternatives and strategies which might prove effective not only in coping with the existing situation but also in creating a more desirable situation for the future. The emphasis was not on "whose fault this is" but on the fact that a situation exists that seems not to be in the best interests of any of the parties concerned.[20]

During the first half of the semester, the class examined the changing market for women in business from a macro point of view by analyzing the changes in the various environments which meaningfully impact that market, i.e., the technological, political/legal, and sociocultural environment. The investigation of the technological environment concentrated on the fact that technology made it possible for women to do many things that their gender may have genuinely prevented their doing in the past (birth control techniques, increasing automation and the decreasing necessity for sheer muscle strength, which of course never was a prerequisite for managerial success). The "biological differences" argument was examined, with the conclusion that there is as much difference within one sex as between the sexes in traits deemed desirable in managers.

The Equal Rights Amendment was being debated in the Virginia General Assembly during the first weeks of the seminar. The lobbyists for both sides made information available to class members, who then debated the issue in class. Existing laws which now protect one's rights, especially those concerning employment, also were discussed.

The discussion of the sociocultural environment centered around the stereotypes that exist about both women and men, how they developed, and how they might be changed. Religion, the family, and the education system were examined as contributing to the development of stereotypes. Especially important to marketers, the image of women in advertisements was considered in some depth, with emphasis on the ability of advertisements to reinforce or create stereotypes and on the responsibility of marketers empowered with such an influential tool.

The second part of the semester was spent on a more micro

level, examining the situation of women in business settings. The Robert Drucker film "51%" was used to introduce this section through three short vignettes, since the film creates an awareness of some of the problems faced by women in their attempts to enter management. Several successful women from New York, Washington, and Richmond spoke to the class, relating problems they had experienced on the way up and the methods they found most useful in hurdling obstacles. The women, representing a banking association, a large pharmaceutical manufacturer, and a law firm, were most candid and were able to bring reality into the classroom. Another film, "Women: Up the Career Ladder," prepared by Theodora Wells at UCLA was used to further document the actual state of affairs. The *Harvard Business Review* study by Rosen and Jerdee was used to provide further examples of the subtle, unconscious types of discrimination the students could expect.[21]

The course concluded with a review of the changing managerial styles which should make the movement of women in management smoother (more emphasis on participatory management, a "theory y" emphasis which should encourage management to consider each employee as an individual, new practices such as flexible time and paired or shared jobs—in short, the humanization of the business environment).

Results

Scores on the AWS scale, both before and after the seminar, indicate that the present sample was quite liberal in its attitudes towards women's changing sex roles. It was more liberal than the college students in Spence and Helmreich's original normative sample,[22] and more liberal than the students in Lunnelong's sample (who were administered the AWS before and after a Psychology of Sex Differences course).[23] Other data (nonsignificant correlations between WAMS and AWS scores for males or females both before and after the seminar) indicated that the present sample of business students differentiated between their attitudes towards women's sex roles in the business environment and their attitudes towards women's sex roles in the home/personal environment. This somewhat surprising finding was in contrast to a highly positive correlation (.58, $p < .05$) obtained between these same two scales in a sample of women enrolled in a consciousness-raising group at VCU. Thus, though the distinction between the personal and business environments is somewhat blurred in this sense for women actively involved in the women's rights movement, both female and male business students differentiate between the two types of situations in terms of their attitudes towards sex roles.

Data for the evaluation of preseminar to postseminar changes in the various attitudes and personality states measured over the course of the seminar are summarized in Exhibit 1. It may be noted in Exhibit 1 that all students who participated in the seminar, as well as males and females as separate groups, expressed more positive attitudes towards women's changing sex roles in the home/personal environment (AWS) after participating in the seminar. Similar findings were obtained for the WAMS scale, which measures attitudes towards women's expanding role in business, although males increased on this scale only to a degree that approached statistical significance. Regarding the Fe scale, there was a tendency for the group as a whole to become more "masculine" in sex-role identity. On the fear of success measure, there was a tendency for the group to decline in reported fear of success from before to after the seminar, with females accounting entirely for the decrease. None of the three mood states which were measured (anxiety, hostility, depression) changed significantly over the course of the seminar for the group as a whole, but there was a tendency for males to be less depressed and also somewhat less anxious and hostile after the seminar.

Implications for Business

The primary purpose of this study was to provide information about a training program geared at informing business students about sex-role related problems they may encounter in their work experiences. The data collected also provided information on some important questions about the effects of moving women more fully into the corporate structure. These questions relate to matters such as family

Exhibit 1: Seminar Effects on Attitudes and Personality

Scale	Males			Females			Males and Females		
	Pre-seminar	Post-seminar	t and p value	Pre-seminar	Post-seminar	t and p value	Pre-seminar	Post-seminar	t and p value
AWS	170.0	185.57	t = 3.47 p < .01	180.07	192.36	t = 3.24 p < .01	176.71	190.09	t = 4.63 p < .01
WAMS	90	98.71	t = 1.68 p < .1	92.64	100.71	t = 2.05 p < .05	91.76	100.05	t = 2.7 p < .01
Fe	16.14	15	NOT SIG.	22.29	21.5	NOT SIG.	20.24	19.33	t = 1.45 p < .1
Fear of success	24.14	23.29	NOT SIG.	23.71	24.43	t = 1.5 p < .1	23.38	24.05	t = 1.42 p < .1
Hostility	9.29	9	NOT SIG.	5.77	5.92	NOT SIG.	7	6.45	NOT SIG.
Anxiety	7.29	5.7	NOT SIG.	6.38	6.46	NOT SIG.	6.7	6.2	NOT SIG.
Depression	12.29	9.7	t = 1.78 p < .1	10.31	11.23	NOT SIG.	11	10.7	NOT SIG.

structure, male ego-threat, and career aspirations of participants. It is emphasized that since no control groups were employed and sample size was small, conclusions must be regarded as tentative.

(1) What are the effects of a seminar on women's changing sex roles on the sex-role attitudes of the participants?

Two measures of sex-role attitude were administered, one measuring acceptance of women's expanding sex roles in the home and personal environment and one measuring that acceptance in the business environment. A significant difference was found for both measures over the course of the seminar, indicating an increased acceptance of changing sex roles for women in both environments. This was true for both males and females.

(2) Are males or females more favorable towards changing sex-role stereotypes for women?

Spence and Helmreich found in their normative sample for the AWS that females were significantly more favorable than males in terms of women expanding their role opportunities.[24] Peters, Terborg, and Taynor also found women more favorably disposed than men toward role expansion for women in business.[25] In the present sample, mean scores for male and female VCU business students were higher (more liberal) on both scales than their respective normative samples. However, in terms of overall magnitude of scores, females were more favorable on the AWS than males, but there was no difference in the sexes on the WAMS. Apparently men and women business students are equally favorably inclined toward women progressing in the business community, but when it comes to women expanding their sex roles at home or in a personal sense male business students are more reluctant than females to voice their approval.

(3) Will women's expanding role in the corporate structure jeopardize the cohesiveness of the family?

Surprisingly, the correlation between the AWS and WAMS scales proved to be nonsignificant for this sample of business students. In other words, business students apparently do not conceptualize women's changing sex roles in the same fashion in the business setting and in the home. Apparently when the students enrolled in the course they felt that some distinction should be made between home and business in terms of expanding sex roles for women. After completing the course, this necessity for differentiating where roles were to be expanded was maintained.

It should also be pointed out that, since there were no overall pre to post seminar changes in the general personality states of anxiety, hostility, or depression, an increased openness in this attitude does not affect basic emotional states, therefore making it much less likely to carry over into family life. In other words, what happens during a business day may not affect personal relationships with family or friends. The suggestion is that male managers who hesitate to open the ranks of management to women for fear of becoming home-wreckers may be concerning themselves with a paper tiger.

(4) What is the effect of such a seminar on the perceived masculinity and femininity of the participants?

There was a trend shown by *all* the students to espouse a more "masculine" sex-role identity. However, this finding only approached statistical significance, and in separate tests for males and females there were no significant pre to post seminar differences on this variable. The slight overall increase in masculine sex-role identity is understandable given that it is the valued identity in our society. Also, a good managerial model is thought to be synonymous with masculine characteristics. It is unfortunate that this myth continues to be perpetuated. A good manager needs many "feminine" skills to be successful. In this study, the males still saw themselves as masculine and the females as basically feminine (despite the slight movement toward masculinity) after taking the course. The common conception that exposure to the type of material covered in this seminar tends to make women hostile and masculine was not supported by our data.

(5) Will males be upset in some ego-threatening manner when enrolled in such a seminar?

There is some evidence in the data that males' feelings would be quite the contrary. First, pre-post measures of anxiety (thought to approximate self-concept) showed no difference. In addition, there was no pre-post difference in hostility. The only difference found for either males or females was a slight ($p < .10$) *decrease* in depression for males. Thus, not only does enrollment in such a seminar not produce ego-threatening or dysphoric emotional feelings in males, but exposure to this material may result in decreased levels of depression. Apparently, when men are apprised of the facts concerning sexual inequality in business, they realize that no one is blaming men for the current state of affairs and that women are interested in equally sharing responsibility without usurping it. Other data indicating that the seminar was not an ego-threatening experience was the finding of no change in males' sex-role identity of masculinity. Also, males showed no change in reported fear of success (if ego-threat was involved an increase in fear of success would be expected).

The apparent lack of ego-threat to males suggested by the data perhaps can be attributed to an "it's no one's fault" approach to the course. Conceivably, a burden was lifted from the men as they realized that women with managerial career goals are not "man-haters" out to destroy the corporate structure. Perhaps the men sensed that women's liberation is really human liberation and that just as all women are not meant to be managers neither are all men. The humanization of the business organization world would mean that men, too, become free to set their own objectives and define their own success.

(6) What is the effect of participation in such a course on a woman's achievement motive and career aspirations?

It may be conjectured that as a result of the increase in positive attitudes towards women's expanding sex roles, especially in the business environment, women have become much more aware of career demands and potentialities; they have learned why they have been hesitant professionally. The data indicated a lowered fear-of-success attitude in women after enrollment in the course. Although this finding only approached statistical significance, it has broad implications in terms of the effectiveness of such a course in helping women crystallize their professional goals. Apparently, when women become more aware of their potentialities in business they become less fearful of actively pursuing business careers. With the decrease in fear of success among females in this study, there was no change in anxiety or hostility. Thus women feel less apprehensive about succeeding yet do not experience any increase in negative emotionality regarding their new professional horizons.

Lowered fear of success might be a reflection of the feeling on the part of women that they now are able to define "success" for themselves on their own terms, rather than in terms of someone else's expectations. When Barbara Boyle conducts seminars connected with the implementation of affirmative action programs, she often finds women choosing not to become managers. The important point is that they have made their own career choice and actually are more productive employees even though they assume no additional responsibilities.[26]

The business literature is replete with references to the idea that men see women entering management as a very real threat to their careers, since the competitive pool becomes larger. Horner and Walsh report that males "find female achievement drives threatening to their highly internalized cultural values and norms . . . some men refuse to take female achievement seriously, while others exhibit more overt hostility."[27] The men in the VCU seminar were surrounded by women with strong and very verbal achievement motives but who did not express greater fear of success at the end of the semester. One young man made his opposition to the women's liberation movement quite clear at the outset of the course. However, during one of the last class meetings he stated: "Now I'd be willing to work with a woman, or even for one." Again, exposure led to understanding and acceptance of a concept that had been opposed.

In summary, the major findings of this study are that students held more positive attitudes towards women's expanding opportunities (both in business and on a more general personal level) after the course than before, and that these attitude changes occurred without any personal emotional threat to the seminar participants. As noted previously, since the present data were not obtained under strictly controlled conditions, they must be interpreted with caution. The following results obtained here should be investigated further with larger samples using appropriate experimental designs: (a) the lack of relationship between AWS and WAMS scores for business students, (b) the increase in perceived masculine sex-role identity for both male and female subjects, and (c) the decrease in reported fear of success for female participants. As for the major finding of a decline in negative attitudes toward women in both the home/personal and the business environment for both male and female subjects, this finding not only needs to be replicated with larger samples but also needs to be further validated. More extensive validation would involve bringing the present methodology directly into the business setting, working with business people, and evaluating program impact using tangible behavioral measures as well as self-report attitudinal measures.

The authors feel that without such attitudinal and attendant behavioral changes, management efforts at recruiting and training women represent wasted resources. Only when women are integrated into the *activity* of management, rather than simply being given token management positions, will true equal opportunity be realized. Only when management recognizes men and women as individuals, each with unique potentials and competencies, will an optimal organizational climate be possible. Investments in short seminars similar to the course offered at VCU appear to be just that—a relatively low-cost investment which should have long-term payoffs. True, the profitability of such endeavors may not be immediately apparent, but the cost of discrimination is too great a threat to ignore. Cooperation and equality of opportunity can only mean a better organization and a better society.

Footnotes

1. S. Daddio, " 'Oh!' the Obstacle to Women in Management," in Dorothy Jongeward and Dru Scott, eds., *Affirmative Action for Women* (Menlo Park, California, Addison-Wesley, 1974), pp. 153-172.

2. D.K. Shah, "Ms. ery Loves Companies," *The National Observer*, May 1973.

3. Benson Rosen and Thomas H. Jerdee, "Sex Stereotyping in the Executive Suite," *Harvard Business Review*, March-April 1974, pp. 45-58.

4. Benson Rosen and Thomas H. Jerdee, "The Influence of Sex-role Stereotypes on

Evaluations of Male and Female Supervisory Behavior," *Journal of Applied Psychology*, 1973, pp. 44-48.

5. Jayne Gackenbach and Stephen Auerbach, "Empirical Evidence for the Phenomenon of the 'Well-Meaning Liberal Male,' " *Journal of Clinical Psychology*, 1975, vol. 31, no. 4, pp. 632-635.

6. See, for example, M. Barbara Boyle, "Equal Opportunity for Women Is Smart Business," *Harvard Business Review*, May-June 1973, pp. 85-95; C.F. Fretz and Joanne Hayman, "Progress for Women—Men Are Still More Equal," *Harvard Business Review*, September-October 1973, pp. 133-139; Eleanor Brantley Schwartz and James J. Rago, Jr., "Beyond Tokenism: Women as True Corporate Peers," *Business Horizons*, December 1970, pp. 69-76; Kristin Anudsen and Karolyn Gould, "The Rise of Womanagement," *Innovation*, September 1971, pp. 14-22; Bette Ann Stead, "Real Equal Opportunity for Women Executives," *Business Horizons*, August 1974, pp. 87-92.

7. Boyle, "Equal Opportunity for Women Is Smart Business," pp. 89-95. For an excellent discussion of the specifics of such seminars, see Jongeward and Scott, *Affirmative Action for Women*.

8. Virginia E. O'Leary, "Some Attitudinal Barriers to Occupational Aspirations in Women," *Psychological Bulletin*, 1974, pp. 809-826.

9. Eleanor E. Maccoby and Carol N. Jacklin, *The Psychology of Sex Differences* (Stanford, California, Stanford University Press, 1974), p. 349.

10. M.M. Paloma and T.N. Garland, "The Myth of the Equalitarian Family: Familial Roles and the Professionally Employed Wife," in A. Theodore, ed., *The Professional Woman* (Cambridge, Massachusetts, Schenkman Publishing Co., Inc., 1971).

11. P. Hawley, "What Women Think Men Think," *Journal of Counseling Psychology*, 1971, pp. 193-199; E.G. French and G.S. Lesser, "Some Characteristics of the Achievement Motive in Women," *Journal of Abnormal and Social Psychology*, 1964, pp. 119-128.

12. Martina Horner, "Why Bright Women Fail," *Psychology Today*, November 1969.

13. David Tresemer, "Fear of Success Popular, But Unproven," *Psychology Today*, March 1974, p. 84.

14. Janet T. Spence and Robert Helmreich, "The Attitudes Toward the Rights and Roles of Women in Contemporary Society," *Selected Documents in Psychology*, Journal Supplement Abstract Service to the American Psychological Association, 1972.

15. Lawrence H. Peters, James R. Terborg, and Janet Taynor, "Women as Managers Scale (WAMS): A Measure in Management Positions," abstracted in the Journal Supplement Abstract Service, *Catalog of Selected Documents in Psychology*, 1974.

16. H.G. Gough, *Manual for the California Psychological Inventory* (Palo Alto, California, Consulting Psychologists Press, 1957).

17. Lawrence R. Good and Katherine C. Good, "An Objective Measure of the Motive to Avoid Success," *Psychological Reports*, 1973, pp. 1009-1010.

18. S.M. Auerbach and Phillip Bowman, "Relationship Among Measured Sex-Role Related Concepts," unpublished manuscript (Richmond, Virginia, Virginia Commonwealth University, 1975).

19. M. Zuckerman and B. Lubin, *Manual for the Multiple Affect Adjective Check List* (San Diego, California, Educational and Industrial Testing Service, 1965).

20. Dr. Estelle Ramey has stated, "To the question: which has the best hormonal basis for leadership and achievement, man or woman? The meaningful answer can only be: which man and which woman?" Estelle R. Ramey, "Sex Hormones and Executive Ability," in Ruth B. Kundsin, ed., *Women and Success: The Anatomy of Achievement* (New York, William Morrow & Co., Inc., 1974), p. 255.

21. Rosen and Jerdee, "Sex Stereotyping in the Executive Suite," p. 56.

22. Spence and Helmreich, "Attitudes Toward Rights and Roles of Women," p. 6.

23. P.W. Lunnelong, "Validity of Attitudes Toward Women Scale," *Psychological Reports*, 1974, pp. 1281-1282.

24. Spence and Helmreich, "Attitudes Toward Rights and Roles of Women," p. 7.

25. Peters, Terborg, and Taynor, "Women as Managers Scale," p. 18.

26. Boyle, "Equal Opportunity for Women," p. 88.

27. Martina S. Horner and Mary R. Walsh, "Psychological Barriers to Success in Women," in Ruth Kundsin, ed., *Women and Success: The Anatomy of Achievement* (New York, William Morrow & Co., Inc., 1974), p. 138.

Dr. Douglas W. Bray *is Director of Management Selection and Development Research with the American Telephone and Telegraph Company, New York.*

This article is reprinted with permission from Atlanta Economic Review, *March-April 1976, pp. 38-43.*

24
Identifying Managerial Talent in Women

Douglas W. Bray

THAT UNTOLD thousands of women with management potential now hold only rank-and-file jobs and that additional numbers with middle- and upper-management ability now languish at lower levels are patent truisms. This gross waste of talent is the residue of overt discrimination and of the social climate of yesterday which persuaded many men that women would not do well in management and many women that they didn't want to be there anyway.

Opening the way for the upward flow of this reservoir of ability will not be easy for any number of reasons, some of which have long impeded the full utilization of male talent. Simply recognizing the existence of a problem, however, even when underscored by governmental commands, is not enough to restructure overnight the complex of traditions and faulty but entrenched methods of management selection and development. Yet the rewards of change will be great. Organizations—private, governmental, and educational—have long lamented shortages of managerial talent. Such shortages now are seen to have been illusory. Organizations which can act appropriately will be more effective than ever before.

The knowledge that there are great numbers of women with more management potential than they now have a chance to use may be a stimulus to action but, standing alone, it is not very helpful. Which of the women in the organization have this potential and to what degree immediately becomes the question. A danger in many affirmative action programs is that this question will not be well answered. Under the pressure of goals and timetables and orders from higher management, managers may select candidates for promotion hastily from readily available female employees and select on inappropriate and unreliable criteria. Some, perhaps many, selections will prove to be unwise, and less than hoped for performance in the new management job will result. Such failures, even if partial, not only are painful experiences for the woman herself but reduce the readiness to make additional promotions of women. "See, I told you so," may well be the reaction.

The problem of identifying those with higher degrees of management ability is not unique to the female employee. Organizations have always struggled with this challenge and often with dubious success. Male managers are not always outstanding! A wide variety of plans and forms for appraising management potential have proliferated over the years but have usually proved disappointing after initial enthusiasm has faded.

Fundamental difficulties stand in the way of supervisors' accurate appraisal of subordinates' promotability. One is that the subordinate's current job may be too limited to reveal the degree of management ability possessed. The file clerk, for example, can scarcely display such characteristics as leadership, oral communication skill, or long-range planning. Employees, furthermore, work at a variety of widely different jobs. It has proved well nigh impossible to devise methods which can enable different supervisors observing different people doing widely different jobs to rate potential validly.

These fundamental difficulties often are compounded by inadequate implementation of appraisal plans. A major weakness is the failure to invest sufficiently in the training of supervisors to use the appraisal plan. After all, a successful plan would have to include the systematic observation of behavior over a period of time and the abstraction from the resulting observations of judgments on carefully defined and applied dimensions of behavior.

The Assessment Center Method

The inadequacies of supervisory appraisal of potential for advancement into and upward within management have led to the ever increasing use of the assessment center method. This method was first applied to the evaluation of management ability in the Bell System in 1956.[1] Although the spread of the method into other businesses was gradual at first, assessment centers now are used in hundreds of business enterprises and in government and education as well.[2]

The assessment center evaluates management ability, and more recently other patterns of ability as well, in an off-the-job situation. In brief, those to be evaluated participate in a variety of simulations designed to evoke managerial behavior. This behavior is expected because the simulations are designed to be relevant to behavioral dimensions important in the target job level. Behavior is observed, reported, and evaluated by a trained staff, usually made up of managers who supervise the level of managerial work in question.

There are a number of variations on the assessment center theme, and centers vary in their purposes, the length of time the assessees spend at the center, and the particular combination of assessment techniques used.[3] A description of the typical center nevertheless will convey the main features of the approach. In such a center assessees are processed in groups of 6 or 12, since most of the group exercises used at assessment centers are constructed to accommodate 6 participants. The assessees, or candidates, usually spend two full days at the center, which often is held at some off-company premises location such as a local motel. The center nearly always is directed by a middle-management person from the organization itself, rather than an outsider, who welcomes the assessees and answers questions about the purpose of the center and the use that will be made of the results.

The aspect that distinguishes assessment centers from other personnel evaluation methods is the use of simulations to elicit behavior relevant to performance on the target job, in this instance managerial work. Few centers use less than three such simulations, and four or five are not uncommon. One such exercise is a business game which occupies the group for several hours. As noted earlier, these games are usually set up for six participants, and their content is designed to be simple enough so that all participants will have sufficient knowledge to enter fully into the exercise. The original Bell System assessment center business game used Tinker Toys as the material. The assessees purchased Tinker Toy parts at various prices, constructed their choice of different prescribed articles from the parts, and sold them back, again at varying prices. Other business games involve the buying and selling of numerical digits printed on metal squares, a greatly simplified version of the stock market, and the trading of shares in imaginary corporations to build conglomerates.

Another ubiquitous assessment center exercise is the leaderless group discussion. Once again, such exercises frequently are designed for six participants and attempt to minimize the possible influence of previous specific experience upon performance. Such exercises are of two types. The more common involves assigning specific roles to the members of the group; that is, they have a prescribed position or point of view which they are to support in the discussion period. For example, they may be told that they are members of the school board of a small city and are meeting to make budgetary decisions. Each of them is given a particular project for which he/she is to seek a maximum of funds from the board. A parallel design has the six participants role play a college scholarship committee, each with a candidate to advocate. In leaderless group discussions without assigned roles the participants are given one or more decisions to make as a group and material to study and use relevant to these decisions. They do not have any prescribed position which they are expected to maintain, however; they develop their own on their analysis of the material and the situation.

Nearly all assessment centers use an exercise known as the in-basket. This is an individual simulation in which the candidate is asked to deal with managerial problems and decisions presented in the form of material which might well come across the desk of a person in the target position. Such material includes correspondence, memos, reports, records of telephone calls, minutes of meetings, and so on. The candidate is given a considerable length of time to deal with the material (up to three hours) and is told to make his/her behavior as close as possible to what it would be in a real life situation. An exception is that fuller notes and records of proposed action are to be made than might be the case if the situation were real. Although the in-basket can be evaluated simply as a written exercise, work on it usually is followed by an intensive interview by one of the assessors. This interview explores the reasons for the particular action taken, or inaction, on at least the more important items in the basket. In addition, more general information can be obtained, such as the candidate's evaluation of the effectiveness of operations in the organization up to this time and plans for the future. As questions move in this direction, the in-basket interview affords a takeoff point for investigating the candidate's perception of the whole managerial role.

Although the foregoing three simulations are the most commonly used, others also have proven valuable. Chief among them are analysis and presentation problems and individual fact-finding and decision-making exercises. In the analysis and presentation type of problem the candidate is given some reasonably complicated material and is allowed up to two hours to study it and prepare to make a presentation. This presentation is made either to the other assessees or to the assessors and may be followed by questioning or by having the candidates advocate their positions in a leaderless group discussion. Individual fact-finding and decision-making exercises require the candidate to dig out the facts and circumstances of a problem situation by questioning and then to present his/her decision orally to one or more assessors. The candidate is then questioned, sometimes even forcefully challenged, on the decision and the reasons therefor.

Although simulations occupy the bulk of the time at assessment centers, ordinarily they are supplemented by one or more of the usual methods of evaluation. One of these, universally found, is the interview. Assessment center interviews cover the candidate's educational and experiential background and, particularly, aspirations and desires for the future. Most assessment centers require the candidate to fill out a personal history form in preparation for the interview. Psychological tests are used in some centers. These may be of the cognitive, mental ability type or, more rarely, of the personality questionnaire or projective technique variety. The latter kinds of instruments are found only when candidates for or incumbents in middle-management positions are being assessed.

Assessees are observed systematically in the assessment exercises, and detailed reports of their behavior in each of them are prepared. These reports are used at the integration session in which the staff reviews and rates each candidate. This process is quite intensive, and it is not at all unusual for the discussion of a candidate to take two hours or more. In the integration session all reports on a candidate are read orally so that every assessor possesses all information on the individual. The staff then rates the candidate on the managerial variables or dimensions. The number of such dimensions varies from center to center, but it is rarely less than 12 or more than 25. Twenty is perhaps the modal number. Examples of dimensions rated are oral communication skill, inner work standards, career ambition, leadership, planning and organizing, decisiveness, energy, flexibility, and judgment.

After the dimensions are rated, discussed, and differences reconciled, the staff proceeds to general recommendations. These recommendations often concern the potential of the individual for promotion into management or for further advancement in management. Some staffs go further and suggest the type of assignment most in line with the abilities of the candidate. Others include developmental recommendations or, at least, point out areas of weakness which might profit from training or experience. Assessment center recommendations and summary reports of performance at the center usually are submitted to local management in written form and are used along with performance appraisal and other indicators in determining future steps in the candidate's career. A nearly universal feature of assessment centers is a private feedback by a member of the assessment staff to the candidate him- or herself. These interviews are confidential and attempt to frankly but supportively convey to the candidate the view of his or her abilities gained at the assessment center and the reasons for the ratings given.

Assessment center ratings and recommendations may be coordinated centrally in the personnel department. Such data are invaluable for human resources planning purposes even if no attempt is made to retain identification of individuals. Just knowing, for example, the number of nonmanagement persons with at least first-level management ability can tell the organization a great deal about what further recruiting or training of lower-level managers is needed. In most cases, however, there is specific interest in the individuals assessed, particularly in those who have been recommended for additional advancement and most particularly in those who are seen as having high levels of managerial ability. It is important to the organization that such people not be lost and that their potential be utilized by appropriate career planning. If centralized monitoring is not conducted, it is likely that even some recommended candidates will get lost in the shuffle.

Many studies of the predictive validity of the assessment center method have been conducted. These studies are reviewed and summarized in a number of sources.[4] The overall assessment rating, made by the staff after the ratings of particular dimensions have been made and discussed, has proven to be more predictive than any other assessment rating or test score. It has been shown to be predictive of advancement in management, job performance, and potential for further promotion.

Although a few studies, notably those done at AT&T,[5] have been basic research studies in which assessment center results were not used in determining the future of the candidates, contamination has been a consistent problem in studying the assessment center method. Since assessment center results are characteristically used as a partial determinant of the next promotion, simple predictive studies of who gets promoted are highly suspect. A number of researchers, however, have gotten around this problem by inventive methods. For example, studies have used demotion after post-assessment promotion as a criterion;[6] others have used two or more promotions as the criterion.[7] This has the effect of reducing or even eliminating contamination. In other instances special supervisory appraisal ratings have been gathered without letting the raters know that the evaluation of assessment center predictions was the purpose of the investigation.[8] Comparisons of ratings by supervisors who knew and those who did not know that the person they were rating had been assessed have shown that assessment results apparently do not seriously contaminate supervisory performance ratings and that the relationship between assessment center ratings and performance ratings are the same for those whose assessment ratings are known and not known.

Bell System Consent Decrees

That the assessment center could be used to facilitate the advancement of women in management was first publicly suggested, by the writer, at a University of Pittsburgh Conference in May 1971.[9] Three advantages of the method were noted. One was that the assessment center would increase the accuracy of the selection of women for managerial assignments and thus maximize their chances of success when advanced into such positions. Second, line managers would be more receptive to assessment center recommendations than to the opinions of coordinates, particularly those in other departments. Third, it was hypothesized that the feedback of assessment center results to successful candidates would enhance their willingness to strive for and accept greater managerial responsibilities.

Not many months after the Pittsburgh conference the Bell System was charged by the EEOC and other governmental agencies with discrimination in its personnel practices. These charges led to a protracted investigation and to testimony before the Federal Communications Commission. Although alleged discrimination against minority groups was a significant part of the case, many charges concerned discrimination against women. The litigation ended in a Consent Decree, agreed to by the Bell System and the government agencies involved, in January 1973. One feature of this agreement is of particular interest since it involved the use of assessment centers to appraise a large group of women managers.

One of the government's charges involved some 2,000 women who had been employed by the Bell System directly into management but who had not been put on the fast-track initial development program that many males had experienced during the same years. This fast-track program was based on the intention that those involved in it had the potential for at least the third-level of management. Thus employment standards for those entering the program were rigorous. In fashioning the aspect of the Consent Decree which concerned management women, the question was how to determine which of the 2,000 women did in fact have third-level or higher management potential. It was this group to which the government insisted that reparation be made. The suggestion was made that an assessment center would be an appropriate method for making such a determination and, after investigation, the government agreed.

In order to assess the large number of candidates as quickly as possible, three centers were set up—one in New York, one in Michigan, and one in California. They were staffed by Bell System middle managers, male and female; all were trained by the same experts in order to achieve uniformity between centers. Assessment was of the two-day variety, following pretty much the typical assessment format outlined previously. In addition, however, several research instruments were administered in order to get additional data on personality and motivational characteristics of the candidates. Scores on these instruments were not available to the assessment staff and played no part in ratings of individual characteristics or of promotability.

Each of the women covered by the Consent Decree received information about the assessment center and its purposes and was asked whether she wished to be assessed. Incentives for attending the assessment center were high. Candidates assessed as having middle-management potential were to receive an immediate $1,200 a year increase in salary and would be put on a special career program to enable them to reach the third level of management as quickly as possible. About 92% of the women managers did volunteer, and some 1,634 were assessed before the program was completed.

The overall staff rating at these special assessment centers was a simple dichotomous one—"does have" or "does not have" the potential for third-level general managerial work. No gradation in rating was possible since a definite decision had to be made in each case. There was no predetermination nor, in fact, was there any clear expectation of what percentage of these first- and second-level management women would receive a "recommended" rating. The assessment staffs were told to pay no attention to such a percentage but to judge each case on its merits. When this was done and the results totaled, 689 of the

1,634 women, or 42%, had been recommended as having potential for third-level or higher management. This percentage was remarkably close to the percentage for a group of male college recruits assessed by a similar process during the late 1950s. These were the college graduate subjects in the Bell System's Management Progress Study. Of that group some 40% were stated clearly to have third-level management ability.

Other Bell System Experience

The special assessment of women candidates under the Consent Decree was far from the first Bell System experience with women in assessment centers. The original operational Bell System assessment program was the so-called Personnel Assessment Program, the purpose of which was to evaluate the management ability of rank-and-file employees who had been nominated for first-line supervisory jobs by their supervisors. The program started in one of the operating telephone companies, Michigan Bell, in 1958. During the next year or two it was also instituted in other telephone companies, such as New York and Southern. These early programs, however, were Plant Department programs, and those examined were telephone installers, linemen, or central office switchmen who were being considered as possible foremen. Because in those days women were essentially never candidates for such jobs, these early centers processed only men. A change occurred in the early 1960s when the Traffic and Commercial Departments, departments highly populated with female employees, decided to try the assessment center method. In the resulting centers all of the candidates examined were women. As time went on it was seen as more logical to have the assessment program administered centrally by the personnel department rather than by separate operating departments. Centers became interdepartmental with consequent mixing of men and women in assessment groups.

From the start of the program in Michigan Bell in 1958 until the end of 1974 nearly 100,000 employees had been processed through such assessment centers, and nearly all of the operating telephone companies were operating them. Almost half of all the candidates assessed were women; about 32,000 had been evaluated in the Personnel Assessment Program through 1974. The success rates, the percentage seen as having high potential, were very comparable for men and women candidates: 33% of the men and 35% of the women were rated as clearly promotable to first-level management.

During the early 1970s a new assessment program was introduced which, it appears, may outstrip the original Personnel Assessment Program as the most popular assessment program in the Bell System. The new application of the assessment center method is called the Early Identification Program. Its purpose is to identify short service nonmanagement employees who have first-level management potential, with the goal of accelerating their development and advancement into such positions. Assessment procedures take one day only and, as a result, it is a high volume program. Even though the program was not introduced until 1971, over 33,000 candidates had been assessed by the end of 1974. More than half of these candidates were women, and, once again, the success rates for men and women were comparable: 25% of the male candidates and 20% of the female candidates were judged to have the potential for first-level supervisory jobs.

In addition to the three programs discussed previously, several other miscellaneous management assessment programs are conducted in the Bell System. When data for all programs are added together, some 132,507 men and women have been assessed from 1958 through 1974. Of this total, more than half, 54%, were women. The success rate in all these programs combined, which amounts to having a rating of good potential for the target level in question, was 33% for men and 30% for women. Although this difference is statistically significant, because of the large number of cases involved, it is of little practical significance. Exhibit 1 shows the data for the various programs.

As noted previously, research on the predictive power of the assessment center method has always been handicapped by criterion contamination. Ways have been found around this difficulty, however, and convincing predictive studies are available for both men and women. These studies have been summarized in several places.[10] Two recent studies focused particularly on women assessees. Huck and Bray used the criterion of performance on the first-level job for women who

Exhibit 1: Numbers Assessed and Success Rates for Women and Men in Bell System Programs

		Number* Rated High	Percent* Rated High
Personnel Assessment Program (1958-1974)			
Women	32,324	11,313	35.0
Men	62,147	21,425	33.4
Total	94,471	32,738	34.6
Early Identification Program (1971-1974)			
Women	18,595	3,774	20.3
Men	14,867	3,761	25.3
Total	33,462	7,535	22.8
Other Management Assessment Programs			
Women	2,064	687	33.3
Men	2,510	772	30.7
Total	4,574	1,459	32.0
All Programs Combined (1958-1974)			
Women	52,938	15,774	29.7
Men	79,524	25,958	32.6
Grand Total	132,507	41,732	31.4

*Approximate

had gone through Michigan Bell's two-day Personnel Assessment Program.[11] This performance criterion was specially obtained from supervisors on a face-to-face basis, using behaviorally anchored rating scales. The correlation between the overall assessment rating and performance on the first-level job was .42 for a sample of 126 women. Moses and Boehm used the criterion of management level of women assessed two years or more before the time the study was conducted.[12] The correlation of the overall assessment rating with this criterion was .37 for 4,846 women. This was not a far different result from that obtained by Moses on a study of 8,085 men, where the comparable correlation was .44.[13]

The same two studies provide data internal to the assessment center process for women candidates. Huck and Bray factor analyzed the ratings of 16 assessment variables (ratings of dimensions made by the assessment center staff) and found 4 underlying factors. These were interpersonal effectiveness, administrative skills, effective intelligence, and sensitivity. Although this analysis did not show all the factors which emerged for men in the Bell System Management Progress Study,[14] three of the factors had emerged in the previous research. They were interpersonal effectiveness, administrative skills, and effective intelligence. Differences between remaining factors were interpreted as being due to the more elaborate nature of the assessment center process in the Management Progress Study rather than any difference between assessment judgments of male and female candidates.

This interpretation is supported by the results of the Moses and Bochm analysis. They compared men and women in the same program, the Personnel Assessment Program, and correlated certain assessment ratings and scores on the School and College Ability Test with management level two years or more after assessment. The same four predictors that correlated most highly for men also correlated most highly for women: overall rating, leadership, decision making, and organizing and planning. The rank order correlation between the men's and women's results for 10 predictors was .75.

In summary, the management assessment center yields highly parallel results for male and female assessees. It is predictive of progress in management for both sexes and of performance in management jobs. Although the data are not yet definitive, it also appears that internal relationships within the assessment center between variables and the overall assessment rating are the same for men and women.

Ever since Women's Lib and Affirmative Action have pressed upon organizations the necessity of moving more and more women into middle and upper management, some have been convinced that special developmental activities for women would be necessary. The implication of the foregoing assessment center data is that this is not true. Data from the Consent Decree assessment centers show that women rated as having middle-management potential are at least equal to their male counterparts on the important managerial characteristics of leadership, planning and organizing, mental ability, and so on. The fact that a high percentage of the women who went through these centers were seen as having middle-management potential says that many women are ready now. The burden of proof is on those who believe that special developmental efforts are necessary. This is not to say that extra training on job content may not be needed, a point that will be discussed later.

Aspects of the Personnel System

The accurate evaluation of women's managerial abilities is a key factor, perhaps *the* key factor, in enabling more of them to rise to the highest level at which they are capable of performing effectively. It would be misleading, however, to leave the impression that the identification of talent is all that is necessary to solve the problem.[15] Other organizational impediments must be overcome. In the first place, there cannot be enough immediate openings to allow for the early promotion of any but a relatively small percentage of capable women. Secondly, it is likely that many women (or men for that matter) with plenty of management potential will not currently possess the job knowledge needed for advancement. This probability is made all the more likely since women currently are not distributed among departments and job families at all proportionately to management openings. This is because of the concentration of women in departments and jobs which were considered particularly appropriate for them. Within the telephone business, for example, past years found women hired in great numbers into the Traffic and Commercial Departments but not into the Plant and technical departments.

The foregoing difficulties dictate systematic attention to career planning and the provision of special job content training where necessary. Bell System experience has demonstrated that career planning proceeds best where a specific target job is identified and agreed upon by the employee and higher supervision. This specificity makes for concreteness in terms of the actual steps needed to be taken before the target job can be reached. It militates against overly general career planning which deteriorates into vague suggestions about overall strengthening of the individual. As has been seen, general strengthening of the individual is not what is needed. It is possible, of course, that the target job chosen for career planning may have to be changed because of a drop in opportunities in that particular job or because the candidate decides that she finds that her interests are somewhat different than that job entails. Even though such changes sometimes will take place, the choice of a specific target keeps both supervision and the candidate focused on occupational realities.

The needed additional ingredient is special job content training to enable promising managers to move between departments or job families, at least laterally. In large organizations such as the Bell System it has been customary for upwardly mobile individuals to progress through a particular type of work. As a result, job knowledge is acquired by months, or even years, of service prior to moving up in that particular function. Were that to remain the only method of learning job content, the advancement of capable women in anywhere near the appropriate numbers would be long delayed.

One of the most positive results of the pressures for equal opportunity and affirmative action has been a trend within organizations toward more effective human resources systems and practices. Organizations would always have been better managed had management ability been accurately evaluated and systematic attention given to the advancement of that talent to its proper level in the organization. These processes become even more important, however, when one is seeking to correct gross imbalances in the utilization of talent. The assessment center has a major contribution to make in identifying those with the needed abilities and in giving organizations a more accurate view of the amount and distribution of managerial talent which they possess.

Footnotes

1. D.W. Bray, R.J. Campbell, and D.L. Grant, *Formative Years in Business: A Long-Term AT&T Study of Managerial Lives* (New York, Wiley-Interscience, 1974), p. 7.

2. J.L. Moses and W.C. Byham, eds., *Applying the Assessment Center Method* (New York, Pergamon Press, Inc., in press).

3. D.W. Bray, "The Assessment Center Method," in R.L. Craig, ed., *Handbook of Training and Development* (New York, McGraw Hill Book Co., in press).

4. A. Howard, "An Assessment of Assessment Centers," *Academy of Management Journal*, 1974, pp. 115-134; B. Cohen, J.L. Moses, and W.C. Byham, *The Validity of Assessment Centers: A Literature Review* (Pittsburgh, Development Dimensions Press, 1974).

5. Bray, Campbell, and Grant, *Formative Years in Business*, p. 69.

6. A.I. Kraut and G.J. Scott, "Validation of an Operational Management Assessment Program," *Journal of Applied Psychology*, 1972, pp. 124-129.

7. J.L. Moses, "Assessment Center Performance and Management Progress," *Studies in Personnel Psychology*, 1972, pp. 7-12.

8. R.J. Campbell and D.W. Bray, "Assessment Centers: An Aid in Management Selection," *Personnel Administration*, 1967, pp. 6-13.

9. D.W. Bray, "The Assessment Center: Opportunities for Women," *Personnel Magazine*, 1971, pp. 30-34.

10. Bray, "The Assessment Center Method"; Howard, "An Assessment of Assessment Centers," pp. 115-134.

11. J.R. Huck and D.W. Bray, "Management Assessment Center Evaluations and Subsequent Job Performance of White and Black Females," *Personnel Psychology*, in press.

12. J.L. Moses and V.R. Boehm, "Relationship of Assessment Center Performance to Management Progress of Women," *Journal of Applied Psychology*, 1975, p. 528.

13. Moses, "Assessment Center Performance and Management Progress," pp. 7-12.

14. Bray, Campbell, and Grant, *Formative Years in Business*, p. 78.

15. D.W. Bray, "Management Development Without Frills," *Conference Board Records*, 1975, pp. 47-50.

M. Barbara Boyle *is President of Boyle/Kirkman Associates, Inc., New York, New York.*

25
Equal Opportunity for Women Is Smart Business

M. Barbara Boyle

"THIS MOVEMENT is not a fad or an aberration, but a major social force with great and growing impact on business and other social, political, and economic institutions. As such, it must be taken seriously by business managers; its future potential must be foreseen and constructive responses must be designed to meet legitimate demands."

The subject in question is the movement for equality in women's rights, and the statement, from a General Electric publication distributed to all managers in the corporation, is typical of many corporate directives now being issued throughout the country. Even those companies that several years ago were rather hoping that the women's movement *was* a fad—and would go away if ignored—are beginning to recognize its importance. Some are still at the stage of merely mouthing their commitment to the elimination of sex discrimination, but others have begun to follow up their words with clearly defined programs designed to improve the utilization of women in all phases of their business.

The effective development of such affirmative action programs is the subject of this article. But let us look first at the reasons why companies are putting such emphasis on women. In talking with executives of several major corporations, I have found these key motivating factors:

Awareness of Social Trends. Today, nearly half the women in the United States work; that amounts to more than 33 million women, representing 40% of the work force. Obviously, women's place is no longer necessarily in the home. Furthermore, women work for essentially the same reasons men do: money (60% of the women in the work force are either single, divorced, widowed, or married to a man who earns less than $7,000 a year), self-satisfaction, and fulfillment. So, no matter what a manager's personal view is concerning "women's place," the fact is that women *are* working and must be considered as a resource that needs to be effectively managed, motivated, and utilized—just like men.

Government Pressure. The federal government is enforcing equal opportunity for women through the following vehicles:
☐ The Equal Pay Act of 1963. This amendment to the Fair Labor Standards Act prohibits discrimination on the basis of sex in the payment of wages for work requiring equal skills, effort, and responsibility, and performed under similar working conditions. Many women employees with legitimate discrimination complaints are finding how easy it is to file charges against their employers. With sufficient evidence they can cause comprehensive discrimination reviews to be initiated without disclosure of their names to the companies.

In the last two years alone, total settlements from these suits amounted to $30,000,000 with individual amounts ranging from $593,000 (Pacific Telephone & Telegraph) to $901,000 (Wheaton Glass). Recently this act was broadened to include executive, administrative, and professional employees.
☐ Title VII, Civil Rights Act of 1964. This act, extremely broad in scope, prohibits discrimination in all phases of employment. Several large awards have been made under this act, and many of the settlements include full back pay, overtime, travel differentials, and interest from the time the complaint was filed.

Recently the Equal Employment Opportunity Commission (EEOC) and American Telephone & Telegraph reached a landmark settlement, under which AT&T agreed to pay $38 million in back pay and restitution charges to thousands of employees, most of them women. "Beyond its importance to the employees involved, this agreement could have far-reaching significance to the entire business world," William H. Brown, EEOC chairman, noted. "We expect AT&T to have a considerable ripple effect. The EEOC lawsuits are designed to turn the ripples into waves where necessary."

☐ Executive Order 11246, Revised Order 4 (1972). This makes it imperative for companies that wish to bid on—or keep—federal contracts to establish affirmative action programs that ensure equal promotion and placement opportunities for women in all ranks. Significant contracts have been withheld in cases where it was decided a company's posture has been discriminatory.

The Women's Equal Rights Movement. Through demonstrations and court suits, women's organizations have been extremely effective in pushing corporations to action. Moreover, Women's Lib groups are raising the consciousness of women within company walls. Women employees are starting to ask these questions:

○ "Why not me?"

○ "Am I really making use of my college degree by sitting here at this typewriter all day?"

○ "Why haven't I been given the experience and development necessary to compete for a vice president's position?"

When they fail to get answers to these questions, groups of dissatisfied women are uniting to express their resentment. In many cases they have organized into committees to meet with top management—or the press—to voice their anger.

It is extremely difficult from a credibility standpoint to react effectively to demands from an internal group. Therefore, many companies are taking positive action before they are *forced* to find answers to these questions.

Public Image. Because women represent 51% of the population, product-based companies are now seriously considering the implications on their marketplace of internal discrimination. The business manager of a leading women's magazine recently told me, "Let's face it—we sell primarily to women and many of them are becoming increasingly aware of discriminatory behavior. Unless we do something to improve the situation of women here on the magazine from a long-range standpoint, our future is in jeopardy."

A General Mills training program consisting of 65 people, 64 of them white males, was recently the target of a formal charge filed by the National Organization for Women (NOW) and the Urban League. Not only was the publicity damaging, but both groups threatened to launch a nationwide boycott against the company's Betty Crocker products, Wheaties, Cheerios, and Gold Medal flour.

Even companies not dealing directly in the consumer market can suffer from bad publicity; college recruiters report situations involving high-potential graduates who have turned down offers because of a company's poor equal opportunity reputation.

Competition and Challenge. Recently, IBM Senior Vice President George S. Beitzel defined industry's biggest problem in the coming years as "a shortage of capable people at all levels of management." If this is true, corporate leaders can no longer ignore half of the population when they are looking for creative and executive talent. It has long been obvious that we are not utilizing the capabilities of the women in our companies. Kept in "women-type" jobs, they have not efficiently used their aptitudes, intelligence, education, and skills. It is a great economic waste. From a dollar standpoint, the female labor force constitutes an important reservoir of talent which is necessary for companies to use to remain competitive in the business world.

Grounds for Action

So much for recognizing the issue. The important question is what can be done about it. For fear of backlash or of disrupting the status quo, several companies have tried to soft-pedal the women's issue and, without fanfare or emphasis, have tried to weave it into their ongoing programs for minorities. In most of the companies where I have seen this done, the results have not been favorable. The problems of women and the problems of minorities are too dissimilar at the *initial* stage of awareness to be treated the same.

For example, I once observed a black woman trying to conduct a general awareness session on equal opportunity. Every time she directed the discussion toward the woman problem, the male participants quickly returned to the minority issue. After several years of consciousness raising, they had finally come to feel comfortable discussing minority problems; but the woman issue was newer, more personal, and more threatening to their male security.

A workable solution, which some major corporations have embraced, is the philosophy that there is *one* equal opportunity umbrella, with individual segments of emphasis. Eventually, companies may have just one total program focusing on managing people—all people—as individuals. Then, ideally, there should not be a need for individual emphasis programs.

"But what do I do if there is a black, a woman, and a Mexican-American equally qualified for a certain job?" the executive may ask. "Whom do I promote?" In most cases this is an unrealistic situation. Especially in the white-collar and management areas, seldom are there enough minorities or women at any one level with the same qualifications to compete for exactly the same job. This philosophical issue is frequently debated, however, by the conference set and persons who in many cases want to smoke-screen the issue and do nothing.

The dozen major companies which I have observed closely have experienced a minimum of conflict because the number and characteristics of the resource have been different. For example, many large corporations just do not have enough black employees—or, depending on the locale, Mexican-Americans—so they must establish high recruiting goals. They do have, however, a large percentage of women—all in low-level jobs—so development and upgrading objectives are of primary importance and recruiting needs to be done only in specialized areas. One company, which did encounter situations where several minorities, women, and "majority" employees were equally qualified for the same promotion, made their decisions based on the particular mix of the area involved.

Some companies initiate one or two parts of a program, such as a personnel selection procedure stipulating that women candidates be considered first for certain openings, and assume that they have now dealt with the female problem. Others make up elaborately detailed goals, objectives, and timetables and then sit back complacently to wait for things to fall into place. They may wait a long time.

What is needed is a total affirmative action program that involves everything from the identification and development of women to management awareness sessions for men. When a company puts such a program into action, it demonstrates its sincerity and commitment to its managers and employees—especially to the women.

One company that has done this is Norton Simon, Inc. When I visit its office now, I am gratified to hear so many women mention how happy they are that management is paying serious attention to the problem. One woman receptionist I met said, "I never saw a need to go back to school and complete the credits necessary for my degree. But now I'm convinced management is sincere in the commitment to equal opportunity, so I'm really working hard to qualify myself for advancement."

So many of the elements in a "women's emphasis program" are simply good management procedures that it can be viewed as a starting point for implementing personnel systems which benefit all employees.

Before I launch into a description of an effective kind of affirmative action program, let me lay to rest a false assumption many people make about such programs. "Why do you want to make all women into managers when they're happy where they are?" I have been asked. "What's wrong with being a secretary anyway?" An affirmative action program is not an attempt to move *all* women into more responsible positions. The goal is, rather, to encourage women and managers not to accept automatically and blindly the traditional assumptions about who should be doing what jobs, and to give women a chance to think about their interests and potential, so they can investigate other possibilities, make an intelligent choice, and then be considered for promotions or openings on an equal basis with men.

After going through this exercise, many women decide that they are not interested or do not have the ability to move into management positions or new areas of responsibility. They are, however, more productive and happier employees after this decision is reached because they have had a choice.

Action Program

A truly comprehensive and viable affirmative action plan should include at least ten basic steps. I shall discuss them in turn.

1. Establishing Responsibility

For the clout and support necessary to ensure success, ultimate responsibility for the program should be at the highest practicable level in a company's organization. Attitude and ability, rather than an organization chart, are the most important factors in deciding which top executive should take on the job.

Then who should have responsibility at the coordination, design, and implementation level? There are at least five possibilities:

☐ A male manager. Originally this was the most popular approach, since it was felt that only a man had the requisite knowledge of the company and firmness to carry out the program. However, men placed in this position have often lacked interest and felt they accomplished little self-development applicable to other areas of the business. They also have found it difficult to thoroughly understand the problem, conduct management awareness sessions, and answer questions about women's motivation.

☐ A top-level woman. When companies have an abundance of talented, professional women, this approach is generally used. But it is not advisable when it means taking a valuable woman out of the mainstream or a functional area where she has the opportunity to advance and be an example to other women. For the woman herself, it may also prove detrimental in the long run; she may find it difficult to shed the "Head of Women's Lib" label after her assignment is completed and she wants to move into other management positions.

☐ Consultants. Some companies are now turning to experienced outside consultants. This approach shortens the start-up phase, demonstrates commitment, and minimizes the risk of initiating programs.

☐ A task force. This approach is usually used when women are dissatisfied and begin to meet on their own to try to work out solutions. After management's attention is focused on the issue, it seems natural to let the group continue functioning. But care must be taken so that the group members can implement their ideas, are accountable to the person with top responsibility, and are not overly distracted from their other jobs.

☐ A combination. From what I have observed, this method is now proving to be the most effective. An example of a combination approach is when a woman currently in personnel is given part-time responsibility for program coordination. Consultants are brought in to make high-level management presentations, develop action plans, design management awareness sessions, and work with the coordinator on implementing procedures. If a task force or advisory committee was involved in the beginning stages, it is reassembled on a quarterly basis to review the program and make suggestions.

2. Problem Definition

Once responsibility is established, the next step is to gather statistics and pinpoint the problem areas.[1] It is extremely important to know how women compare in the organization with men in level of jobs, area of employment, educational achievement, tenure, salary, and attrition rate (the latter broken down by position classification and reason for leaving). These data should be supplemented by interviews.

Statistical studies can be enlightening, if sometimes embarrassing. Many corporate executives are confident that the woman problem "can't happen here" because they are such good equal opportunity employers and the women have such good jobs. But even in their organizations, evidence of discrimination can often be found.

An executive of a large women's wear company declared proudly that his company's position was "different" from that of others. "Women have the best jobs in the company," he said. When I cited the facts, he was surprised and chagrined to learn that while women *were* highly visible in the business, accounting for some 65% of employment, the majority of the better-paying and more responsible jobs went to men.

Salary is the area in which it is easiest to identify discriminatory behavior. The average salary of a working woman in this country is less than 60% that of a man—even among professional workers with five years or more of college. If you think things are a lot different in your organization, you may be surprised.

One large, service-oriented company did a study comparing the average salaries of men and women who had the same appraisal ratings and who were in their positions for approximately the same length of time. The results caused the president to exclaim, "I knew most of the women were in lower levels than they deserved to be. But I'm really shocked to see that even within their level, when I know they're the best in that category, their salaries are less than that of the average man."

But many middle managers are not convinced that this is inequitable. Not long ago, a personnel manager (female) asked a department manager to give a raise to one of his women employees, who was the lowest paid of the 12 engineers in his office though she had the highest efficiency, performance, and aptitude ratings. He turned red at the collar. "Let me tell you something," he exclaimed. "That girl drives a red Porsche and I run around in a used Ford. She takes three weeks' vacation in Europe every year, and I take my family to a cottage on Cape Cod that isn't even on the beach. Now why does she need more money?" The personnel manager asked quietly whether one of his male engineers shouldn't be paid more money than he, since the engineer had two more children than the manager.

Discrimination also exists in the kinds of work men and women do. Women have traditionally been channeled into certain areas and "protected" from the stressful or dirty positions. But this chivalry has worked more against than for them. Not only do these "unfeminine" jobs often pay well; they also can offer more upward mobility. Unless a woman has worked in the "dirty" areas of a plant, for instance, she can never be a plant manager. In many companies, unless she has aggressively knocked on doors as a sales representative, she cannot qualify for the more responsible and rewarding positions.

Finally, there is the question of job development. Many training programs and job assignments in a company are traditionally, and often unconsciously, reserved "for men only." At a recent equal opportunity conference, a woman asked a top executive if he had ever considered naming a woman as his administrative assistant. "You don't understand the nature of that position," he replied. "The idea is to bring a man in for a year or two, to give him the experience of working with a top executive. . . . In short, to give him exposure to the entire company. . . . To let him see. . . . To develop him for increasing responsibility. . . ." He went on for several minutes, employing the words "man," "he," and "him" at least 17 times. Then he stopped and blushed faintly at what he was saying. "I guess maybe some of us here ought to rethink that program," he said.

Some managers rationalize that it is not worth the effort to develop a young woman's potential because "after all, she'll leave after a couple of years to get married." It is generally true that women's attrition rate is higher than men's. But, as in the other areas of discrimination, going beyond the surface statistics reveals interesting facts. Within a given job level there is often no significant difference between the percentages of men and women leaving a company; attrition is higher in low-level jobs, and that is where most women are.

A recent university study indicates that many women rush into marriage simply because they are unhappy and frustrated in their jobs. A large manufacturer recently reviewed its separation statistics and discovered that fewer than half of the women leaving each year resigned for family-related reasons. The company then decided to initiate development programs so that women with potential would see that they could have a future in the company and would weigh that fact when considering other possibilities.

Sufficient analysis can save spending unnecessary dollars. For example, a major pharmaceutical company had established a large recruiting program for college graduates in order to improve its utilization of women. When the company analyzed its work force, however, it discovered that more than 20% of the secretaries had college degrees that were appropriate to the business. So the company placed emphasis on upgrading and development, doing recruiting only in specialized areas.

3. Executive Involvement

Top-management participation is the key to the success of any affirmative action effort. Participation can be conveyed through personal letters to each manager from the president or chairman of the board, or through presentations by the president or chairman at management meetings. Middle echelons have to *know* that top management is serious about the issue and that part of their performance appraisal includes results in the area of women's equality. (This attitude should be communicated repeatedly to the stockholders and the public as well.)

Rawleigh Warner, Jr., the chairman and chief executive officer of Mobil Oil, made a film clip which was shown to all managers in the company. When a divisional director was asked at the end of one session whether he planned to establish a women's program, he remarked, "What do you expect me to say? After hearing Mr. Warner up there telling me that it's a high-priority item, do you think I'd say no? Of course we're going to do it."

General Electric is another good example of commitment beyond the motherhood words on paper. In one division, middle managers constantly complained that it was difficult to promote women and minority members because (a) they could not locate qualified people, and (b) they did not have the funds to pay them. Top management promptly removed these two ancient excuses. It provided the necessary budget and head count and told the personnel department to find the qualified candidates, which it did.

A small manufacturing company, which was unable to augment its head count, established a system whereby no promotion could be made into the white, male-dominated, exempt group until the list of minority and women candidates had been exhausted or approval given by the senior vice president of operations.

Consistency and Sincerity. Top-executive commitment and awareness has to be consistent and evident on a day-to-day basis or credibility is lost. One senior executive spent the better part of one day making a videotape concerning the expanding role of women in the business. But he undid himself that evening when he delivered a speech at an employee dinner. At the conclusion of his talk, he launched into a thank-you to "all the women in the audience" for being understanding when their husbands worked long hours and for standing squarely behind the men behind the product. Obviously he did not know that most of the women in the audience were employees (systems analysts and marketing representatives) who were there with their husbands. If he had known, would he have thanked the men behind the women behind the product?

To demonstrate sincerity, the corporate office also must set an example. A middle manager of a large travel company, after reading a formal "we must put women in responsible positions" statement from his president, remarked, "I'll believe he means it when I see a woman on one of the executive floors." Appointing capable, qualified women to the highest levels is much more than tokenism; women who have the potential to advance in an organization need role models at the top. So far these role models have been few and far between.

A metropolitan bank realized the fruits of this within a short period of time when it made several women branch managers—a position heretofore held only by men. Several months later bank officers were amazed by the number of younger women in the bank who were establishing personal development plans.

But how does top management acquire this understanding and commitment? This area of personnel management is so new that many top corporate officers do not realize the scope of the problem and know little about it except the radical viewpoints expressed in the media. They honestly believe the equal opportunity words but do not know what to be committed to. However, when they are made aware of business-like approaches to the problem that detail ways in which they can participate, they often get "turned on" and sufficiently involved to ensure success.

4. Identification and Tracking

A formal mechanism is necessary whereby women with potential can be identified, jobs pinpointed, development plans established, and promotional opportunities reviewed. Under this procedure, many personnel departments have sent out forms to each manager which require this detail on female employees: prior experience, interests, next two possible positions, long-range potential, and personal development plans to ensure progress. All requisitions for personnel have to be first reviewed against this file before other applicants can be considered.

This practice has been quite successful, since it forces the managers to discuss career plans seriously with their women employees. It also provides a mechanism to keep track of women with potential who may get trapped later under a biased manager.

Many organizations already have a procedure to identify high-potential persons and establish replacement lists, but somehow women are often left out because managers fail to recognize their ability. When a utility discovered, for example, that not one woman was included in the high-potential pool of 300 persons, it lowered the level of eligibility and set up a separate procedure for the identification and tracking of talented women.

As part of their resource development system, some organizations are establishing personalized "fast-track" procedures for a few top-notch women who have had a variety of business experiences but who lack necessary exposure in a particular area, such as manufacturing, finance, or sales, to qualify for management positions.

5. Job Restructuring

A large chemical company recently addressed the problem of too few female chemical engineers. In examining several positions, the top executives discovered that the real problem was overstatement of qualifications; the jobs could be filled by intelligent nonengineers.

In other areas they found that a portion of the job was nonengineering-oriented, so they combined and restructured certain functions and came up with several meaningful paraprofessional jobs. This made it possible for some women to be far more productive for the company, while they were gaining experience and insights necessary in order to climb professional and managerial ladders.

In the secretarial realm, a new concept called "word processing" is gaining favor in some organizations that want to upgrade women employees and also benefit from improved efficiency. Under this system the typewriter is removed from the woman outside the boss's office and all dictating is telephoned to an in-house word-processing center where it is transcribed and returned in a short time. The former secretary becomes an administrative assistant, performing the nontranscription portion of the traditional job plus taking on additional responsibilities. Job ladders are established in both areas, and the secretaries have the opportunity to choose in which portion of their current functions they prefer to specialize and advance.

This is the kind of job analysis and restructuring which has enabled many employers to discover a wealth of resources in women filling such positions as administrative assistant and manager of the word-processing center. The employees have an opportunity to prove their organizational talents, and this experience will make them candidates for other positions in their organizations which previously were beyond their reach.

6. Setting Objectives

Three years ago, when I was setting up an affirmative action plan at IBM, I initially opposed the idea of goals. But a veteran manufacturing manager said, "Barbara, I really believe in your program, but you have to understand the climate you're working in. We have all sorts of priorities and unless you give us numbers and dates, nothing will ever get accomplished. It's just easier to fill a job with a male applicant than to go out of your way to look for a woman."

He was right. After nine months of persuasion and "good faith," which resulted in minimal progress, the company established goals that were realistic, measurable, and challenging. These started with input from the first-level managers. During the corporate review, however, they were stretched to meet company objectives. Within another nine months the overall annual goal was nearly reached.

The company also added to its formal planning structure an "equal opportunity" section, in which each division must submit annually a plan stating the objectives for the next two and five years. About that time, a section was added to every manager's appraisal form which deals with objectives and performance in the equal opportunity area. These appraisals are, of course, tied to salary and advancement.

7. Recruiting

"We've advertised for months for a product manager and no woman has ever applied," an executive may say. Or, "I'd be happy to promote a woman if she'd do what the men do: knock on my door and say, 'I want to be a manager.' "

Edward D. Goldstein, president of Glass Containers Corporation, stated a different approach to the situation: "We're not going to wait for women to knock on our doors. I'm serious about solving the problem. We're going out and search for qualified women who have the talent and potential to advance in our company. I know their qualifications won't always be the same as the men's; in sales, for example, just add 'ten years of experience' as an important criterion and you've eliminated most women."

More companies are establishing action programs to recruit women for a broader range of positions. The implementation of these programs, however, sometimes leaves something to be desired. An outstanding MBA student in California described her interview with a representative of a large corporation. The recruiter, evidently unaware of the company's affirmative action program, said, "You'll like this position. It's a good job for a girl, **and it pays an excellent salary for a girl.**" When she asked where she could go in the company, he replied, "Oh, most of the girls stay in this position—they really love it. It offers a lot of challenge and it's a glamourous job." Needless to say, she did not accept the position.

It is also important to make sure your recruiting material portrays the image you want to convey. AT&T has received extremely favorable reaction to its advertisement showing a woman climbing a telephone pole. TRW and General Electric have pioneered in featuring professional women in their ads. One company was successful in attracting women candidates merely by stating in an ad, "We are interested in *both* men and women applicants."

8. Development and Training

Because half the problem lies in the attitudes of the women themselves—their lack of motivation and ambitious career objectives—many companies have developed special awareness and career planning sessions for them. In some cases these seminars have been cited as the turning point to a change in self-image.

The sessions include discussions on stereotypes that women have traditionally accepted and also focus on problems that women face in business. Members of the group share experiences and give each other advice on handling difficult situations, such as how to work with a chauvinistic manager or how to manage a subordinate who refuses to work for a woman. Questions of business style and image arise, such as, "Should a woman act like one of the boys, or be coy and 'feminine'?"

The procedure of investigating traditionally nonfemale job opportunities also gets emphasis; each session begins with reports by group members on various positions within the company. These reports not only increase practical knowledge of the company but also give each person an opportunity to develop her presentation skills.

Women, like men, have to become accustomed to working with women, and here the awareness sessions can help. One engineer who had spent nearly all her business life in strictly male departments remarked that after the sessions she found she enjoyed the association with other women. The sessions had given her a chance to meet intelligent women whom she could respect, use as role models, and with whom she could share experiences.

In addition to specialized seminars, many companies have specified that every regular management training and development program include some qualified minority and women participants. Other companies without internal training opportunities have concentrated on getting women enrolled in outside development courses such as those sponsored by the American Management Association, Katharine Gibbs, or Dale Carnegie.

A discussion leader at one of these conferences commented that he was amazed at the quality of females in attendance—most of them secretaries. One young woman explained the situation succinctly: "It's not surprising that so many secretaries have so much ability; we've learned from working with our bosses. We've had exposure to top-level problem solving and decision making, and in many cases we do most of their work and recommend solutions. The poor management trainees are three floors below and don't get that kind of experience or exposure."

9. Management Awareness

Development of awareness on the part of lower-level managers is a crucial aspect of the program, without which the other steps can be fruitless. Discrimination against women is often unconscious behavior resulting from traditional upbringing and the influence of our culture.

In-house awareness seminars give managers a chance to bring out and examine their attitudes and assumptions so that they can change their behavior. The sessions usually start with a discussion of typical remarks such as "women can't travel with our salesmen," "they belong in the home," "they're too emotional," and "they'll leave and get married." Then they proceed to deeper matters, such as societal role changes, fear of competition, and backlash.

An expert discussion leader can bring these things to the surface (see ruled insert on page 404). Myths about attrition and

When the shoe is on the other foot

Management awareness sessions can sometimes modify behavior, if not change basic attitudes. Here is a tape of a discussion of an issue raised by the discussion leader at one such session.

Leader: Suppose you're the manager of a division of a large organization based in New York. A management opening occurs in your Denver office for which one of your New York women is the best qualified candidate. It would be a very good opportunity for her. However, she is married to a rising young executive in a local company; they have a three-year-old child and a newly purchased home in Chappaqua. Not only that, you play poker with the husband every other week. How many of you would offer her the job? Raise your hands. Hmm, only 2 out of 20. What are your reasons?

Manager A: I wouldn't offer it to her because I wouldn't want to be the cause of a divorce.

Manager B: Right. Anyway, her husband's job is more important than hers. He's the one who's likely to be making the most money for the family in the future as well as now.

Manager C: I know she wouldn't take the job, for all those reasons you mentioned in your question. So why offer it to her? It will only cause conflict.

Manager D: I should probably have been developing her and keeping close enough tabs on her to *know* whether she'd accept it or not.

Manager E: I don't know. How can you be absolutely sure until you actually ask?

Manager F: I might offer her the job—she should be the one to decide, and she could always ask her husband's advice.

Manager G: Well, I wouldn't want to put myself in the position of bringing up a divisive issue. Our job as managers is not to break up families.

Leader: Now let me ask you another question. Suppose that you work for me in this same New York-based company. I know that you moved to New York in the first place because your wife has a serious disease that can be treated only by a certain specialist here. She's now under treatment. An excellent opening comes up in San Francisco for which you'd be ideal. How many of you would like me to offer you that position? Let's see your hands. Now almost all of you would want me to. Why?

Manager G: I must admit that even if I knew I couldn't take it, I'd like you to offer it. Then I'd know you thought a lot of me.

Manager H: Also, even if I couldn't take this particular job at this particular time, my situation might change later. And if you thought I was good enough for this job, I'd be encouraged to think I'd have another good opportunity in the future.

Manager I: How do you really know I wouldn't take it? It's up to me to investigate what kind of medical assistance I can get for my wife in San Francisco.

Manager J: And if you offer the job to me but I can't take it, at least the company gets some mileage out of the offer itself.

Manager F: And who knows? Maybe that person you thought wouldn't take the job will surprise you and accept. Come to think of it, there *is* a woman I've been considering for a great position involving relocation. I think I'll at least give her the opportunity to accept it.

Manager D: I guess the answer is, it's not up to us as managers to make personal decisions for our employees no matter how well we *think* we know them. In the first example you gave us, maybe the woman's husband is dissatisfied with his job and can get a better one in Denver. The position should be offered to the person who's the best qualified. Then it's up to him—uh, her—to make the decision.

absenteeism are vulnerable to demolition by statistics. Stereotypes are handled via case studies. Behavior issues are treated through discussion of management techniques; for example, participants answer the question, "What do you do if a woman cries during her appraisal?" Or "What do you do if a talented woman says she's not interested in advancement?" The last part of the session concentrates on motivation and career counseling of female employees.

There are several industrial programs available to complement internal management awareness procedures. Films and videotape series can be obtained from commercial sources. Not all of them need skilled discussion leaders to make them effective.

10. Personnel Policies Study

An organization's personnel practices need to be explored in order to ensure that discrimination does not exist and to create a climate fostering the utilization of women to their full potential. Some of the critical areas are personnel forms, part-time employment, day-care centers, job descriptions, entrance exams, benefits, and policies on overtime, travel, and working conditions.

Sometimes such a study must go beyond policy to interpretation. For example, the employment form of a major oil company included the question, "Can this employee relocate?" On examining the completed forms of 300 women employees, the company officials found the appropriate box marked "no" in every case. On probing further, they discovered that no one had actually asked the women whether they would relocate; it had simply been assumed that they would not.

During personnel reviews, several companies have become aware of *reverse* discrimination practices—such as that of the chivalrous manager who arranged for taxis to drive up at midnight to take the women keypunchers home—and have revised them accordingly. In other cases, policies that affect women have been liberalized; IBM and Polaroid, for example, have followed EEOC guidelines and now treat pregnancy as a temporary disability covered under their regular sickness and accident plans. (This helps reduce costly attrition and attracts feminine talent necessary to the business.)

Reservoir of Skills

The ten steps I have listed here by no means comprise a complete program, and many of these ideas need to be tailored to the particular company environment. However, even some small companies have successfully initiated many of these programs on a limited basis and have experienced a significant increase in the morale and work quality of their women employees.

The establishment of an affirmative action program is not costly—its absence is—and the most important ingredient to its success is commitment. Not only is it the law; it is also smart business. From an economic point of view women are a valuable resource, and it is up to managers to make use of women's creative talent, education, and skills to help meet the challenges of the marketplace.

In the words of George R. Vila, chairman and president of Uniroyal, Inc., "In the decades ahead any organization which ignores or underestimates the potential of women—or overlooks any source of talent for that matter—will be making a fatal mistake."

A study prepared in 1970 for internal consumption at one of the largest U.S. corporations concerned the significant labor force developments anticipated in the United States up to 1979. The study revealed:

"It will be an increasingly female labor force. Women will account for more than half of the 15.5 million growth in the labor force in the decade to 1979. Furthermore, society is not presently making fully effective use of the aptitudes, intelligence, and education of many women in the labor force. The female labor force, therefore, constitutes an important reservoir of skills needed by business. Competitive, political, and social pressures will force greater equality of opportunity for working women and this corporation could gain considerable competitive advantage by prompt and creative moves in this area."

Footnote

1. For more on this aspect, see Charles D. Orth, 3rd, and Frederic Jacobs, "Women in Management: Pattern for Change," *Harvard Business Review*, July-August 1971, p. 139.

Sources for
Further Reading

Acker, J. and D.R. Van Houten. "Differential Recruitment and Control: The Sex Structuring of Organizations." *Administrative Science Quarterly*, vol. 19, no. 2, pp. 152-163.

Baruch, R.W. "The Achievement Motive in Women: A Study of the Implications for Career Development." *Research in Education*, 1969, vol. 4, no. 8.

Burstiner, Irving. "Comparing Male and Female Department Heads for Self Confidence and Job Adjustment." *College Student Journal*, vol. 8, no. 4, pp. 61-63.

Careers for Women in the Seventies. Washington, D.C.: Employment Standards Administration, Women's Bureau, 1973.

Chernik, Doris A. and Joseph G. Phelan. "Attitudes of Women in Management: I. Job Satisfaction: A Study of Perceived Need Satisfaction as a Function of Job Level." *International Journal of Social Psychiatry*, Spring-Summer 1974, pp. 94-98.

Dimarco, Nicholas and Susan E. Whitsitt. "A Comparison of Female Supervisors in Business and Government Organizations." *Journal of Vocational Behavior*, vol. 6, no. 2, pp. 185-196.

Dragoslav, Slezska. "Problems of Activity of Women's Participation in Managing an Industrial Plant." *Sociological Abstracts*, 1967, vol. 15, no. 7.

Echternacht, Gary J. and Ann L. Hussein. "Survey of Women Interested in Management." Prepared by Educational Testing Service for the Graduate Business Admissions Council.

Epstein, Cynthia F. "Encountering the Male Establishment: Sex-Status Limits on Women's Careers in the Professions." *American Journal of Sociology*, vol. 75, no. 6, pp. 965-982.

Epstein, C.F. "Reflections on the Women's Movement: An Assessment of Change and its Limits." *Resources in Education*, 1976.

Epstein, Cynthia Fuchs. *Woman's Place*. Berkeley: University of California Press, 1973.

Eyde, L.D. "Eliminating Barriers to Career Development of Women." *Personnel Guidance Journal*, vol. 49, no. 1, pp. 24-27.

Garland, T. Neal and Margaret M. Poloma. "Cribs or Careers? Professionally Employed Married Women's Attitudes Toward Motherhood." *Sociological Abstracts*, 1971.

Gaskell, J. "Explaining the Aspirations of Working Class Girls." Paper presented at the Annual Meeting of the American Education Association, Boston, Massachusetts, July 1-4, 1975.

Geach, L. "Why Are More Women Not in Management?" *Current Index Journal of Education*, 1974.

Goldberg, Philip. "Are Women Prejudiced Against Women?" *Trans-Action*, vol. 5, no. 5, pp. 28-30.

Gordon, Francine E. and Myra Strober. *Bringing Women into Management*. New York: McGraw-Hill, 1975.

Hardy, Richard E. and John G. Cull. *Career Guidance for Young Women: Considerations in Planning Professional Careers*. Springfield, Illinois: Charles C. Thomas, 1974.

Helson, Ravenna. "The Changing Image of the Career Woman." *Journal of Social Issues*, vol. 28, no. 2, pp. 33-46.

Herman, D.D. "More Career Opportunities for Women: Whose Responsibility?" *Personnel Journal*, vol. 53, no. 6, p. 414.

Homall, Geraldine M., Suzanne Juhasz, and Joseph Juhasz. "Differences in Self-Perception and Vocational Aspirations of College Women." *California Journal of Educational Research*, vol. 26, no. 1, pp. 6-10.

Hora, Stefan. "On the Problem of Low Participation by Women in Managerial Activities." *Synteza*, June 1973, pp. 81-86.

Kanowitz, Lee. *Women and the Law: The Unfinished Revolution*. Albuquerque: University of New Mexico Press, 1969.

Kaplan, F.B. and M.E. Meade. "American Women, The Report of the President's Commission on the Status of Women and Other Publications of the Commission." *Research in Education*, 1968, vol. 3, no. 10.

Keller, Suzanne. "The Future Role of Women." *Annals of the American Academy of Political and Social Science*, July 1973, pp. 1-12.

Klemmack, D.L. and J.N. Edwards. "Women's Acquisition of Stereotyped Occupational Aspirations." *Sociology and Social Research*, vol. 57, no. 4, pp. 510-525.

Kohen, A.I. et al. *Women and the Economy: A Bibliography and a Review of the Literature on Sex Differentiation in the Labor Market*. Columbus: Ohio State University, Center for Human Resource Research, 1976.

Loring, Rosalind and Theodora Wells. *Breakthrough: Women into Management*. New York: Van Nostrand Reinhold Company, 1972.

Marchak, Patricia. "Women Workers and White-Collar Unions." *Canadian Review of Sociology and Anthropology*, vol. 10, no. 2, pp. 134-147.

Medvene, A.M. and A. Collins. "Occupational Prestige and its Relationships to Traditional and Nontraditional Views of Women's Roles." *Journal of Counseling Psychology*, vol. 21, no. 2, pp. 139-143.

Moses, Joseph L. and Virginia R. Boehm. "Relationship of Assessment-Center Performance to Management Progress of Women." *Journal of Applied Psychology*, vol. 60, no. 4, pp. 527-529.

Odiorne, George S. "The Corporation and the Women's Revolution." *Training and Development Journal*, vol. 29, no. 5, pp. 3-11.

Osipow, Samuel H. *Emerging Woman: Career Analysis and*

Outlooks. Columbus, Ohio: Charles E. Merrill, 1975.

Peoples, Vickie Y. "Measuring the Vocational Interest of Women," in S.H. Osipow (ed.), *Emerging Woman: Career Analysis and Outlooks*. Columbus, Ohio: Charles E. Merrill, 1975.

Quinn, Francis X. "Women at Work—(1)—The Facts." *Sociological Abstracts*, 1964, vol. 12, no. 2.

Reinfeld, P.M. "Woman: Yesterday, Today, Tomorrow." *Research in Education*, 1974.

Richardson, Mary S. "The Dimensions of Career and Work Orientation in College Women." *Journal of Vocational Behavior*, vol. 5, no. 1, pp. 161-172.

Rogalin, Wilma C. and Arthur R. Pell. *Women's Guide to Management Positions*. New York: Simon and Schuster, 1975.

Rosen, B. et al. "Dual-Career Marital Adjustment: Potential Effects of Discriminatory Managerial Attitudes." *Journal of Marriage and the Family*, vol. 37, no. 3, pp. 565-572.

Rosenthal, G. "Move Over, Jack—Here Comes Jill." *Journal of College Placement*, vol. 34, no. 3, pp. 58-62.

Rothstein, S.W. "What Does the Future Hold for Women?" *Integrated Education*, vol. 13, no. 4, pp. 36-37.

Sandler, B. "Discrimination Is Immoral, Illegal and, Offenders Find, Costly." *College and University Business*, vol. 56, no. 2, pp. 27-30.

Sandler, B. "Women: The Last Minority." *Journal of College Placement*, vol. 32, no. 2, pp. 49-52.

Schab, F. "What Jobs Do High School Girls Want?" *Integrated Education*, vol. 11, no. 6, pp. 29-30.

Schein, Virginia E. "Relationships Between Sex Role Stereotypes and Requisite Management Characteristics Among Female Managers." *Journal of Applied Psychology*, vol. 60, no. 3, pp. 340-344.

Schoonover, Jean Way. "Why Corporate America Fears Women." *Vital Speeches of the Day*, vol. XL, no. 13, pp. 414-416.

Sex Discrimination in Employment: What to Know About It, What to Do About It. 2nd edition. Boston: National Organization for Women, 1974.

Shafer, S.M. "Factors Affecting the Utilization of Women in Professional and Managerial Roles." *Comparative Education*, vol. 10, no. 1, pp. 1-11.

Standley, Kay and Bradley Soule. "Women in Professions: Historic Antecedents and Current Lifestyles," in R.E. Hardy and J.G. Cull (eds.), *Career Guidance for Young Women: Considerations in Planning Professional Careers.* Springfield, Illinois: Charles C. Thomas, 1974.

Taylor, G. "Who Will Do the Women's Work?" *Current Index Journal of Education*, 1974.

Theodore, Athena. "Professional Women: The Unchanging Scene." *Sociological Abstracts*, vol. 19, 1971.

Wasserman, E.R. "Changing Aspirations of College Women." *Journal of the American College Health Association*, vol. 21, no. 4, pp. 333-335.

Wells, T. "Equalizing Advancement Between Women and Men." *Training and Development Journal*, vol. 27, no. 8, pp. 20-24.

Wheeler, H.R. "Alice in Wonderland, Or, Through the Looking Glass: Resources for Implementing Principles of Affirmative Action Employment of Women." *Resources in Education*, 1976.

Winters, Carol J. and Janet Sorensen. "Individual Factors Related to Career Orientation in Women," in S.H. Osipow (ed.), *Emerging Woman: Career Analysis and Outlooks.* Columbus, Ohio: Charles E. Merrill, 1975.

"Women on Women." *American Scholar*, Autumn 1972, vol. 41, no. 4, pp. 599-627.